PostgreSQL 9.4 Vol6: Internals

A catalogue record for this book is available from the Hong Kong Public Libraries.

Published in Hong Kong by Samurai Media Limited.

Email: info@samuraimedia.org

ISBN 978-988-8381-36-4

Table of Contents

VII. Internals

This part contains assorted information that might be of use to PostgreSQL developers.

postmaster

1876

Chapter 47. Overview of PostgreSQL Internals

Author: This chapter originated as part of *Enhancement of the ANSI SQL Implementation of Post-greSQL*, Stefan Simkovics' Master's Thesis prepared at Vienna University of Technology under the direction of O.Univ.Prof.Dr. Georg Gottlob and Univ.Ass. Mag. Katrin Seyr.

This chapter gives an overview of the internal structure of the backend of PostgreSQL. After having read the following sections you should have an idea of how a query is processed. This chapter does not aim to provide a detailed description of the internal operation of PostgreSQL, as such a document would be very extensive. Rather, this chapter is intended to help the reader understand the general sequence of operations that occur within the backend from the point at which a query is received, to the point at which the results are returned to the client.

47.1. The Path of a Query

Here we give a short overview of the stages a query has to pass in order to obtain a result.

1. A connection from an application program to the PostgreSQL server has to be established. The application program transmits a query to the server and waits to receive the results sent back by the server.

2. The *parser stage* checks the query transmitted by the application program for correct syntax and creates a *query tree*.

3. The *rewrite system* takes the query tree created by the parser stage and looks for any *rules* (stored in the *system catalogs*) to apply to the query tree. It performs the transformations given in the *rule bodies*.

    One application of the rewrite system is in the realization of *views*. Whenever a query against a view (i.e., a *virtual table*) is made, the rewrite system rewrites the user's query to a query that accesses the *base tables* given in the *view definition* instead.

4. The *planner/optimizer* takes the (rewritten) query tree and creates a *query plan* that will be the input to the *executor*.

    It does so by first creating all possible *paths* leading to the same result. For example if there is an index on a relation to be scanned, there are two paths for the scan. One possibility is a simple sequential scan and the other possibility is to use the index. Next the cost for the execution of each path is estimated and the cheapest path is chosen. The cheapest path is expanded into a complete plan that the executor can use.

5. The executor recursively steps through the *plan tree* and retrieves rows in the way represented by the plan. The executor makes use of the *storage system* while scanning relations, performs *sorts* and *joins*, evaluates *qualifications* and finally hands back the rows derived.

In the following sections we will cover each of the above listed items in more detail to give a better understanding of PostgreSQL's internal control and data structures.

47.2. How Connections are Established

PostgreSQL is implemented using a simple "process per user" client/server model. In this model there is one *client process* connected to exactly one *server process*. As we do not know ahead of time how many connections will be made, we have to use a *master process* that spawns a new server process every time a connection is requested. This master process is called postgres and listens at a specified TCP/IP port for incoming connections. Whenever a request for a connection is detected the postgres process spawns a new server process. The server tasks communicate with each other using *semaphores* and *shared memory* to ensure data integrity throughout concurrent data access.

The client process can be any program that understands the PostgreSQL protocol described in Chapter 49. Many clients are based on the C-language library libpq, but several independent implementations of the protocol exist, such as the Java JDBC driver.

Once a connection is established the client process can send a query to the *backend* (server). The query is transmitted using plain text, i.e., there is no parsing done in the *frontend* (client). The server parses the query, creates an *execution plan*, executes the plan and returns the retrieved rows to the client by transmitting them over the established connection.

47.3. The Parser Stage

The *parser stage* consists of two parts:

- The *parser* defined in gram.y and scan.l is built using the Unix tools bison and flex.
- The *transformation process* does modifications and augmentations to the data structures returned by the parser.

47.3.1. Parser

The parser has to check the query string (which arrives as plain text) for valid syntax. If the syntax is correct a *parse tree* is built up and handed back; otherwise an error is returned. The parser and lexer are implemented using the well-known Unix tools bison and flex.

The *lexer* is defined in the file scan.l and is responsible for recognizing *identifiers*, the *SQL key words* etc. For every key word or identifier that is found, a *token* is generated and handed to the parser.

The parser is defined in the file gram.y and consists of a set of *grammar rules* and *actions* that are executed whenever a rule is fired. The code of the actions (which is actually C code) is used to build up the parse tree.

The file scan.l is transformed to the C source file scan.c using the program flex and gram.y is transformed to gram.c using bison. After these transformations have taken place a normal C compiler can be used to create the parser. Never make any changes to the generated C files as they will be overwritten the next time flex or bison is called.

Note: The mentioned transformations and compilations are normally done automatically using the *makefiles* shipped with the PostgreSQL source distribution.

A detailed description of bison or the grammar rules given in `gram.y` would be beyond the scope of this paper. There are many books and documents dealing with flex and bison. You should be familiar with bison before you start to study the grammar given in `gram.y` otherwise you won't understand what happens there.

47.3.2. Transformation Process

The parser stage creates a parse tree using only fixed rules about the syntactic structure of SQL. It does not make any lookups in the system catalogs, so there is no possibility to understand the detailed semantics of the requested operations. After the parser completes, the *transformation process* takes the tree handed back by the parser as input and does the semantic interpretation needed to understand which tables, functions, and operators are referenced by the query. The data structure that is built to represent this information is called the *query tree*.

The reason for separating raw parsing from semantic analysis is that system catalog lookups can only be done within a transaction, and we do not wish to start a transaction immediately upon receiving a query string. The raw parsing stage is sufficient to identify the transaction control commands (`BEGIN`, `ROLLBACK`, etc), and these can then be correctly executed without any further analysis. Once we know that we are dealing with an actual query (such as `SELECT` or `UPDATE`), it is okay to start a transaction if we're not already in one. Only then can the transformation process be invoked.

The query tree created by the transformation process is structurally similar to the raw parse tree in most places, but it has many differences in detail. For example, a `FuncCall` node in the parse tree represents something that looks syntactically like a function call. This might be transformed to either a `FuncExpr` or `Aggref` node depending on whether the referenced name turns out to be an ordinary function or an aggregate function. Also, information about the actual data types of columns and expression results is added to the query tree.

47.4. The PostgreSQL Rule System

PostgreSQL supports a powerful *rule system* for the specification of *views* and ambiguous *view updates*. Originally the PostgreSQL rule system consisted of two implementations:

- The first one worked using *row level* processing and was implemented deep in the *executor*. The rule system was called whenever an individual row had been accessed. This implementation was removed in 1995 when the last official release of the Berkeley Postgres project was transformed into Postgres95.

- The second implementation of the rule system is a technique called *query rewriting*. The *rewrite system* is a module that exists between the *parser stage* and the *planner/optimizer*. This technique is still implemented.

The query rewriter is discussed in some detail in Chapter 38, so there is no need to cover it here. We will only point out that both the input and the output of the rewriter are query trees, that is, there is no change in the representation or level of semantic detail in the trees. Rewriting can be thought of as a form of macro expansion.

47.5. Planner/Optimizer

The task of the *planner/optimizer* is to create an optimal execution plan. A given SQL query (and hence, a query tree) can be actually executed in a wide variety of different ways, each of which will produce the same set of results. If it is computationally feasible, the query optimizer will examine each of these possible execution plans, ultimately selecting the execution plan that is expected to run the fastest.

> **Note:** In some situations, examining each possible way in which a query can be executed would take an excessive amount of time and memory space. In particular, this occurs when executing queries involving large numbers of join operations. In order to determine a reasonable (not necessarily optimal) query plan in a reasonable amount of time, PostgreSQL uses a *Genetic Query Optimizer* (see Chapter 54) when the number of joins exceeds a threshold (see geqo_threshold).

The planner's search procedure actually works with data structures called *paths*, which are simply cut-down representations of plans containing only as much information as the planner needs to make its decisions. After the cheapest path is determined, a full-fledged *plan tree* is built to pass to the executor. This represents the desired execution plan in sufficient detail for the executor to run it. In the rest of this section we'll ignore the distinction between paths and plans.

47.5.1. Generating Possible Plans

The planner/optimizer starts by generating plans for scanning each individual relation (table) used in the query. The possible plans are determined by the available indexes on each relation. There is always the possibility of performing a sequential scan on a relation, so a sequential scan plan is always created. Assume an index is defined on a relation (for example a B-tree index) and a query contains the restriction `relation.attribute OPR constant`. If `relation.attribute` happens to match the key of the B-tree index and `OPR` is one of the operators listed in the index's *operator class*, another plan is created using the B-tree index to scan the relation. If there are further indexes present and the restrictions in the query happen to match a key of an index, further plans will be considered. Index scan plans are also generated for indexes that have a sort ordering that can match the query's `ORDER BY` clause (if any), or a sort ordering that might be useful for merge joining (see below).

If the query requires joining two or more relations, plans for joining relations are considered after all feasible plans have been found for scanning single relations. The three available join strategies are:

- *nested loop join*: The right relation is scanned once for every row found in the left relation. This strategy is easy to implement but can be very time consuming. (However, if the right relation can be scanned with an index scan, this can be a good strategy. It is possible to use values from the current row of the left relation as keys for the index scan of the right.)

- *merge join*: Each relation is sorted on the join attributes before the join starts. Then the two relations are scanned in parallel, and matching rows are combined to form join rows. This kind of join is more attractive because each relation has to be scanned only once. The required sorting might be achieved either by an explicit sort step, or by scanning the relation in the proper order using an index on the join key.

- *hash join*: the right relation is first scanned and loaded into a hash table, using its join attributes as hash keys. Next the left relation is scanned and the appropriate values of every row found are used as hash keys to locate the matching rows in the table.

When the query involves more than two relations, the final result must be built up by a tree of join steps, each with two inputs. The planner examines different possible join sequences to find the cheapest one.

If the query uses fewer than geqo_threshold relations, a near-exhaustive search is conducted to find the best join sequence. The planner preferentially considers joins between any two relations for which there exist a corresponding join clause in the WHERE qualification (i.e., for which a restriction like `where rel1.attr1=rel2.attr2` exists). Join pairs with no join clause are considered only when there is no other choice, that is, a particular relation has no available join clauses to any other relation. All possible plans are generated for every join pair considered by the planner, and the one that is (estimated to be) the cheapest is chosen.

When `geqo_threshold` is exceeded, the join sequences considered are determined by heuristics, as described in Chapter 54. Otherwise the process is the same.

The finished plan tree consists of sequential or index scans of the base relations, plus nested-loop, merge, or hash join nodes as needed, plus any auxiliary steps needed, such as sort nodes or aggregate-function calculation nodes. Most of these plan node types have the additional ability to do *selection* (discarding rows that do not meet a specified Boolean condition) and *projection* (computation of a derived column set based on given column values, that is, evaluation of scalar expressions where needed). One of the responsibilities of the planner is to attach selection conditions from the WHERE clause and computation of required output expressions to the most appropriate nodes of the plan tree.

47.6. Executor

The *executor* takes the plan created by the planner/optimizer and recursively processes it to extract the required set of rows. This is essentially a demand-pull pipeline mechanism. Each time a plan node is called, it must deliver one more row, or report that it is done delivering rows.

To provide a concrete example, assume that the top node is a MergeJoin node. Before any merge can be done two rows have to be fetched (one from each subplan). So the executor recursively calls itself to process the subplans (it starts with the subplan attached to lefttree). The new top node (the top node of the left subplan) is, let's say, a Sort node and again recursion is needed to obtain an input row. The child node of the Sort might be a SeqScan node, representing actual reading of a table. Execution of this node causes the executor to fetch a row from the table and return it up to the calling node. The Sort node will repeatedly call its child to obtain all the rows to be sorted. When the input is exhausted (as indicated by the child node returning a NULL instead of a row), the Sort code performs the sort, and finally is able to return its first output row, namely the first one in sorted order. It keeps the remaining rows stored so that it can deliver them in sorted order in response to later demands.

The `MergeJoin` node similarly demands the first row from its right subplan. Then it compares the two rows to see if they can be joined; if so, it returns a join row to its caller. On the next call, or immediately if it cannot join the current pair of inputs, it advances to the next row of one table or the other (depending on how the comparison came out), and again checks for a match. Eventually, one subplan or the other is exhausted, and the `MergeJoin` node returns NULL to indicate that no more join rows can be formed.

Complex queries can involve many levels of plan nodes, but the general approach is the same: each node computes and returns its next output row each time it is called. Each node is also responsible for applying any selection or projection expressions that were assigned to it by the planner.

The executor mechanism is used to evaluate all four basic SQL query types: SELECT, INSERT, UPDATE, and DELETE. For SELECT, the top-level executor code only needs to send each row returned by the query plan tree off to the client. For INSERT, each returned row is inserted into the target table specified for the INSERT. This is done in a special top-level plan node called `ModifyTable`. (A simple INSERT ... VALUES command creates a trivial plan tree consisting of a single `Result` node, which computes just one result row, and `ModifyTable` above it to perform the insertion. But INSERT ... SELECT can demand the full power of the executor mechanism.) For UPDATE, the planner arranges that each computed row includes all the updated column values, plus the *TID* (tuple ID, or row ID) of the original target row; this data is fed into a `ModifyTable` node, which uses the information to create a new updated row and mark the old row deleted. For DELETE, the only column that is actually returned by the plan is the TID, and the `ModifyTable` node simply uses the TID to visit each target row and mark it deleted.

Chapter 48. System Catalogs

The system catalogs are the place where a relational database management system stores schema meta-data, such as information about tables and columns, and internal bookkeeping information. PostgreSQL's system catalogs are regular tables. You can drop and recreate the tables, add columns, insert and update values, and severely mess up your system that way. Normally, one should not change the system catalogs by hand, there are always SQL commands to do that. (For example, CREATE DATABASE inserts a row into the pg_database catalog — and actually creates the database on disk.) There are some exceptions for particularly esoteric operations, such as adding index access methods.

48.1. Overview

Table 48-1 lists the system catalogs. More detailed documentation of each catalog follows below.

Most system catalogs are copied from the template database during database creation and are thereafter database-specific. A few catalogs are physically shared across all databases in a cluster; these are noted in the descriptions of the individual catalogs.

Table 48-1. System Catalogs

Catalog Name	Purpose
pg_aggregate	aggregate functions
pg_am	index access methods
pg_amop	access method operators
pg_amproc	access method support procedures
pg_attrdef	column default values
pg_attribute	table columns ("attributes")
pg_authid	authorization identifiers (roles)
pg_auth_members	authorization identifier membership relationships
pg_cast	casts (data type conversions)
pg_class	tables, indexes, sequences, views ("relations")
pg_collation	collations (locale information)
pg_constraint	check constraints, unique constraints, primary key constraints, foreign key constraints
pg_conversion	encoding conversion information
pg_database	databases within this database cluster
pg_db_role_setting	per-role and per-database settings
pg_default_acl	default privileges for object types
pg_depend	dependencies between database objects
pg_description	descriptions or comments on database objects

Catalog Name	Purpose
pg_enum	enum label and value definitions
pg_event_trigger	event triggers
pg_extension	installed extensions
pg_foreign_data_wrapper	foreign-data wrapper definitions
pg_foreign_server	foreign server definitions
pg_foreign_table	additional foreign table information
pg_index	additional index information
pg_inherits	table inheritance hierarchy
pg_language	languages for writing functions
pg_largeobject	data pages for large objects
pg_largeobject_metadata	metadata for large objects
pg_namespace	schemas
pg_opclass	access method operator classes
pg_operator	operators
pg_opfamily	access method operator families
pg_pltemplate	template data for procedural languages
pg_proc	functions and procedures
pg_range	information about range types
pg_rewrite	query rewrite rules
pg_replication_slots	replication slot information
pg_seclabel	security labels on database objects
pg_shdepend	dependencies on shared objects
pg_shdescription	comments on shared objects
pg_shseclabel	security labels on shared database objects
pg_statistic	planner statistics
pg_tablespace	tablespaces within this database cluster
pg_trigger	triggers
pg_ts_config	text search configurations
pg_ts_config_map	text search configurations' token mappings
pg_ts_dict	text search dictionaries
pg_ts_parser	text search parsers
pg_ts_template	text search templates
pg_type	data types
pg_user_mapping	mappings of users to foreign servers

48.2. pg_aggregate

The catalog pg_aggregate stores information about aggregate functions. An aggregate function is a function that operates on a set of values (typically one column from each row that matches a query condition) and returns a single value computed from all these values. Typical aggregate functions are sum, count, and max. Each entry in pg_aggregate is an extension of an entry in pg_proc. The pg_proc entry carries the aggregate's name, input and output data types, and other information that is similar to ordinary functions.

Table 48-2. pg_aggregate Columns

Name	Type	References	Description
aggfnoid	regproc	pg_proc.oid	pg_proc OID of the aggregate function
aggkind	char		Aggregate kind: n for "normal" aggregates, o for "ordered-set" aggregates, or h for "hypothetical-set" aggregates
aggnumdirectargs	int2		Number of direct (non-aggregated) arguments of an ordered-set or hypothetical-set aggregate, counting a variadic array as one argument. If equal to pronargs, the aggregate must be variadic and the variadic array describes the aggregated arguments as well as the final direct arguments. Always zero for normal aggregates.
aggtransfn	regproc	pg_proc.oid	Transition function
aggfinalfn	regproc	pg_proc.oid	Final function (zero if none)
aggmtransfn	regproc	pg_proc.oid	Forward transition function for moving-aggregate mode (zero if none)
aggminvtransfn	regproc	pg_proc.oid	Inverse transition function for moving-aggregate mode (zero if none)

Name	Type	References	Description
aggmfinalfn	regproc	pg_proc.oid	Final function for moving-aggregate mode (zero if none)
aggfinalextra	bool		True to pass extra dummy arguments to aggfinalfn
aggmfinalextra	bool		True to pass extra dummy arguments to aggmfinalfn
aggsortop	oid	pg_operator.oid	Associated sort operator (zero if none)
aggtranstype	oid	pg_type.oid	Data type of the aggregate function's internal transition (state) data
aggtransspace	int4		Approximate average size (in bytes) of the transition state data, or zero to use a default estimate
aggmtranstype	oid	pg_type.oid	Data type of the aggregate function's internal transition (state) data for moving-aggregate mode (zero if none)
aggmtransspace	int4		Approximate average size (in bytes) of the transition state data for moving-aggregate mode, or zero to use a default estimate
agginitval	text		The initial value of the transition state. This is a text field containing the initial value in its external string representation. If this field is null, the transition state value starts out null.

Name	Type	References	Description
aggminitval	text		The initial value of the transition state for moving-aggregate mode. This is a text field containing the initial value in its external string representation. If this field is null, the transition state value starts out null.

New aggregate functions are registered with the CREATE AGGREGATE command. See Section 35.10 for more information about writing aggregate functions and the meaning of the transition functions, etc.

48.3. pg_am

The catalog pg_am stores information about index access methods. There is one row for each index access method supported by the system. The contents of this catalog are discussed in detail in Chapter 55.

Table 48-3. pg_am Columns

Name	Type	References	Description
oid	oid		Row identifier (hidden attribute; must be explicitly selected)
amname	name		Name of the access method
amstrategies	int2		Number of operator strategies for this access method, or zero if access method does not have a fixed set of operator strategies
amsupport	int2		Number of support routines for this access method
amcanorder	bool		Does the access method support ordered scans sorted by the indexed column's value?

Name	Type	References	Description
amcanorderbyop	bool		Does the access method support ordered scans sorted by the result of an operator on the indexed column?
amcanbackward	bool		Does the access method support backward scanning?
amcanunique	bool		Does the access method support unique indexes?
amcanmulticol	bool		Does the access method support multicolumn indexes?
amoptionalkey	bool		Does the access method support a scan without any constraint for the first index column?
amsearcharray	bool		Does the access method support `ScalarArrayOpExpr` searches?
amsearchnulls	bool		Does the access method support IS NULL/NOT NULL searches?
amstorage	bool		Can index storage data type differ from column data type?
amclusterable	bool		Can an index of this type be clustered on?
ampredlocks	bool		Does an index of this type manage fine-grained predicate locks?
amkeytype	oid	pg_type.oid	Type of data stored in index, or zero if not a fixed type
aminsert	regproc	pg_proc.oid	"Insert this tuple" function
ambeginscan	regproc	pg_proc.oid	"Prepare for index scan" function
amgettuple	regproc	pg_proc.oid	"Next valid tuple" function, or zero if none

Name	Type	References	Description
amgetbitmap	regproc	pg_proc.oid	"Fetch all valid tuples" function, or zero if none
amrescan	regproc	pg_proc.oid	"(Re)start index scan" function
amendscan	regproc	pg_proc.oid	"Clean up after index scan" function
ammarkpos	regproc	pg_proc.oid	"Mark current scan position" function
amrestrpos	regproc	pg_proc.oid	"Restore marked scan position" function
ambuild	regproc	pg_proc.oid	"Build new index" function
ambuildempty	regproc	pg_proc.oid	"Build empty index" function
ambulkdelete	regproc	pg_proc.oid	Bulk-delete function
amvacuumcleanup	regproc	pg_proc.oid	Post-VACUUM cleanup function
amcanreturn	regproc	pg_proc.oid	Function to check whether index supports index-only scans, or zero if none
amcostestimate	regproc	pg_proc.oid	Function to estimate cost of an index scan
amoptions	regproc	pg_proc.oid	Function to parse and validate reloptions for an index

48.4. pg_amop

The catalog pg_amop stores information about operators associated with access method operator families. There is one row for each operator that is a member of an operator family. A family member can be either a *search* operator or an *ordering* operator. An operator can appear in more than one family, but cannot appear in more than one search position nor more than one ordering position within a family. (It is allowed, though unlikely, for an operator to be used for both search and ordering purposes.)

Table 48-4. pg_amop Columns

Name	Type	References	Description
oid	oid		Row identifier (hidden attribute; must be explicitly selected)

Name	Type	References	Description
amopfamily	oid	pg_opfamily.oid	The operator family this entry is for
amoplefttype	oid	pg_type.oid	Left-hand input data type of operator
amoprighttype	oid	pg_type.oid	Right-hand input data type of operator
amopstrategy	int2		Operator strategy number
amoppurpose	char		Operator purpose, either s for search or o for ordering
amopopr	oid	pg_operator.oid	OID of the operator
amopmethod	oid	pg_am.oid	Index access method operator family is for
amopsortfamily	oid	pg_opfamily.oid	The B-tree operator family this entry sorts according to, if an ordering operator; zero if a search operator

A "search" operator entry indicates that an index of this operator family can be searched to find all rows satisfying WHERE *indexed_column operator constant*. Obviously, such an operator must return boolean, and its left-hand input type must match the index's column data type.

An "ordering" operator entry indicates that an index of this operator family can be scanned to return rows in the order represented by ORDER BY *indexed_column operator constant*. Such an operator could return any sortable data type, though again its left-hand input type must match the index's column data type. The exact semantics of the ORDER BY are specified by the amopsortfamily column, which must reference a B-tree operator family for the operator's result type.

> **Note:** At present, it's assumed that the sort order for an ordering operator is the default for the referenced operator family, i.e., ASC NULLS LAST. This might someday be relaxed by adding additional columns to specify sort options explicitly.

An entry's amopmethod must match the opfmethod of its containing operator family (including amopmethod here is an intentional denormalization of the catalog structure for performance reasons). Also, amoplefttype and amoprighttype must match the oprleft and oprright fields of the referenced pg_operator entry.

48.5. pg_amproc

The catalog pg_amproc stores information about support procedures associated with access method operator families. There is one row for each support procedure belonging to an operator family.

Table 48-5. `pg_amproc` Columns

Name	Type	References	Description
oid	oid		Row identifier (hidden attribute; must be explicitly selected)
amprocfamily	oid	pg_opfamily.oid	The operator family this entry is for
amproclefttype	oid	pg_type.oid	Left-hand input data type of associated operator
amprocrighttype	oid	pg_type.oid	Right-hand input data type of associated operator
amprocnum	int2		Support procedure number
amproc	regproc	pg_proc.oid	OID of the procedure

The usual interpretation of the `amproclefttype` and `amprocrighttype` fields is that they identify the left and right input types of the operator(s) that a particular support procedure supports. For some access methods these match the input data type(s) of the support procedure itself, for others not. There is a notion of "default" support procedures for an index, which are those with `amproclefttype` and `amprocrighttype` both equal to the index operator class's `opcintype`.

48.6. `pg_attrdef`

The catalog `pg_attrdef` stores column default values. The main information about columns is stored in `pg_attribute` (see below). Only columns that explicitly specify a default value (when the table is created or the column is added) will have an entry here.

Table 48-6. `pg_attrdef` Columns

Name	Type	References	Description
oid	oid		Row identifier (hidden attribute; must be explicitly selected)
adrelid	oid	pg_class.oid	The table this column belongs to
adnum	int2	pg_attribute.attnum	The number of the column
adbin	pg_node_tree		The internal representation of the column default value

Name	Type	References	Description
adsrc	text		A human-readable representation of the default value

The `adsrc` field is historical, and is best not used, because it does not track outside changes that might affect the representation of the default value. Reverse-compiling the `adbin` field (with `pg_get_expr` for example) is a better way to display the default value.

48.7. `pg_attribute`

The catalog `pg_attribute` stores information about table columns. There will be exactly one `pg_attribute` row for every column in every table in the database. (There will also be attribute entries for indexes, and indeed all objects that have `pg_class` entries.)

The term attribute is equivalent to column and is used for historical reasons.

Table 48-7. `pg_attribute` Columns

Name	Type	References	Description
attrelid	oid	pg_class.oid	The table this column belongs to
attname	name		The column name
atttypid	oid	pg_type.oid	The data type of this column

Name	Type	References	Description
attstattarget	int4		attstattarget controls the level of detail of statistics accumulated for this column by ANALYZE. A zero value indicates that no statistics should be collected. A negative value says to use the system default statistics target. The exact meaning of positive values is data type-dependent. For scalar data types, attstattarget is both the target number of "most common values" to collect, and the target number of histogram bins to create.
attlen	int2		A copy of pg_type.typlen of this column's type
attnum	int2		The number of the column. Ordinary columns are numbered from 1 up. System columns, such as oid, have (arbitrary) negative numbers.
attndims	int4		Number of dimensions, if the column is an array type; otherwise 0. (Presently, the number of dimensions of an array is not enforced, so any nonzero value effectively means "it's an array".)

Name	Type	References	Description
attcacheoff	int4		Always -1 in storage, but when loaded into a row descriptor in memory this might be updated to cache the offset of the attribute within the row
atttypmod	int4		`atttypmod` records type-specific data supplied at table creation time (for example, the maximum length of a `varchar` column). It is passed to type-specific input functions and length coercion functions. The value will generally be -1 for types that do not need `atttypmod`.
attbyval	bool		A copy of `pg_type.typbyval` of this column's type
attstorage	char		Normally a copy of `pg_type.typstorage` of this column's type. For TOAST-able data types, this can be altered after column creation to control storage policy.
attalign	char		A copy of `pg_type.typalign` of this column's type
attnotnull	bool		This represents a not-null constraint. It is possible to change this column to enable or disable the constraint.
atthasdef	bool		This column has a default value, in which case there will be a corresponding entry in the `pg_attrdef` catalog that actually defines the value.

Name	Type	References	Description
attisdropped	bool		This column has been dropped and is no longer valid. A dropped column is still physically present in the table, but is ignored by the parser and so cannot be accessed via SQL.
attislocal	bool		This column is defined locally in the relation. Note that a column can be locally defined and inherited simultaneously.
attinhcount	int4		The number of direct ancestors this column has. A column with a nonzero number of ancestors cannot be dropped nor renamed.
attcollation	oid	pg_collation.oid	The defined collation of the column, or zero if the column is not of a collatable data type.
attacl	aclitem[]		Column-level access privileges, if any have been granted specifically on this column
attoptions	text[]		Attribute-level options, as "keyword=value" strings
attfdwoptions	text[]		Attribute-level foreign data wrapper options, as "keyword=value" strings

In a dropped column's `pg_attribute` entry, `atttypid` is reset to zero, but `attlen` and the other fields copied from `pg_type` are still valid. This arrangement is needed to cope with the situation where the dropped column's data type was later dropped, and so there is no `pg_type` row anymore. `attlen` and the other fields can be used to interpret the contents of a row of the table.

48.8. `pg_authid`

The catalog `pg_authid` contains information about database authorization identifiers (roles). A role subsumes the concepts of "users" and "groups". A user is essentially just a role with the `rolcanlogin` flag set. Any role (with or without `rolcanlogin`) can have other roles as members; see `pg_auth_members`.

Since this catalog contains passwords, it must not be publicly readable. `pg_roles` is a publicly readable view on `pg_authid` that blanks out the password field.

Chapter 20 contains detailed information about user and privilege management.

Because user identities are cluster-wide, `pg_authid` is shared across all databases of a cluster: there is only one copy of `pg_authid` per cluster, not one per database.

Table 48-8. `pg_authid` Columns

Name	Type	Description
oid	oid	Row identifier (hidden attribute; must be explicitly selected)
rolname	name	Role name
rolsuper	bool	Role has superuser privileges
rolinherit	bool	Role automatically inherits privileges of roles it is a member of
rolcreaterole	bool	Role can create more roles
rolcreatedb	bool	Role can create databases
rolcatupdate	bool	Role can update system catalogs directly. (Even a superuser cannot do this unless this column is true)
rolcanlogin	bool	Role can log in. That is, this role can be given as the initial session authorization identifier
rolreplication	bool	Role is a replication role. That is, this role can initiate streaming replication (see Section 25.2.5) and set/unset the system backup mode using `pg_start_backup` and `pg_stop_backup`
rolconnlimit	int4	For roles that can log in, this sets maximum number of concurrent connections this role can make. -1 means no limit.

Name	Type	Description
rolpassword	text	Password (possibly encrypted); null if none. If the password is encrypted, this column will begin with the string md5 followed by a 32-character hexadecimal MD5 hash. The MD5 hash will be of the user's password concatenated to their user name. For example, if user joe has password xyzzy, PostgreSQL will store the md5 hash of xyzzyjoe. A password that does not follow that format is assumed to be unencrypted.
rolvaliduntil	timestamptz	Password expiry time (only used for password authentication); null if no expiration

48.9. `pg_auth_members`

The catalog pg_auth_members shows the membership relations between roles. Any non-circular set of relationships is allowed.

Because user identities are cluster-wide, pg_auth_members is shared across all databases of a cluster: there is only one copy of pg_auth_members per cluster, not one per database.

Table 48-9. `pg_auth_members` Columns

Name	Type	References	Description
roleid	oid	pg_authid.oid	ID of a role that has a member
member	oid	pg_authid.oid	ID of a role that is a member of roleid
grantor	oid	pg_authid.oid	ID of the role that granted this membership
admin_option	bool		True if member can grant membership in roleid to others

48.10. `pg_cast`

The catalog pg_cast stores data type conversion paths, both built-in and user-defined.

It should be noted that pg_cast does not represent every type conversion that the system knows how to perform; only those that cannot be deduced from some generic rule. For example, casting between a domain and its base type is not explicitly represented in pg_cast. Another important exception is that "automatic I/O conversion casts", those performed using a data type's own I/O functions to convert to or from text or other string types, are not explicitly represented in pg_cast.

Table 48-10. pg_cast Columns

Name	Type	References	Description
oid	oid		Row identifier (hidden attribute; must be explicitly selected)
castsource	oid	pg_type.oid	OID of the source data type
casttarget	oid	pg_type.oid	OID of the target data type
castfunc	oid	pg_proc.oid	The OID of the function to use to perform this cast. Zero is stored if the cast method doesn't require a function.
castcontext	char		Indicates what contexts the cast can be invoked in. e means only as an explicit cast (using CAST or :: syntax). a means implicitly in assignment to a target column, as well as explicitly. i means implicitly in expressions, as well as the other cases.
castmethod	char		Indicates how the cast is performed. f means that the function specified in the castfunc field is used. i means that the input/output functions are used. b means that the types are binary-coercible, thus no conversion is required.

The cast functions listed in pg_cast must always take the cast source type as their first argument type, and return the cast destination type as their result type. A cast function can have up to three arguments. The second argument, if present, must be type integer; it receives the type modifier associated with the destination type, or -1 if there is none. The third argument, if present, must be type `boolean`; it receives `true` if the cast is an explicit cast, `false` otherwise.

It is legitimate to create a `pg_cast` entry in which the source and target types are the same, if the associated function takes more than one argument. Such entries represent "length coercion functions" that coerce values of the type to be legal for a particular type modifier value.

When a `pg_cast` entry has different source and target types and a function that takes more than one argument, it represents converting from one type to another and applying a length coercion in a single step. When no such entry is available, coercion to a type that uses a type modifier involves two steps, one to convert between data types and a second to apply the modifier.

48.11. `pg_class`

The catalog `pg_class` catalogs tables and most everything else that has columns or is otherwise similar to a table. This includes indexes (but see also `pg_index`), sequences, views, materialized views, composite types, and TOAST tables; see `relkind`. Below, when we mean all of these kinds of objects we speak of "relations". Not all columns are meaningful for all relation types.

Table 48-11. `pg_class` Columns

Name	Type	References	Description
oid	oid		Row identifier (hidden attribute; must be explicitly selected)
relname	name		Name of the table, index, view, etc.
relnamespace	oid	pg_namespace.oid	The OID of the namespace that contains this relation
reltype	oid	pg_type.oid	The OID of the data type that corresponds to this table's row type, if any (zero for indexes, which have no pg_type entry)
reloftype	oid	pg_type.oid	For typed tables, the OID of the underlying composite type, zero for all other relations
relowner	oid	pg_authid.oid	Owner of the relation
relam	oid	pg_am.oid	If this is an index, the access method used (B-tree, hash, etc.)

Name	Type	References	Description
relfilenode	oid		Name of the on-disk file of this relation; zero means this is a "mapped" relation whose disk file name is determined by low-level state
reltablespace	oid	pg_tablespace.oid	The tablespace in which this relation is stored. If zero, the database's default tablespace is implied. (Not meaningful if the relation has no on-disk file.)
relpages	int4		Size of the on-disk representation of this table in pages (of size BLCKSZ). This is only an estimate used by the planner. It is updated by VACUUM, ANALYZE, and a few DDL commands such as CREATE INDEX.
reltuples	float4		Number of rows in the table. This is only an estimate used by the planner. It is updated by VACUUM, ANALYZE, and a few DDL commands such as CREATE INDEX.
relallvisible	int4		Number of pages that are marked all-visible in the table's visibility map. This is only an estimate used by the planner. It is updated by VACUUM, ANALYZE, and a few DDL commands such as CREATE INDEX.

Name	Type	References	Description
reltoastrelid	oid	pg_class.oid	OID of the TOAST table associated with this table, 0 if none. The TOAST table stores large attributes "out of line" in a secondary table.
relhasindex	bool		True if this is a table and it has (or recently had) any indexes
relisshared	bool		True if this table is shared across all databases in the cluster. Only certain system catalogs (such as pg_database) are shared.
relpersistence	char		p = permanent table, u = unlogged table, t = temporary table
relkind	char		r = ordinary table, i = index, S = sequence, v = view, m = materialized view, c = composite type, t = TOAST table, f = foreign table
relnatts	int2		Number of user columns in the relation (system columns not counted). There must be this many corresponding entries in pg_attribute. See also pg_attribute.attnum.
relchecks	int2		Number of CHECK constraints on the table; see pg_constraint catalog
relhasoids	bool		True if we generate an OID for each row of the relation

Name	Type	References	Description
relhaspkey	bool		True if the table has (or once had) a primary key
relhasrules	bool		True if table has (or once had) rules; see `pg_rewrite` catalog
relhastriggers	bool		True if table has (or once had) triggers; see `pg_trigger` catalog
relhassubclass	bool		True if table has (or once had) any inheritance children
relispopulated	bool		True if relation is populated (this is true for all relations other than some materialized views)
relreplident	char		Columns used to form "replica identity" for rows: d = default (primary key, if any), n = nothing, f = all columns i = index with `indisreplident` set, or default
relfrozenxid	xid		All transaction IDs before this one have been replaced with a permanent ("frozen") transaction ID in this table. This is used to track whether the table needs to be vacuumed in order to prevent transaction ID wraparound or to allow `pg_clog` to be shrunk. Zero (`InvalidTransactionI` if the relation is not a table.

Name	Type	References	Description
relminmxid	xid		All multixact IDs before this one have been replaced by a transaction ID in this table. This is used to track whether the table needs to be vacuumed in order to prevent multixact ID wraparound or to allow `pg_multixact` to be shrunk. Zero (`InvalidMultiXactId`) if the relation is not a table.
relacl	aclitem[]		Access privileges; see **GRANT** and **REVOKE** for details
reloptions	text[]		Access-method-specific options, as "keyword=value" strings

Several of the Boolean flags in `pg_class` are maintained lazily: they are guaranteed to be true if that's the correct state, but may not be reset to false immediately when the condition is no longer true. For example, `relhasindex` is set by CREATE INDEX, but it is never cleared by DROP INDEX. Instead, VACUUM clears `relhasindex` if it finds the table has no indexes. This arrangement avoids race conditions and improves concurrency.

48.12. `pg_collation`

The catalog `pg_collation` describes the available collations, which are essentially mappings from an SQL name to operating system locale categories. See Section 22.2 for more information.

Table 48-12. `pg_collation` Columns

Name	Type	References	Description
oid	oid		Row identifier (hidden attribute; must be explicitly selected)
collname	name		Collation name (unique per namespace and encoding)

Name	Type	References	Description
collnamespace	oid	pg_namespace.oid	The OID of the namespace that contains this collation
collowner	oid	pg_authid.oid	Owner of the collation
collencoding	int4		Encoding in which the collation is applicable, or -1 if it works for any encoding
collcollate	name		LC_COLLATE for this collation object
collctype	name		LC_CTYPE for this collation object

Note that the unique key on this catalog is (collname, collencoding, collnamespace) not just (collname, collnamespace). PostgreSQL generally ignores all collations that do not have collencoding equal to either the current database's encoding or -1, and creation of new entries with the same name as an entry with collencoding = -1 is forbidden. Therefore it is sufficient to use a qualified SQL name (*schema.name*) to identify a collation, even though this is not unique according to the catalog definition. The reason for defining the catalog this way is that initdb fills it in at cluster initialization time with entries for all locales available on the system, so it must be able to hold entries for all encodings that might ever be used in the cluster.

In the template0 database, it could be useful to create collations whose encoding does not match the database encoding, since they could match the encodings of databases later cloned from template0. This would currently have to be done manually.

48.13. pg_constraint

The catalog pg_constraint stores check, primary key, unique, foreign key, and exclusion constraints on tables. (Column constraints are not treated specially. Every column constraint is equivalent to some table constraint.) Not-null constraints are represented in the pg_attribute catalog, not here.

User-defined constraint triggers (created with CREATE CONSTRAINT TRIGGER) also give rise to an entry in this table.

Check constraints on domains are stored here, too.

Table 48-13. pg_constraint Columns

Name	Type	References	Description
oid	oid		Row identifier (hidden attribute; must be explicitly selected)
conname	name		Constraint name (not necessarily unique!)

Name	Type	References	Description
connamespace	oid	pg_namespace.oid	The OID of the namespace that contains this constraint
contype	char		c = check constraint, f = foreign key constraint, p = primary key constraint, u = unique constraint, t = constraint trigger, x = exclusion constraint
condeferrable	bool		Is the constraint deferrable?
condeferred	bool		Is the constraint deferred by default?
convalidated	bool		Has the constraint been validated? Currently, can only be false for foreign keys and CHECK constraints
conrelid	oid	pg_class.oid	The table this constraint is on; 0 if not a table constraint
contypid	oid	pg_type.oid	The domain this constraint is on; 0 if not a domain constraint
conindid	oid	pg_class.oid	The index supporting this constraint, if it's a unique, primary key, foreign key, or exclusion constraint; else 0
confrelid	oid	pg_class.oid	If a foreign key, the referenced table; else 0
confupdtype	char		Foreign key update action code: a = no action, r = restrict, c = cascade, n = set null, d = set default
confdeltype	char		Foreign key deletion action code: a = no action, r = restrict, c = cascade, n = set null, d = set default

Name	Type	References	Description
confmatchtype	char		Foreign key match type: f = full, p = partial, s = simple
conislocal	bool	.	This constraint is defined locally for the relation. Note that a constraint can be locally defined and inherited simultaneously.
coninhcount	int4		The number of direct inheritance ancestors this constraint has. A constraint with a nonzero number of ancestors cannot be dropped nor renamed.
connoinherit	bool		This constraint is defined locally for the relation. It is a non-inheritable constraint.
conkey	int2[]	pg_attribute.attnum	If a table constraint (including foreign keys, but not constraint triggers), list of the constrained columns
confkey	int2[]	pg_attribute.attnum	If a foreign key, list of the referenced columns
conpfeqop	oid[]	pg_operator.oid	If a foreign key, list of the equality operators for PK = FK comparisons
conppeqop	oid[]	pg_operator.oid	If a foreign key, list of the equality operators for PK = PK comparisons
conffeqop	oid[]	pg_operator.oid	If a foreign key, list of the equality operators for FK = FK comparisons
conexclop	oid[]	pg_operator.oid	If an exclusion constraint, list of the per-column exclusion operators

Name	Type	References	Description
conbin	pg_node_tree		If a check constraint, an internal representation of the expression
consrc	text		If a check constraint, a human-readable representation of the expression

In the case of an exclusion constraint, conkey is only useful for constraint elements that are simple column references. For other cases, a zero appears in conkey and the associated index must be consulted to discover the expression that is constrained. (conkey thus has the same contents as pg_index.indkey for the index.)

Note: consrc is not updated when referenced objects change; for example, it won't track renaming of columns. Rather than relying on this field, it's best to use pg_get_constraintdef() to extract the definition of a check constraint.

Note: pg_class.relchecks needs to agree with the number of check-constraint entries found in this table for each relation.

48.14. pg_conversion

The catalog pg_conversion describes encoding conversion procedures. See CREATE CONVERSION for more information.

Table 48-14. pg_conversion Columns

Name	Type	References	Description
oid	oid		Row identifier (hidden attribute; must be explicitly selected)
conname	name		Conversion name (unique within a namespace)
connamespace	oid	pg_namespace.oid	The OID of the namespace that contains this conversion
conowner	oid	pg_authid.oid	Owner of the conversion
conforencoding	int4		Source encoding ID

Name	Type	References	Description
contoencoding	int4		Destination encoding ID
conproc	regproc	pg_proc.oid	Conversion procedure
condefault	bool		True if this is the default conversion

48.15. pg_database

The catalog pg_database stores information about the available databases. Databases are created with the CREATE DATABASE command. Consult Chapter 21 for details about the meaning of some of the parameters.

Unlike most system catalogs, pg_database is shared across all databases of a cluster: there is only one copy of pg_database per cluster, not one per database.

Table 48-15. pg_database Columns

Name	Type	References	Description
oid	oid		Row identifier (hidden attribute; must be explicitly selected)
datname	name		Database name
datdba	oid	pg_authid.oid	Owner of the database, usually the user who created it
encoding	int4		Character encoding for this database (pg_encoding_to_char can translate this number to the encoding name)
datcollate	name		LC_COLLATE for this database
datctype	name		LC_CTYPE for this database
datistemplate	bool		If true, then this database can be cloned by any user with CREATEDB privileges; if false, then only superusers or the owner of the database can clone it.

Name	Type	References	Description
datallowconn	bool		If false then no one can connect to this database. This is used to protect the `template0` database from being altered.
datconnlimit	int4		Sets maximum number of concurrent connections that can be made to this database. -1 means no limit.
datlastsysoid	oid		Last system OID in the database; useful particularly to pg_dump
datfrozenxid	xid		All transaction IDs before this one have been replaced with a permanent ("frozen") transaction ID in this database. This is used to track whether the database needs to be vacuumed in order to prevent transaction ID wraparound or to allow `pg_clog` to be shrunk. It is the minimum of the per-table `pg_class.relfrozenxi` values.

Name	Type	References	Description
datminmxid	xid		All multixact IDs before this one have been replaced with a transaction ID in this database. This is used to track whether the database needs to be vacuumed in order to prevent multixact ID wraparound or to allow `pg_multixact` to be shrunk. It is the minimum of the per-table `pg_class.relminmxid` values.
dattablespace	oid	pg_tablespace.oid	The default tablespace for the database. Within this database, all tables for which `pg_class.reltablespa` is zero will be stored in this tablespace; in particular, all the non-shared system catalogs will be there.
datacl	aclitem[]		Access privileges; see GRANT and REVOKE for details

48.16. `pg_db_role_setting`

The catalog `pg_db_role_setting` records the default values that have been set for run-time configuration variables, for each role and database combination.

Unlike most system catalogs, `pg_db_role_setting` is shared across all databases of a cluster: there is only one copy of `pg_db_role_setting` per cluster, not one per database.

Table 48-16. `pg_db_role_setting` Columns

Name	Type	References	Description

Name	Type	References	Description
setdatabase	oid	pg_database.oid	The OID of the database the setting is applicable to, or zero if not database-specific
setrole	oid	pg_authid.oid	The OID of the role the setting is applicable to, or zero if not role-specific
setconfig	text[]		Defaults for run-time configuration variables

48.17. `pg_default_acl`

The catalog `pg_default_acl` stores initial privileges to be assigned to newly created objects.

Table 48-17. `pg_default_acl` Columns

Name	Type	References	Description
oid	oid		Row identifier (hidden attribute; must be explicitly selected)
defaclrole	oid	pg_authid.oid	The OID of the role associated with this entry
defaclnamespace	oid	pg_namespace.oid	The OID of the namespace associated with this entry, or 0 if none
defaclobjtype	char		Type of object this entry is for: r = relation (table, view), S = sequence, f = function, T = type
defaclacl	aclitem[]		Access privileges that this type of object should have on creation

A `pg_default_acl` entry shows the initial privileges to be assigned to an object belonging to the indicated user. There are currently two types of entry: "global" entries with `defaclnamespace` = 0, and "per-schema" entries that reference a particular schema. If a global entry is present then it *overrides* the normal hard-wired default privileges for the object type. A per-schema entry, if present, represents privileges to be *added to* the global or hard-wired default privileges.

Note that when an ACL entry in another catalog is null, it is taken to represent the hard-wired default privileges for its object, *not* whatever might be in `pg_default_acl` at the moment. `pg_default_acl` is only consulted during object creation.

48.18. `pg_depend`

The catalog `pg_depend` records the dependency relationships between database objects. This information allows DROP commands to find which other objects must be dropped by DROP CASCADE or prevent dropping in the DROP RESTRICT case.

See also `pg_shdepend`, which performs a similar function for dependencies involving objects that are shared across a database cluster.

Table 48-18. `pg_depend` Columns

Name	Type	References	Description
classid	oid	pg_class.oid	The OID of the system catalog the dependent object is in
objid	oid	any OID column	The OID of the specific dependent object
objsubid	int4		For a table column, this is the column number (the `objid` and `classid` refer to the table itself). For all other object types, this column is zero.
refclassid	oid	pg_class.oid	The OID of the system catalog the referenced object is in
refobjid	oid	any OID column	The OID of the specific referenced object
refobjsubid	int4		For a table column, this is the column number (the `refobjid` and `refclassid` refer to the table itself). For all other object types, this column is zero.
deptype	char		A code defining the specific semantics of this dependency relationship; see text

In all cases, a `pg_depend` entry indicates that the referenced object cannot be dropped without also dropping the dependent object. However, there are several subflavors identified by `deptype`:

DEPENDENCY_NORMAL (n)

A normal relationship between separately-created objects. The dependent object can be dropped without affecting the referenced object. The referenced object can only be dropped by specifying CASCADE, in which case the dependent object is dropped, too. Example: a table column has a normal dependency on its data type.

DEPENDENCY_AUTO (a)

The dependent object can be dropped separately from the referenced object, and should be automatically dropped (regardless of RESTRICT or CASCADE mode) if the referenced object is dropped. Example: a named constraint on a table is made autodependent on the table, so that it will go away if the table is dropped.

DEPENDENCY_INTERNAL (i)

The dependent object was created as part of creation of the referenced object, and is really just a part of its internal implementation. A DROP of the dependent object will be disallowed outright (we'll tell the user to issue a DROP against the referenced object, instead). A DROP of the referenced object will be propagated through to drop the dependent object whether CASCADE is specified or not. Example: a trigger that's created to enforce a foreign-key constraint is made internally dependent on the constraint's pg_constraint entry.

DEPENDENCY_EXTENSION (e)

The dependent object is a member of the *extension* that is the referenced object (see pg_extension). The dependent object can be dropped only via DROP EXTENSION on the referenced object. Functionally this dependency type acts the same as an internal dependency, but it's kept separate for clarity and to simplify pg_dump.

DEPENDENCY_PIN (p)

There is no dependent object; this type of entry is a signal that the system itself depends on the referenced object, and so that object must never be deleted. Entries of this type are created only by initdb. The columns for the dependent object contain zeroes.

Other dependency flavors might be needed in future.

48.19. pg_description

The catalog pg_description stores optional descriptions (comments) for each database object. Descriptions can be manipulated with the COMMENT command and viewed with psql's \d commands. Descriptions of many built-in system objects are provided in the initial contents of pg_description.

See also pg_shdescription, which performs a similar function for descriptions involving objects that are shared across a database cluster.

Table 48-19. pg_description Columns

Name	Type	References	Description
objoid	oid	any OID column	The OID of the object this description pertains to

Name	Type	References	Description
classoid	oid	pg_class.oid	The OID of the system catalog this object appears in
objsubid	int4		For a comment on a table column, this is the column number (the objoid and classoid refer to the table itself). For all other object types, this column is zero.
description	text		Arbitrary text that serves as the description of this object

48.20. pg_enum

The pg_enum catalog contains entries showing the values and labels for each enum type. The internal representation of a given enum value is actually the OID of its associated row in pg_enum.

Table 48-20. pg_enum Columns

Name	Type	References	Description
oid	oid		Row identifier (hidden attribute; must be explicitly selected)
enumtypid	oid	pg_type.oid	The OID of the pg_type entry owning this enum value
enumsortorder	float4		The sort position of this enum value within its enum type
enumlabel	name		The textual label for this enum value

The OIDs for pg_enum rows follow a special rule: even-numbered OIDs are guaranteed to be ordered in the same way as the sort ordering of their enum type. That is, if two even OIDs belong to the same enum type, the smaller OID must have the smaller enumsortorder value. Odd-numbered OID values need bear no relationship to the sort order. This rule allows the enum comparison routines to avoid catalog lookups in many common cases. The routines that create and alter enum types attempt to assign even OIDs to enum values whenever possible.

When an enum type is created, its members are assigned sort-order positions 1..*n*. But members added later might be given negative or fractional values of enumsortorder. The only requirement on these values is that they be correctly ordered and unique within each enum type.

48.21. `pg_event_trigger`

The catalog `pg_event_trigger` stores event triggers. See Chapter 37 for more information.

Table 48-21. `pg_event_trigger` Columns

Name	Type	References	Description
evtname	name		Trigger name (must be unique)
evtevent	name		Identifies the event for which this trigger fires
evtowner	oid	pg_authid.oid	Owner of the event trigger
evtfoid	oid	pg_proc.oid	The function to be called
evtenabled	char		Controls in which session_replication_role modes the event trigger fires. O = trigger fires in "origin" and "local" modes, D = trigger is disabled, R = trigger fires in "replica" mode, A = trigger fires always.
evttags	text[]		Command tags for which this trigger will fire. If NULL, the firing of this trigger is not restricted on the basis of the command tag.

48.22. `pg_extension`

The catalog `pg_extension` stores information about the installed extensions. See Section 35.15 for details about extensions.

Table 48-22. `pg_extension` Columns

Name	Type	References	Description

Name	Type	References	Description
oid	oid		Row identifier (hidden attribute; must be explicitly selected)
extname	name		Name of the extension
extowner	oid	pg_authid.oid	Owner of the extension
extnamespace	oid	pg_namespace.oid	Schema containing the extension's exported objects
extrelocatable	bool		True if extension can be relocated to another schema
extversion	text		Version name for the extension
extconfig	oid[]	pg_class.oid	Array of regclass OIDs for the extension's configuration table(s), or NULL if none
extcondition	text[]		Array of WHERE-clause filter conditions for the extension's configuration table(s), or NULL if none

Note that unlike most catalogs with a "namespace" column, extnamespace is not meant to imply that the extension belongs to that schema. Extension names are never schema-qualified. Rather, extnamespace indicates the schema that contains most or all of the extension's objects. If extrelocatable is true, then this schema must in fact contain all schema-qualifiable objects belonging to the extension.

48.23. pg_foreign_data_wrapper

The catalog pg_foreign_data_wrapper stores foreign-data wrapper definitions. A foreign-data wrapper is the mechanism by which external data, residing on foreign servers, is accessed.

Table 48-23. pg_foreign_data_wrapper Columns

Name	Type	References	Description
oid	oid		Row identifier (hidden attribute; must be explicitly selected)
fdwname	name		Name of the foreign-data wrapper
fdwowner	oid	pg_authid.oid	Owner of the foreign-data wrapper

Name	Type	References	Description
fdwhandler	oid	pg_proc.oid	References a handler function that is responsible for supplying execution routines for the foreign-data wrapper. Zero if no handler is provided
fdwvalidator	oid	pg_proc.oid	References a validator function that is responsible for checking the validity of the options given to the foreign-data wrapper, as well as options for foreign servers and user mappings using the foreign-data wrapper. Zero if no validator is provided
fdwacl	aclitem[]		Access privileges; see GRANT and REVOKE for details
fdwoptions	text[]		Foreign-data wrapper specific options, as "keyword=value" strings

48.24. `pg_foreign_server`

The catalog `pg_foreign_server` stores foreign server definitions. A foreign server describes a source of external data, such as a remote server. Foreign servers are accessed via foreign-data wrappers.

Table 48-24. `pg_foreign_server` Columns

Name	Type	References	Description
oid	oid		Row identifier (hidden attribute; must be explicitly selected)
srvname	name		Name of the foreign server
srvowner	oid	pg_authid.oid	Owner of the foreign server

Name	Type	References	Description
srvfdw	oid	pg_foreign_data_wrapper.oid	OID of the foreign-data wrapper of this foreign server
srvtype	text		Type of the server (optional)
srvversion	text		Version of the server (optional)
srvacl	aclitem[]		Access privileges; see GRANT and REVOKE for details
srvoptions	text[]		Foreign server specific options, as "keyword=value" strings

48.25. `pg_foreign_table`

The catalog `pg_foreign_table` contains auxiliary information about foreign tables. A foreign table is primarily represented by a `pg_class` entry, just like a regular table. Its `pg_foreign_table` entry contains the information that is pertinent only to foreign tables and not any other kind of relation.

Table 48-25. `pg_foreign_table` Columns

Name	Type	References	Description
ftrelid	oid	pg_class.oid	OID of the pg_class entry for this foreign table
ftserver	oid	pg_foreign_server.oid	OID of the foreign server for this foreign table
ftoptions	text[]		Foreign table options, as "keyword=value" strings

48.26. `pg_index`

The catalog `pg_index` contains part of the information about indexes. The rest is mostly in `pg_class`.

Table 48-26. `pg_index` Columns

Name	Type	References	Description

Name	Type	References	Description
indexrelid	oid	pg_class.oid	The OID of the pg_class entry for this index
indrelid	oid	pg_class.oid	The OID of the pg_class entry for the table this index is for
indnatts	int2		The number of columns in the index (duplicates pg_class.relnatts)
indisunique	bool		If true, this is a unique index
indisprimary	bool		If true, this index represents the primary key of the table (indisunique should always be true when this is true)
indisexclusion	bool		If true, this index supports an exclusion constraint
indimmediate	bool		If true, the uniqueness check is enforced immediately on insertion (irrelevant if indisunique is not true)
indisclustered	bool		If true, the table was last clustered on this index
indisvalid	bool		If true, the index is currently valid for queries. False means the index is possibly incomplete: it must still be modified by INSERT/UPDATE operations, but it cannot safely be used for queries. If it is unique, the uniqueness property is not guaranteed true either.

Name	Type	References	Description
indcheckxmin	bool		If true, queries must not use the index until the `xmin` of this `pg_index` row is below their `TransactionXmin` event horizon, because the table may contain broken HOT chains with incompatible rows that they can see
indisready	bool		If true, the index is currently ready for inserts. False means the index must be ignored by `INSERT`/`UPDATE` operations.
indislive	bool		If false, the index is in process of being dropped, and should be ignored for all purposes (including HOT-safety decisions)
indisreplident	bool		If true this index has been chosen as "replica identity" using `ALTER TABLE ... REPLICA IDENTITY USING INDEX ...`
indkey	int2vector	pg_attribute.attnum	This is an array of `indnatts` values that indicate which table columns this index indexes. For example a value of 1 3 would mean that the first and the third table columns make up the index key. A zero in this array indicates that the corresponding index attribute is an expression over the table columns, rather than a simple column reference.

Name	Type	References	Description
indcollation	oidvector	pg_collation.oid	For each column in the index key, this contains the OID of the collation to use for the index.
indclass	oidvector	pg_opclass.oid	For each column in the index key, this contains the OID of the operator class to use. See pg_opclass for details.
indoption	int2vector		This is an array of indnatts values that store per-column flag bits. The meaning of the bits is defined by the index's access method.
indexprs	pg_node_tree		Expression trees (in nodeToString() representation) for index attributes that are not simple column references. This is a list with one element for each zero entry in indkey. Null if all index attributes are simple references.
indpred	pg_node_tree		Expression tree (in nodeToString() representation) for partial index predicate. Null if not a partial index.

48.27. pg_inherits

The catalog pg_inherits records information about table inheritance hierarchies. There is one entry for each direct child table in the database. (Indirect inheritance can be determined by following chains of entries.)

Table 48-27. pg_inherits Columns

Name	Type	References	Description

Name	Type	References	Description
inhrelid	oid	pg_class.oid	The OID of the child table
inhparent	oid	pg_class.oid	The OID of the parent table
inhseqno	int4		If there is more than one direct parent for a child table (multiple inheritance), this number tells the order in which the inherited columns are to be arranged. The count starts at 1.

48.28. pg_language

The catalog pg_language registers languages in which you can write functions or stored procedures. See CREATE LANGUAGE and Chapter 39 for more information about language handlers.

Table 48-28. pg_language Columns

Name	Type	References	Description
oid	oid		Row identifier (hidden attribute; must be explicitly selected)
lanname	name		Name of the language
lanowner	oid	pg_authid.oid	Owner of the language
lanispl	bool		This is false for internal languages (such as SQL) and true for user-defined languages. Currently, pg_dump still uses this to determine which languages need to be dumped, but this might be replaced by a different mechanism in the future.

Name	Type	References	Description
lanpltrusted	bool		True if this is a trusted language, which means that it is believed not to grant access to anything outside the normal SQL execution environment. Only superusers can create functions in untrusted languages.
lanplcallfoid	oid	pg_proc.oid	For noninternal languages this references the language handler, which is a special function that is responsible for executing all functions that are written in the particular language
laninline	oid	pg_proc.oid	This references a function that is responsible for executing "inline" anonymous code blocks (DO blocks). Zero if inline blocks are not supported.
lanvalidator	oid	pg_proc.oid	This references a language validator function that is responsible for checking the syntax and validity of new functions when they are created. Zero if no validator is provided.
lanacl	aclitem[]		Access privileges; see GRANT and REVOKE for details

48.29. `pg_largeobject`

The catalog `pg_largeobject` holds the data making up "large objects". A large object is identified by an OID assigned when it is created. Each large object is broken into segments or "pages" small enough to be conveniently stored as rows in `pg_largeobject`. The amount of data per page is defined to be

LOBLKSIZE (which is currently BLCKSZ/4, or typically 2 kB).

Prior to PostgreSQL 9.0, there was no permission structure associated with large objects. As a result, pg_largeobject was publicly readable and could be used to obtain the OIDs (and contents) of all large objects in the system. This is no longer the case; use pg_largeobject_metadata to obtain a list of large object OIDs.

Table 48-29. pg_largeobject Columns

Name	Type	References	Description
loid	oid	pg_largeobject_metadata	Identifier of the large object that includes this page
pageno	int4		Page number of this page within its large object (counting from zero)
data	bytea		Actual data stored in the large object. This will never be more than LOBLKSIZE bytes and might be less.

Each row of pg_largeobject holds data for one page of a large object, beginning at byte offset (pageno * LOBLKSIZE) within the object. The implementation allows sparse storage: pages might be missing, and might be shorter than LOBLKSIZE bytes even if they are not the last page of the object. Missing regions within a large object read as zeroes.

48.30. pg_largeobject_metadata

The catalog pg_largeobject_metadata holds metadata associated with large objects. The actual large object data is stored in pg_largeobject.

Table 48-30. pg_largeobject_metadata Columns

Name	Type	References	Description
oid	oid		Row identifier (hidden attribute; must be explicitly selected)
lomowner	oid	pg_authid.oid	Owner of the large object
lomacl	aclitem[]		Access privileges; see GRANT and REVOKE for details

48.31. `pg_namespace`

The catalog `pg_namespace` stores namespaces. A namespace is the structure underlying SQL schemas: each namespace can have a separate collection of relations, types, etc. without name conflicts.

Table 48-31. `pg_namespace` Columns

Name	Type	References	Description
oid	oid		Row identifier (hidden attribute; must be explicitly selected)
nspname	name		Name of the namespace
nspowner	oid	pg_authid.oid	Owner of the namespace
nspacl	aclitem[]		Access privileges; see GRANT and REVOKE for details

48.32. `pg_opclass`

The catalog `pg_opclass` defines index access method operator classes. Each operator class defines semantics for index columns of a particular data type and a particular index access method. An operator class essentially specifies that a particular operator family is applicable to a particular indexable column data type. The set of operators from the family that are actually usable with the indexed column are whichever ones accept the column's data type as their left-hand input.

Operator classes are described at length in Section 35.14.

Table 48-32. `pg_opclass` Columns

Name	Type	References	Description
oid	oid		Row identifier (hidden attribute; must be explicitly selected)
opcmethod	oid	pg_am.oid	Index access method operator class is for
opcname	name		Name of this operator class
opcnamespace	oid	pg_namespace.oid	Namespace of this operator class
opcowner	oid	pg_authid.oid	Owner of the operator class

Name	Type	References	Description
opcfamily	oid	pg_opfamily.oid	Operator family containing the operator class
opcintype	oid	pg_type.oid	Data type that the operator class indexes
opcdefault	bool		True if this operator class is the default for opcintype
opckeytype	oid	pg_type.oid	Type of data stored in index, or zero if same as opcintype

An operator class's opcmethod must match the opfmethod of its containing operator family. Also, there must be no more than one pg_opclass row having opcdefault true for any given combination of opcmethod and opcintype.

48.33. pg_operator

The catalog pg_operator stores information about operators. See CREATE OPERATOR and Section 35.12 for more information.

Table 48-33. pg_operator Columns

Name	Type	References	Description
oid	oid		Row identifier (hidden attribute; must be explicitly selected)
oprname	name		Name of the operator
oprnamespace	oid	pg_namespace.oid	The OID of the namespace that contains this operator
oprowner	oid	pg_authid.oid	Owner of the operator
oprkind	char		b = infix ("both"), l = prefix ("left"), r = postfix ("right")
oprcanmerge	bool		This operator supports merge joins
oprcanhash	bool		This operator supports hash joins
oprleft	oid	pg_type.oid	Type of the left operand
oprright	oid	pg_type.oid	Type of the right operand

Name	Type	References	Description
oprresult	oid	pg_type.oid	Type of the result
oprcom	oid	pg_operator.oid	Commutator of this operator, if any
oprnegate	oid	pg_operator.oid	Negator of this operator, if any
oprcode	regproc	pg_proc.oid	Function that implements this operator
oprrest	regproc	pg_proc.oid	Restriction selectivity estimation function for this operator
oprjoin	regproc	pg_proc.oid	Join selectivity estimation function for this operator

Unused column contain zeroes. For example, `oprleft` is zero for a prefix operator.

48.34. `pg_opfamily`

The catalog `pg_opfamily` defines operator families. Each operator family is a collection of operators and associated support routines that implement the semantics specified for a particular index access method. Furthermore, the operators in a family are all "compatible", in a way that is specified by the access method. The operator family concept allows cross-data-type operators to be used with indexes and to be reasoned about using knowledge of access method semantics.

Operator families are described at length in Section 35.14.

Table 48-34. `pg_opfamily` Columns

Name	Type	References	Description
oid	oid		Row identifier (hidden attribute; must be explicitly selected)
opfmethod	oid	pg_am.oid	Index access method operator family is for
opfname	name		Name of this operator family
opfnamespace	oid	pg_namespace.oid	Namespace of this operator family
opfowner	oid	pg_authid.oid	Owner of the operator family

The majority of the information defining an operator family is not in its `pg_opfamily` row, but in the associated rows in `pg_amop`, `pg_amproc`, and `pg_opclass`.

48.35. `pg_pltemplate`

The catalog `pg_pltemplate` stores "template" information for procedural languages. A template for a language allows the language to be created in a particular database by a simple CREATE LANGUAGE command, with no need to specify implementation details.

Unlike most system catalogs, `pg_pltemplate` is shared across all databases of a cluster: there is only one copy of `pg_pltemplate` per cluster, not one per database. This allows the information to be accessible in each database as it is needed.

Table 48-35. `pg_pltemplate` Columns

Name	Type	Description
tmplname	name	Name of the language this template is for
tmpltrusted	boolean	True if language is considered trusted
tmpldbacreate	boolean	True if language may be created by a database owner
tmplhandler	text	Name of call handler function
tmplinline	text	Name of anonymous-block handler function, or null if none
tmplvalidator	text	Name of validator function, or null if none
tmpllibrary	text	Path of shared library that implements language
tmplacl	aclitem[]	Access privileges for template (not actually used)

There are not currently any commands that manipulate procedural language templates; to change the built-in information, a superuser must modify the table using ordinary INSERT, DELETE, or UPDATE commands.

> **Note:** It is likely that `pg_pltemplate` will be removed in some future release of PostgreSQL, in favor of keeping this knowledge about procedural languages in their respective extension installation scripts.

48.36. `pg_proc`

The catalog `pg_proc` stores information about functions (or procedures). See CREATE FUNCTION and Section 35.3 for more information.

The table contains data for aggregate functions as well as plain functions. If `proisagg` is true, there should be a matching row in `pg_aggregate`.

Table 48-36. `pg_proc` Columns

Name	Type	References	Description
oid	oid		Row identifier (hidden attribute; must be explicitly selected)
proname	name		Name of the function
pronamespace	oid	pg_namespace.oid	The OID of the namespace that contains this function
proowner	oid	pg_authid.oid	Owner of the function
prolang	oid	pg_language.oid	Implementation language or call interface of this function
procost	float4		Estimated execution cost (in units of cpu_operator_cost); if `proretset`, this is cost per row returned
prorows	float4		Estimated number of result rows (zero if not `proretset`)
provariadic	oid	pg_type.oid	Data type of the variadic array parameter's elements, or zero if the function does not have a variadic parameter
protransform	regproc	pg_proc.oid	Calls to this function can be simplified by this other function (see Section 35.9.11)
proisagg	bool		Function is an aggregate function
proiswindow	bool		Function is a window function
prosecdef	bool		Function is a security definer (i.e., a "setuid" function)

Name	Type	References	Description
proleakproof	bool		The function has no side effects. No information about the arguments is conveyed except via the return value. Any function that might throw an error depending on the values of its arguments is not leak-proof.
proisstrict	bool		Function returns null if any call argument is null. In that case the function won't actually be called at all. Functions that are not "strict" must be prepared to handle null inputs.
proretset	bool		Function returns a set (i.e., multiple values of the specified data type)
provolatile	char		provolatile tells whether the function's result depends only on its input arguments, or is affected by outside factors. It is i for "immutable" functions, which always deliver the same result for the same inputs. It is s for "stable" functions, whose results (for fixed inputs) do not change within a scan. It is v for "volatile" functions, whose results might change at any time. (Use v also for functions with side-effects, so that calls to them cannot get optimized away.)
pronargs	int2		Number of input arguments

Name	Type	References	Description
pronargdefaults	int2		Number of arguments that have defaults
prorettype	oid	pg_type.oid	Data type of the return value
proargtypes	oidvector	pg_type.oid	An array with the data types of the function arguments. This includes only input arguments (including INOUT and VARIADIC arguments), and thus represents the call signature of the function.
proallargtypes	oid[]	pg_type.oid	An array with the data types of the function arguments. This includes all arguments (including OUT and INOUT arguments); however, if all the arguments are IN arguments, this field will be null. Note that subscripting is 1-based, whereas for historical reasons proargtypes is subscripted from 0.
proargmodes	char[]		An array with the modes of the function arguments, encoded as i for IN arguments, o for OUT arguments, b for INOUT arguments, v for VARIADIC arguments, t for TABLE arguments. If all the arguments are IN arguments, this field will be null. Note that subscripts correspond to positions of proallargtypes not proargtypes.

Name	Type	References	Description
proargnames	text[]		An array with the names of the function arguments. Arguments without a name are set to empty strings in the array. If none of the arguments have a name, this field will be null. Note that subscripts correspond to positions of proallargtypes not proargtypes.
proargdefaults	pg_node_tree		Expression trees (in nodeToString() representation) for default values. This is a list with pronargdefaults elements, corresponding to the last *N input* arguments (i.e., the last *N* proargtypes positions). If none of the arguments have defaults, this field will be null.
prosrc	text		This tells the function handler how to invoke the function. It might be the actual source code of the function for interpreted languages, a link symbol, a file name, or just about anything else, depending on the implementation language/call convention.
probin	text		Additional information about how to invoke the function. Again, the interpretation is language-specific.
proconfig	text[]		Function's local settings for run-time configuration variables

Name	Type	References	Description
proacl	aclitem[]		Access privileges; see GRANT and REVOKE for details

For compiled functions, both built-in and dynamically loaded, prosrc contains the function's C-language name (link symbol). For all other currently-known language types, prosrc contains the function's source text. probin is unused except for dynamically-loaded C functions, for which it gives the name of the shared library file containing the function.

48.37. pg_range

The catalog pg_range stores information about range types. This is in addition to the types' entries in pg_type.

Table 48-37. pg_range Columns

Name	Type	References	Description
rngtypid	oid	pg_type.oid	OID of the range type
rngsubtype	oid	pg_type.oid	OID of the element type (subtype) of this range type
rngcollation	oid	pg_collation.oid	OID of the collation used for range comparisons, or 0 if none
rngsubopc	oid	pg_opclass.oid	OID of the subtype's operator class used for range comparisons
rngcanonical	regproc	pg_proc.oid	OID of the function to convert a range value into canonical form, or 0 if none
rngsubdiff	regproc	pg_proc.oid	OID of the function to return the difference between two element values as double precision, or 0 if none

rngsubopc (plus rngcollation, if the element type is collatable) determines the sort ordering used by the range type. rngcanonical is used when the element type is discrete. rngsubdiff is optional but should be supplied to improve performance of GiST indexes on the range type.

48.38. `pg_rewrite`

The catalog `pg_rewrite` stores rewrite rules for tables and views.

Table 48-38. `pg_rewrite` Columns

Name	Type	References	Description
oid	oid		Row identifier (hidden attribute; must be explicitly selected)
rulename	name		Rule name
ev_class	oid	pg_class.oid	The table this rule is for
ev_type	char		Event type that the rule is for: 1 = SELECT, 2 = UPDATE, 3 = INSERT, 4 = DELETE
ev_enabled	char		Controls in which session_replication_role modes the rule fires. O = rule fires in "origin" and "local" modes, D = rule is disabled, R = rule fires in "replica" mode, A = rule fires always.
is_instead	bool		True if the rule is an INSTEAD rule
ev_qual	pg_node_tree		Expression tree (in the form of a nodeToString() representation) for the rule's qualifying condition
ev_action	pg_node_tree		Query tree (in the form of a nodeToString() representation) for the rule's action

Note: `pg_class.relhasrules` must be true if a table has any rules in this catalog.

48.39. `pg_replication_slots`

The `pg_replication_slots` view provides a listing of all replication slots that currently exist on the database cluster, along with their current state.

For more on replication slots, see Section 25.2.6 and Chapter 46.

Table 48-39. `pg_replication_slots` Columns

Name	Type	References	Description
slot_name	name		A unique, cluster-wide identifier for the replication slot
plugin	name		The base name of the shared object containing the output plugin this logical slot is using, or null for physical slots.
slot_type	text		The slot type - physical or logical
datoid	oid	pg_database.oid	The OID of the database this slot is associated with, or null. Only logical slots have an associated database.
database	text	pg_database.datname	The name of the database this slot is associated with, or null. Only logical slots have an associated database.
active	boolean		True if this slot is currently actively being used
xmin	xid		The oldest transaction that this slot needs the database to retain. VACUUM cannot remove tuples deleted by any later transaction.
catalog_xmin	xid		The oldest transaction affecting the system catalogs that this slot needs the database to retain. VACUUM cannot remove catalog tuples deleted by any later transaction.

Name	Type	References	Description
restart_lsn	pg_lsn		The address (LSN) of oldest WAL which still might be required by the consumer of this slot and thus won't be automatically removed during checkpoints.

48.40. pg_seclabel

The catalog pg_seclabel stores security labels on database objects. Security labels can be manipulated with the SECURITY LABEL command. For an easier way to view security labels, see Section 48.66.

See also pg_shseclabel, which performs a similar function for security labels of database objects that are shared across a database cluster.

Table 48-40. pg_seclabel Columns

Name	Type	References	Description
objoid	oid	any OID column	The OID of the object this security label pertains to
classoid	oid	pg_class.oid	The OID of the system catalog this object appears in
objsubid	int4		For a security label on a table column, this is the column number (the objoid and classoid refer to the table itself). For all other object types, this column is zero.
provider	text		The label provider associated with this label.
label	text		The security label applied to this object.

48.41. pg_shdepend

The catalog pg_shdepend records the dependency relationships between database objects and shared objects, such as roles. This information allows PostgreSQL to ensure that those objects are unreferenced before attempting to delete them.

See also `pg_depend`, which performs a similar function for dependencies involving objects within a single database.

Unlike most system catalogs, `pg_shdepend` is shared across all databases of a cluster: there is only one copy of `pg_shdepend` per cluster, not one per database.

Table 48-41. `pg_shdepend` Columns

Name	Type	References	Description
dbid	oid	pg_database.oid	The OID of the database the dependent object is in, or zero for a shared object
classid	oid	pg_class.oid	The OID of the system catalog the dependent object is in
objid	oid	any OID column	The OID of the specific dependent object
objsubid	int4		For a table column, this is the column number (the `objid` and `classid` refer to the table itself). For all other object types, this column is zero.
refclassid	oid	pg_class.oid	The OID of the system catalog the referenced object is in (must be a shared catalog)
refobjid	oid	any OID column	The OID of the specific referenced object
deptype	char		A code defining the specific semantics of this dependency relationship; see text

In all cases, a `pg_shdepend` entry indicates that the referenced object cannot be dropped without also dropping the dependent object. However, there are several subflavors identified by `deptype`:

SHARED_DEPENDENCY_OWNER (o)

The referenced object (which must be a role) is the owner of the dependent object.

SHARED_DEPENDENCY_ACL (a)

The referenced object (which must be a role) is mentioned in the ACL (access control list, i.e., privileges list) of the dependent object. (A SHARED_DEPENDENCY_ACL entry is not made for the owner of the object, since the owner will have a SHARED_DEPENDENCY_OWNER entry anyway.)

SHARED_DEPENDENCY_PIN (p)

There is no dependent object; this type of entry is a signal that the system itself depends on the referenced object, and so that object must never be deleted. Entries of this type are created only by initdb. The columns for the dependent object contain zeroes.

Other dependency flavors might be needed in future. Note in particular that the current definition only supports roles as referenced objects.

48.42. `pg_shdescription`

The catalog `pg_shdescription` stores optional descriptions (comments) for shared database objects. Descriptions can be manipulated with the COMMENT command and viewed with psql's \d commands.

See also `pg_description`, which performs a similar function for descriptions involving objects within a single database.

Unlike most system catalogs, `pg_shdescription` is shared across all databases of a cluster: there is only one copy of `pg_shdescription` per cluster, not one per database.

Table 48-42. `pg_shdescription` Columns

Name	Type	References	Description
objoid	oid	any OID column	The OID of the object this description pertains to
classoid	oid	pg_class.oid	The OID of the system catalog this object appears in
description	text		Arbitrary text that serves as the description of this object

48.43. `pg_shseclabel`

The catalog `pg_shseclabel` stores security labels on shared database objects. Security labels can be manipulated with the SECURITY LABEL command. For an easier way to view security labels, see Section 48.66.

See also `pg_seclabel`, which performs a similar function for security labels involving objects within a single database.

Unlike most system catalogs, `pg_shseclabel` is shared across all databases of a cluster: there is only one copy of `pg_shseclabel` per cluster, not one per database.

Table 48-43. `pg_shseclabel` Columns

Name	Type	References	Description
objoid	oid	any OID column	The OID of the object this security label pertains to
classoid	oid	pg_class.oid	The OID of the system catalog this object appears in
provider	text		The label provider associated with this label.
label	text		The security label applied to this object.

48.44. `pg_statistic`

The catalog `pg_statistic` stores statistical data about the contents of the database. Entries are created by ANALYZE and subsequently used by the query planner. Note that all the statistical data is inherently approximate, even assuming that it is up-to-date.

Normally there is one entry, with `stainherit` = `false`, for each table column that has been analyzed. If the table has inheritance children, a second entry with `stainherit` = `true` is also created. This row represents the column's statistics over the inheritance tree, i.e., statistics for the data you'd see with SELECT *column* FROM *table**, whereas the `stainherit` = `false` row represents the results of SELECT *column* FROM ONLY *table*.

`pg_statistic` also stores statistical data about the values of index expressions. These are described as if they were actual data columns; in particular, `starelid` references the index. No entry is made for an ordinary non-expression index column, however, since it would be redundant with the entry for the underlying table column. Currently, entries for index expressions always have `stainherit` = `false`.

Since different kinds of statistics might be appropriate for different kinds of data, `pg_statistic` is designed not to assume very much about what sort of statistics it stores. Only extremely general statistics (such as nullness) are given dedicated columns in `pg_statistic`. Everything else is stored in "slots", which are groups of associated columns whose content is identified by a code number in one of the slot's columns. For more information see `src/include/catalog/pg_statistic.h`.

`pg_statistic` should not be readable by the public, since even statistical information about a table's contents might be considered sensitive. (Example: minimum and maximum values of a salary column might be quite interesting.) `pg_stats` is a publicly readable view on `pg_statistic` that only exposes information about those tables that are readable by the current user.

Table 48-44. `pg_statistic` Columns

Name	Type	References	Description

Name	Type	References	Description
starelid	oid	pg_class.oid	The table or index that the described column belongs to
staattnum	int2	pg_attribute.attnum	The number of the described column
stainherit	bool		If true, the stats include inheritance child columns, not just the values in the specified relation
stanullfrac	float4		The fraction of the column's entries that are null
stawidth	int4		The average stored width, in bytes, of nonnull entries
stadistinct	float4		The number of distinct nonnull data values in the column. A value greater than zero is the actual number of distinct values. A value less than zero is the negative of a multiplier for the number of rows in the table; for example, a column in which values appear about twice on the average could be represented by stadistinct = -0.5. A zero value means the number of distinct values is unknown.
stakind$N$	int2		A code number indicating the kind of statistics stored in the Nth "slot" of the pg_statistic row.

Name	Type	References	Description
staop*N*	oid	pg_operator.oid	An operator used to derive the statistics stored in the *N*th "slot". For example, a histogram slot would show the < operator that defines the sort order of the data.
stanumbers*N*	float4[]		Numerical statistics of the appropriate kind for the *N*th "slot", or null if the slot kind does not involve numerical values
stavalues*N*	anyarray		Column data values of the appropriate kind for the *N*th "slot", or null if the slot kind does not store any data values. Each array's element values are actually of the specific column's data type, or a related type such as an array's element type, so there is no way to define these columns' type more specifically than anyarray.

48.45. pg_tablespace

The catalog pg_tablespace stores information about the available tablespaces. Tables can be placed in particular tablespaces to aid administration of disk layout.

Unlike most system catalogs, pg_tablespace is shared across all databases of a cluster: there is only one copy of pg_tablespace per cluster, not one per database.

Table 48-45. pg_tablespace Columns

Name	Type	References	Description
oid	oid		Row identifier (hidden attribute; must be explicitly selected)

Name	Type	References	Description
spcname	name		Tablespace name
spcowner	oid	pg_authid.oid	Owner of the tablespace, usually the user who created it
spcacl	aclitem[]		Access privileges; see GRANT and REVOKE for details
spcoptions	text[]		Tablespace-level options, as "keyword=value" strings

48.46. `pg_trigger`

The catalog `pg_trigger` stores triggers on tables and views. See CREATE TRIGGER for more information.

Table 48-46. `pg_trigger` Columns

Name	Type	References	Description
oid	oid		Row identifier (hidden attribute; must be explicitly selected)
tgrelid	oid	pg_class.oid	The table this trigger is on
tgname	name		Trigger name (must be unique among triggers of same table)
tgfoid	oid	pg_proc.oid	The function to be called
tgtype	int2		Bit mask identifying trigger firing conditions
tgenabled	char		Controls in which session_replication_role modes the trigger fires. O = trigger fires in "origin" and "local" modes, D = trigger is disabled, R = trigger fires in "replica" mode, A = trigger fires always.

Name	Type	References	Description
tgisinternal	bool		True if trigger is internally generated (usually, to enforce the constraint identified by tgconstraint)
tgconstrrelid	oid	pg_class.oid	The table referenced by a referential integrity constraint
tgconstrindid	oid	pg_class.oid	The index supporting a unique, primary key, referential integrity, or exclusion constraint
tgconstraint	oid	pg_constraint.oid	The pg_constraint entry associated with the trigger, if any
tgdeferrable	bool		True if constraint trigger is deferrable
tginitdeferred	bool		True if constraint trigger is initially deferred
tgnargs	int2		Number of argument strings passed to trigger function
tgattr	int2vector	pg_attribute.attnum	Column numbers, if trigger is column-specific; otherwise an empty array
tgargs	bytea		Argument strings to pass to trigger, each NULL-terminated
tgqual	pg_node_tree		Expression tree (in nodeToString() representation) for the trigger's WHEN condition, or null if none

Currently, column-specific triggering is supported only for UPDATE events, and so tgattr is relevant only for that event type. tgtype might contain bits for other event types as well, but those are presumed to be table-wide regardless of what is in tgattr.

> **Note:** When tgconstraint is nonzero, tgconstrrelid, tgconstrindid, tgdeferrable, and tginitdeferred are largely redundant with the referenced pg_constraint entry. However, it is possible for a non-deferrable trigger to be associated with a deferrable constraint: foreign key constraints can have some deferrable and some non-deferrable triggers.

Note: `pg_class.relhastriggers` must be true if a relation has any triggers in this catalog.

48.47. `pg_ts_config`

The `pg_ts_config` catalog contains entries representing text search configurations. A configuration specifies a particular text search parser and a list of dictionaries to use for each of the parser's output token types. The parser is shown in the `pg_ts_config` entry, but the token-to-dictionary mapping is defined by subsidiary entries in `pg_ts_config_map`.

PostgreSQL's text search features are described at length in Chapter 12.

Table 48-47. `pg_ts_config` Columns

Name	Type	References	Description
oid	oid		Row identifier (hidden attribute; must be explicitly selected)
cfgname	name		Text search configuration name
cfgnamespace	oid	pg_namespace.oid	The OID of the namespace that contains this configuration
cfgowner	oid	pg_authid.oid	Owner of the configuration
cfgparser	oid	pg_ts_parser.oid	The OID of the text search parser for this configuration

48.48. `pg_ts_config_map`

The `pg_ts_config_map` catalog contains entries showing which text search dictionaries should be consulted, and in what order, for each output token type of each text search configuration's parser.

PostgreSQL's text search features are described at length in Chapter 12.

Table 48-48. `pg_ts_config_map` Columns

Name	Type	References	Description

Name	Type	References	Description
mapcfg	oid	pg_ts_config.oid	The OID of the pg_ts_config entry owning this map entry
maptokentype	integer		A token type emitted by the configuration's parser
mapseqno	integer		Order in which to consult this entry (lower mapseqnos first)
mapdict	oid	pg_ts_dict.oid	The OID of the text search dictionary to consult

48.49. `pg_ts_dict`

The pg_ts_dict catalog contains entries defining text search dictionaries. A dictionary depends on a text search template, which specifies all the implementation functions needed; the dictionary itself provides values for the user-settable parameters supported by the template. This division of labor allows dictionaries to be created by unprivileged users. The parameters are specified by a text string dictinitoption, whose format and meaning vary depending on the template.

PostgreSQL's text search features are described at length in Chapter 12.

Table 48-49. `pg_ts_dict` Columns

Name	Type	References	Description
oid	oid		Row identifier (hidden attribute; must be explicitly selected)
dictname	name		Text search dictionary name
dictnamespace	oid	pg_namespace.oid	The OID of the namespace that contains this dictionary
dictowner	oid	pg_authid.oid	Owner of the dictionary
dicttemplate	oid	pg_ts_template.oid	The OID of the text search template for this dictionary
dictinitoption	text		Initialization option string for the template

48.50. `pg_ts_parser`

The `pg_ts_parser` catalog contains entries defining text search parsers. A parser is responsible for splitting input text into lexemes and assigning a token type to each lexeme. Since a parser must be implemented by C-language-level functions, creation of new parsers is restricted to database superusers.

PostgreSQL's text search features are described at length in Chapter 12.

Table 48-50. `pg_ts_parser` Columns

Name	Type	References	Description
oid	oid		Row identifier (hidden attribute; must be explicitly selected)
prsname	name		Text search parser name
prsnamespace	oid	pg_namespace.oid	The OID of the namespace that contains this parser
prsstart	regproc	pg_proc.oid	OID of the parser's startup function
prstoken	regproc	pg_proc.oid	OID of the parser's next-token function
prsend	regproc	pg_proc.oid	OID of the parser's shutdown function
prsheadline	regproc	pg_proc.oid	OID of the parser's headline function
prslextype	regproc	pg_proc.oid	OID of the parser's lextype function

48.51. `pg_ts_template`

The `pg_ts_template` catalog contains entries defining text search templates. A template is the implementation skeleton for a class of text search dictionaries. Since a template must be implemented by C-language-level functions, creation of new templates is restricted to database superusers.

PostgreSQL's text search features are described at length in Chapter 12.

Table 48-51. `pg_ts_template` Columns

Name	Type	References	Description
oid	oid		Row identifier (hidden attribute; must be explicitly selected)
tmplname	name		Text search template name

Name	Type	References	Description
tmplnamespace	oid	pg_namespace.oid	The OID of the namespace that contains this template
tmplinit	regproc	pg_proc.oid	OID of the template's initialization function
tmpllexize	regproc	pg_proc.oid	OID of the template's lexize function

48.52. pg_type

The catalog pg_type stores information about data types. Base types and enum types (scalar types) are created with CREATE TYPE, and domains with CREATE DOMAIN. A composite type is automatically created for each table in the database, to represent the row structure of the table. It is also possible to create composite types with CREATE TYPE AS.

Table 48-52. pg_type Columns

Name	Type	References	Description
oid	oid		Row identifier (hidden attribute; must be explicitly selected)
typname	name		Data type name
typnamespace	oid	pg_namespace.oid	The OID of the namespace that contains this type
typowner	oid	pg_authid.oid	Owner of the type
typlen	int2		For a fixed-size type, typlen is the number of bytes in the internal representation of the type. But for a variable-length type, typlen is negative. -1 indicates a "varlena" type (one that has a length word), -2 indicates a null-terminated C string.

Name	Type	References	Description
typbyval	bool		typbyval determines whether internal routines pass a value of this type by value or by reference. typbyval had better be false if typlen is not 1, 2, or 4 (or 8 on machines where Datum is 8 bytes). Variable-length types are always passed by reference. Note that typbyval can be false even if the length would allow pass-by-value.
typtype	char		typtype is b for a base type, c for a composite type (e.g., a table's row type), d for a domain, e for an enum type, p for a pseudo-type, or r for a range type. See also typrelid and typbasetype.
typcategory	char		typcategory is an arbitrary classification of data types that is used by the parser to determine which implicit casts should be "preferred". See Table 48-53.
typispreferred	bool		True if the type is a preferred cast target within its typcategory
typisdefined	bool		True if the type is defined, false if this is a placeholder entry for a not-yet-defined type. When typisdefined is false, nothing except the type name, namespace, and OID can be relied on.

Name	Type	References	Description
typdelim	char		Character that separates two values of this type when parsing array input. Note that the delimiter is associated with the array element data type, not the array data type.
typrelid	oid	pg_class.oid	If this is a composite type (see typtype), then this column points to the pg_class entry that defines the corresponding table. (For a free-standing composite type, the pg_class entry doesn't really represent a table, but it is needed anyway for the type's pg_attribute entries to link to.) Zero for non-composite types.

Name	Type	References	Description
typelem	oid	pg_type.oid	If typelem is not 0 then it identifies another row in pg_type. The current type can then be subscripted like an array yielding values of type typelem. A "true" array type is variable length (typlen = -1), but some fixed-length (typlen > 0) types also have nonzero typelem, for example name and point. If a fixed-length type has a typelem then its internal representation must be some number of values of the typelem data type with no other data. Variable-length array types have a header defined by the array subroutines.
typarray	oid	pg_type.oid	If typarray is not 0 then it identifies another row in pg_type, which is the "true" array type having this type as element
typinput	regproc	pg_proc.oid	Input conversion function (text format)
typoutput	regproc	pg_proc.oid	Output conversion function (text format)
typreceive	regproc	pg_proc.oid	Input conversion function (binary format), or 0 if none
typsend	regproc	pg_proc.oid	Output conversion function (binary format), or 0 if none
typmodin	regproc	pg_proc.oid	Type modifier input function, or 0 if type does not support modifiers

Name	Type	References	Description
typmodout	regproc	pg_proc.oid	Type modifier output function, or 0 to use the standard format
typanalyze	regproc	pg_proc.oid	Custom ANALYZE function, or 0 to use the standard function

Name	Type	References	Description
typalign	char		typalign is the alignment required when storing a value of this type. It applies to storage on disk as well as most representations of the value inside PostgreSQL. When multiple values are stored consecutively, such as in the representation of a complete row on disk, padding is inserted before a datum of this type so that it begins on the specified boundary. The alignment reference is the beginning of the first datum in the sequence. Possible values are: • c = char alignment, i.e., no alignment needed. • s = short alignment (2 bytes on most machines). • i = int alignment (4 bytes on most machines). • d = double alignment (8 bytes on many machines, but by no means all). **Note:** For types used in system tables, it is critical that the size and alignment defined in pg_type agree with the way that the compiler will lay out the column in a structure representing a table row. *1952*

Name	Type	References	Description
typstorage	char		typstorage tells for varlena types (those with typlen = -1) if the type is prepared for toasting and what the default strategy for attributes of this type should be. Possible values are • p: Value must always be stored plain. • e: Value can be stored in a "secondary" relation (if relation has one, see pg_class.reltoast • m: Value can be stored compressed inline. • x: Value can be stored compressed inline or stored in "secondary" storage. Note that m columns can also be moved out to secondary storage, but only as a last resort (e and x columns are moved first).
typnotnull	bool		typnotnull represents a not-null constraint on a type. Used for domains only.
typbasetype	oid	pg_type.oid	If this is a domain (see typtype), then typbasetype identifies the type that this one is based on. Zero if this type is not a domain.

Name	Type	References	Description
typtypmod	int4		Domains use typtypmod to record the typmod to be applied to their base type (-1 if base type does not use a typmod). -1 if this type is not a domain.
typndims	int4		typndims is the number of array dimensions for a domain over an array (that is, typbasetype is an array type). Zero for types other than domains over array types.
typcollation	oid	pg_collation.oid	typcollation specifies the collation of the type. If the type does not support collations, this will be zero. A base type that supports collations will have DEFAULT_COLLATION_O here. A domain over a collatable type can have some other collation OID, if one was specified for the domain.
typdefaultbin	pg_node_tree		If typdefaultbin is not null, it is the nodeToString() representation of a default expression for the type. This is only used for domains.

Name	Type	References	Description
typdefault	text		typdefault is null if the type has no associated default value. If typdefaultbin is not null, typdefault must contain a human-readable version of the default expression represented by typdefaultbin. If typdefaultbin is null and typdefault is not, then typdefault is the external representation of the type's default value, which can be fed to the type's input converter to produce a constant.
typacl	aclitem[]		Access privileges; see **GRANT** and **REVOKE** for details

Table 48-53 lists the system-defined values of typcategory. Any future additions to this list will also be upper-case ASCII letters. All other ASCII characters are reserved for user-defined categories.

Table 48-53. typcategory Codes

Code	Category
A	Array types
B	Boolean types
C	Composite types
D	Date/time types
E	Enum types
G	Geometric types
I	Network address types
N	Numeric types
P	Pseudo-types
R	Range types
S	String types
T	Timespan types
U	User-defined types
V	Bit-string types

Code	Category
X	unknown type

48.53. `pg_user_mapping`

The catalog `pg_user_mapping` stores the mappings from local user to remote. Access to this catalog is restricted from normal users, use the view `pg_user_mappings` instead.

Table 48-54. `pg_user_mapping` Columns

Name	Type	References	Description
oid	oid		Row identifier (hidden attribute; must be explicitly selected)
umuser	oid	pg_authid.oid	OID of the local role being mapped, 0 if the user mapping is public
umserver	oid	pg_foreign_server.oid	The OID of the foreign server that contains this mapping
umoptions	text[]		User mapping specific options, as "keyword=value" strings

48.54. System Views

In addition to the system catalogs, PostgreSQL provides a number of built-in views. Some system views provide convenient access to some commonly used queries on the system catalogs. Other views provide access to internal server state.

The information schema (Chapter 34) provides an alternative set of views which overlap the functionality of the system views. Since the information schema is SQL-standard whereas the views described here are PostgreSQL-specific, it's usually better to use the information schema if it provides all the information you need.

Table 48-55 lists the system views described here. More detailed documentation of each view follows below. There are some additional views that provide access to the results of the statistics collector; they are described in Table 27-1.

Except where noted, all the views described here are read-only.

Table 48-55. System Views

View Name	Purpose
pg_available_extensions	available extensions
pg_available_extension_versions	available versions of extensions
pg_cursors	open cursors
pg_group	groups of database users
pg_indexes	indexes
pg_locks	currently held locks
pg_matviews	materialized views
pg_prepared_statements	prepared statements
pg_prepared_xacts	prepared transactions
pg_roles	database roles
pg_rules	rules
pg_seclabels	security labels
pg_settings	parameter settings
pg_shadow	database users
pg_stats	planner statistics
pg_tables	tables
pg_timezone_abbrevs	time zone abbreviations
pg_timezone_names	time zone names
pg_user	database users
pg_user_mappings	user mappings
pg_views	views

48.55. `pg_available_extensions`

The `pg_available_extensions` view lists the extensions that are available for installation. See also the `pg_extension` catalog, which shows the extensions currently installed.

Table 48-56. `pg_available_extensions` Columns

Name	Type	Description
name	name	Extension name
default_version	text	Name of default version, or NULL if none is specified
installed_version	text	Currently installed version of the extension, or NULL if not installed
comment	text	Comment string from the extension's control file

The `pg_available_extensions` view is read only.

48.56. `pg_available_extension_versions`

The `pg_available_extension_versions` view lists the specific extension versions that are available for installation. See also the `pg_extension` catalog, which shows the extensions currently installed.

Table 48-57. `pg_available_extension_versions` Columns

Name	Type	Description
name	name	Extension name
version	text	Version name
installed	bool	True if this version of this extension is currently installed
superuser	bool	True if only superusers are allowed to install this extension
relocatable	bool	True if extension can be relocated to another schema
schema	name	Name of the schema that the extension must be installed into, or NULL if partially or fully relocatable
requires	name[]	Names of prerequisite extensions, or NULL if none
comment	text	Comment string from the extension's control file

The `pg_available_extension_versions` view is read only.

48.57. `pg_cursors`

The `pg_cursors` view lists the cursors that are currently available. Cursors can be defined in several ways:

- via the DECLARE statement in SQL

- via the Bind message in the frontend/backend protocol, as described in Section 49.2.3

- via the Server Programming Interface (SPI), as described in Section 44.1

The `pg_cursors` view displays cursors created by any of these means. Cursors only exist for the duration of the transaction that defines them, unless they have been declared WITH HOLD. Therefore non-holdable cursors are only present in the view until the end of their creating transaction.

> **Note:** Cursors are used internally to implement some of the components of PostgreSQL, such as procedural languages. Therefore, the `pg_cursors` view might include cursors that have not been explicitly created by the user.

Table 48-58. `pg_cursors` Columns

Name	Type	Description
name	text	The name of the cursor
statement	text	The verbatim query string submitted to declare this cursor
is_holdable	boolean	`true` if the cursor is holdable (that is, it can be accessed after the transaction that declared the cursor has committed); `false` otherwise
is_binary	boolean	`true` if the cursor was declared `BINARY`; `false` otherwise
is_scrollable	boolean	`true` if the cursor is scrollable (that is, it allows rows to be retrieved in a nonsequential manner); `false` otherwise
creation_time	timestamptz	The time at which the cursor was declared

The `pg_cursors` view is read only.

48.58. `pg_group`

The view `pg_group` exists for backwards compatibility: it emulates a catalog that existed in PostgreSQL before version 8.1. It shows the names and members of all roles that are marked as not `rolcanlogin`, which is an approximation to the set of roles that are being used as groups.

Table 48-59. `pg_group` Columns

Name	Type	References	Description
groname	name	pg_authid.rolname	Name of the group
grosysid	oid	pg_authid.oid	ID of this group
grolist	oid[]	pg_authid.oid	An array containing the IDs of the roles in this group

48.59. `pg_indexes`

The view `pg_indexes` provides access to useful information about each index in the database.

Table 48-60. `pg_indexes` Columns

Name	Type	References	Description
schemaname	name	pg_namespace.nspname	Name of schema containing table and index
tablename	name	pg_class.relname	Name of table the index is for
indexname	name	pg_class.relname	Name of index
tablespace	name	pg_tablespace.spcname	Name of tablespace containing index (null if default for database)
indexdef	text		Index definition (a reconstructed CREATE INDEX command)

48.60. `pg_locks`

The view `pg_locks` provides access to information about the locks held by open transactions within the database server. See Chapter 13 for more discussion of locking.

`pg_locks` contains one row per active lockable object, requested lock mode, and relevant transaction. Thus, the same lockable object might appear many times, if multiple transactions are holding or waiting for locks on it. However, an object that currently has no locks on it will not appear at all.

There are several distinct types of lockable objects: whole relations (e.g., tables), individual pages of relations, individual tuples of relations, transaction IDs (both virtual and permanent IDs), and general database objects (identified by class OID and object OID, in the same way as in `pg_description` or `pg_depend`). Also, the right to extend a relation is represented as a separate lockable object. Also, "advisory" locks can be taken on numbers that have user-defined meanings.

Table 48-61. `pg_locks` Columns

Name	Type	References	Description
locktype	text		Type of the lockable object: relation, extend, page, tuple, transactionid, virtualxid, object, userlock, or advisory

Name	Type	References	Description
database	oid	pg_database.oid	OID of the database in which the lock target exists, or zero if the target is a shared object, or null if the target is a transaction ID
relation	oid	pg_class.oid	OID of the relation targeted by the lock, or null if the target is not a relation or part of a relation
page	integer		Page number targeted by the lock within the relation, or null if the target is not a relation page or tuple
tuple	smallint		Tuple number targeted by the lock within the page, or null if the target is not a tuple
virtualxid	text		Virtual ID of the transaction targeted by the lock, or null if the target is not a virtual transaction ID
transactionid	xid		ID of the transaction targeted by the lock, or null if the target is not a transaction ID
classid	oid	pg_class.oid	OID of the system catalog containing the lock target, or null if the target is not a general database object
objid	oid	any OID column	OID of the lock target within its system catalog, or null if the target is not a general database object

Name	Type	References	Description
objsubid	smallint		Column number targeted by the lock (the `classid` and `objid` refer to the table itself), or zero if the target is some other general database object, or null if the target is not a general database object
virtualtransaction	text		Virtual ID of the transaction that is holding or awaiting this lock
pid	integer		Process ID of the server process holding or awaiting this lock, or null if the lock is held by a prepared transaction
mode	text		Name of the lock mode held or desired by this process (see Section 13.3.1 and Section 13.2.3)
granted	boolean		True if lock is held, false if lock is awaited
fastpath	boolean		True if lock was taken via fast path, false if taken via main lock table

granted is true in a row representing a lock held by the indicated transaction. False indicates that this transaction is currently waiting to acquire this lock, which implies that some other transaction is holding a conflicting lock mode on the same lockable object. The waiting transaction will sleep until the other lock is released (or a deadlock situation is detected). A single transaction can be waiting to acquire at most one lock at a time.

Every transaction holds an exclusive lock on its virtual transaction ID for its entire duration. If a permanent ID is assigned to the transaction (which normally happens only if the transaction changes the state of the database), it also holds an exclusive lock on its permanent transaction ID until it ends. When one transaction finds it necessary to wait specifically for another transaction, it does so by attempting to acquire share lock on the other transaction ID (either virtual or permanent ID depending on the situation). That will succeed only when the other transaction terminates and releases its locks.

Although tuples are a lockable type of object, information about row-level locks is stored on disk, not in memory, and therefore row-level locks normally do not appear in this view. If a transaction is waiting for a row-level lock, it will usually appear in the view as waiting for the permanent transaction ID of the current holder of that row lock.

Advisory locks can be acquired on keys consisting of either a single `bigint` value or two integer values. A `bigint` key is displayed with its high-order half in the `classid` column, its low-order half in the `objid` column, and `objsubid` equal to 1. The original `bigint` value can be reassembled with the expression `(classid::bigint << 32) | objid::bigint`. Integer keys are displayed with the first key in the `classid` column, the second key in the `objid` column, and `objsubid` equal to 2. The actual meaning of the keys is up to the user. Advisory locks are local to each database, so the `database` column is meaningful for an advisory lock.

`pg_locks` provides a global view of all locks in the database cluster, not only those relevant to the current database. Although its `relation` column can be joined against `pg_class.oid` to identify locked relations, this will only work correctly for relations in the current database (those for which the `database` column is either the current database's OID or zero).

The `pid` column can be joined to the `pid` column of the `pg_stat_activity` view to get more information on the session holding or waiting to hold each lock, for example

```
SELECT * FROM pg_locks pl LEFT JOIN pg_stat_activity psa
    ON pl.pid = psa.pid;
```

Also, if you are using prepared transactions, the `virtualtransaction` column can be joined to the `transaction` column of the `pg_prepared_xacts` view to get more information on prepared transactions that hold locks. (A prepared transaction can never be waiting for a lock, but it continues to hold the locks it acquired while running.) For example:

```
SELECT * FROM pg_locks pl LEFT JOIN pg_prepared_xacts ppx
    ON pl.virtualtransaction = '-1/' || ppx.transaction;
```

The `pg_locks` view displays data from both the regular lock manager and the predicate lock manager, which are separate systems; in addition, the regular lock manager subdivides its locks into regular and *fast-path* locks. This data is not guaranteed to be entirely consistent. When the view is queried, data on fast-path locks (with `fastpath = true`) is gathered from each backend one at a time, without freezing the state of the entire lock manager, so it is possible for locks to be taken or released while information is gathered. Note, however, that these locks are known not to conflict with any other lock currently in place. After all backends have been queried for fast-path locks, the remainder of the regular lock manager is locked as a unit, and a consistent snapshot of all remaining locks is collected as an atomic action. After unlocking the regular lock manager, the predicate lock manager is similarly locked and all predicate locks are collected as an atomic action. Thus, with the exception of fast-path locks, each lock manager will deliver a consistent set of results, but as we do not lock both lock managers simultaneously, it is possible for locks to be taken or released after we interrogate the regular lock manager and before we interrogate the predicate lock manager.

Locking the regular and/or predicate lock manager could have some impact on database performance if this view is very frequently accessed. The locks are held only for the minimum amount of time necessary to obtain data from the lock managers, but this does not completely eliminate the possibility of a performance impact.

48.61. `pg_matviews`

The view `pg_matviews` provides access to useful information about each materialized view in the database.

Table 48-62. `pg_matviews` Columns

Name	Type	References	Description
schemaname	name	pg_namespace.nspname	Name of schema containing materialized view
matviewname	name	pg_class.relname	Name of materialized view
matviewowner	name	pg_authid.rolname	Name of materialized view's owner
tablespace	name	pg_tablespace.spcname	Name of tablespace containing materialized view (null if default for database)
hasindexes	boolean		True if materialized view has (or recently had) any indexes
ispopulated	boolean		True if materialized view is currently populated
definition	text		Materialized view definition (a reconstructed SELECT query)

48.62. `pg_prepared_statements`

The `pg_prepared_statements` view displays all the prepared statements that are available in the current session. See PREPARE for more information about prepared statements.

`pg_prepared_statements` contains one row for each prepared statement. Rows are added to the view when a new prepared statement is created and removed when a prepared statement is released (for example, via the DEALLOCATE command).

Table 48-63. `pg_prepared_statements` Columns

Name	Type	Description
name	text	The identifier of the prepared statement

Name	Type	Description
statement	text	The query string submitted by the client to create this prepared statement. For prepared statements created via SQL, this is the PREPARE statement submitted by the client. For prepared statements created via the frontend/backend protocol, this is the text of the prepared statement itself.
prepare_time	timestamptz	The time at which the prepared statement was created
parameter_types	regtype[]	The expected parameter types for the prepared statement in the form of an array of regtype. The OID corresponding to an element of this array can be obtained by casting the regtype value to oid.
from_sql	boolean	true if the prepared statement was created via the PREPARE SQL statement; false if the statement was prepared via the frontend/backend protocol

The pg_prepared_statements view is read only.

48.63. pg_prepared_xacts

The view pg_prepared_xacts displays information about transactions that are currently prepared for two-phase commit (see PREPARE TRANSACTION for details).

pg_prepared_xacts contains one row per prepared transaction. An entry is removed when the transaction is committed or rolled back.

Table 48-64. pg_prepared_xacts Columns

Name	Type	References	Description
transaction	xid		Numeric transaction identifier of the prepared transaction

Name	Type	References	Description
gid	text		Global transaction identifier that was assigned to the transaction
prepared	timestamp with time zone		Time at which the transaction was prepared for commit
owner	name	pg_authid.rolname	Name of the user that executed the transaction
database	name	pg_database.datname	Name of the database in which the transaction was executed

When the pg_prepared_xacts view is accessed, the internal transaction manager data structures are momentarily locked, and a copy is made for the view to display. This ensures that the view produces a consistent set of results, while not blocking normal operations longer than necessary. Nonetheless there could be some impact on database performance if this view is frequently accessed.

48.64. pg_roles

The view pg_roles provides access to information about database roles. This is simply a publicly readable view of pg_authid that blanks out the password field.

This view explicitly exposes the OID column of the underlying table, since that is needed to do joins to other catalogs.

Table 48-65. pg_roles Columns

Name	Type	References	Description
rolname	name		Role name
rolsuper	bool		Role has superuser privileges
rolinherit	bool		Role automatically inherits privileges of roles it is a member of
rolcreaterole	bool		Role can create more roles
rolcreatedb	bool		Role can create databases

Name	Type	References	Description
rolcatupdate	bool		Role can update system catalogs directly. (Even a superuser cannot do this unless this column is true)
rolcanlogin	bool		Role can log in. That is, this role can be given as the initial session authorization identifier
rolreplication	bool		Role is a replication role. That is, this role can initiate streaming replication (see Section 25.2.5) and set/unset the system backup mode using `pg_start_backup` and `pg_stop_backup`
rolconnlimit	int4		For roles that can log in, this sets maximum number of concurrent connections this role can make. -1 means no limit.
rolpassword	text		Not the password (always reads as `********`)
rolvaliduntil	timestamptz		Password expiry time (only used for password authentication); null if no expiration
rolconfig	text[]		Role-specific defaults for run-time configuration variables
oid	oid	pg_authid.oid	ID of role

48.65. `pg_rules`

The view `pg_rules` provides access to useful information about query rewrite rules.

Table 48-66. `pg_rules` Columns

Name	Type	References	Description

Name	Type	References	Description
schemaname	name	pg_namespace.nspname	Name of schema containing table
tablename	name	pg_class.relname	Name of table the rule is for
rulename	name	pg_rewrite.rulename	Name of rule
definition	text		Rule definition (a reconstructed creation command)

The pg_rules view excludes the ON SELECT rules of views and materialized views; those can be seen in pg_views and pg_matviews.

48.66. pg_seclabels

The view pg_seclabels provides information about security labels. It as an easier-to-query version of the pg_seclabel catalog.

Table 48-67. pg_seclabels Columns

Name	Type	References	Description
objoid	oid	any OID column	The OID of the object this security label pertains to
classoid	oid	pg_class.oid	The OID of the system catalog this object appears in
objsubid	int4		For a security label on a table column, this is the column number (the objoid and classoid refer to the table itself). For all other object types, this column is zero.
objtype	text		The type of object to which this label applies, as text.
objnamespace	oid	pg_namespace.oid	The OID of the namespace for this object, if applicable; otherwise NULL.

Name	Type	References	Description
objname	text		The name of the object to which this label applies, as text.
provider	text	pg_seclabel.provider	The label provider associated with this label.
label	text	pg_seclabel.label	The security label applied to this object.

48.67. pg_settings

The view pg_settings provides access to run-time parameters of the server. It is essentially an alternative interface to the SHOW and SET commands. It also provides access to some facts about each parameter that are not directly available from SHOW, such as minimum and maximum values.

Table 48-68. pg_settings Columns

Name	Type	Description
name	text	Run-time configuration parameter name
setting	text	Current value of the parameter
unit	text	Implicit unit of the parameter
category	text	Logical group of the parameter
short_desc	text	A brief description of the parameter
extra_desc	text	Additional, more detailed, description of the parameter
context	text	Context required to set the parameter's value (see below)
vartype	text	Parameter type (bool, enum, integer, real, or string)
source	text	Source of the current parameter value
min_val	text	Minimum allowed value of the parameter (null for non-numeric values)
max_val	text	Maximum allowed value of the parameter (null for non-numeric values)

Name	Type	Description
enumvals	text[]	Allowed values of an enum parameter (null for non-enum values)
boot_val	text	Parameter value assumed at server startup if the parameter is not otherwise set
reset_val	text	Value that RESET would reset the parameter to in the current session
sourcefile	text	Configuration file the current value was set in (null for values set from sources other than configuration files, or when examined by a non-superuser); helpful when using include directives in configuration files
sourceline	integer	Line number within the configuration file the current value was set at (null for values set from sources other than configuration files, or when examined by a non-superuser)

There are several possible values of context. In order of decreasing difficulty of changing the setting, they are:

internal

> These settings cannot be changed directly; they reflect internally determined values. Some of them may be adjustable by rebuilding the server with different configuration options, or by changing options supplied to initdb.

postmaster

> These settings can only be applied when the server starts, so any change requires restarting the server. Values for these settings are typically stored in the postgresql.conf file, or passed on the command line when starting the server. Of course, settings with any of the lower context types can also be set at server start time.

sighup

> Changes to these settings can be made in postgresql.conf without restarting the server. Send a SIGHUP signal to the postmaster to cause it to re-read postgresql.conf and apply the changes. The postmaster will also forward the SIGHUP signal to its child processes so that they all pick up the new value.

backend

> Changes to these settings can be made in postgresql.conf without restarting the server; they can also be set for a particular session in the connection request packet (for example, via libpq's

PGOPTIONS environment variable). However, these settings never change in a session after it is started. If you change them in `postgresql.conf`, send a SIGHUP signal to the postmaster to cause it to re-read `postgresql.conf`. The new values will only affect subsequently-launched sessions.

superuser

> These settings can be set from `postgresql.conf`, or within a session via the SET command; but only superusers can change them via SET. Changes in `postgresql.conf` will affect existing sessions only if no session-local value has been established with SET.

user

> These settings can be set from `postgresql.conf`, or within a session via the SET command. Any user is allowed to change his session-local value. Changes in `postgresql.conf` will affect existing sessions only if no session-local value has been established with SET.

See Section 18.1 for more information about the various ways to change these parameters.

The `pg_settings` view cannot be inserted into or deleted from, but it can be updated. An UPDATE applied to a row of `pg_settings` is equivalent to executing the SET command on that named parameter. The change only affects the value used by the current session. If an UPDATE is issued within a transaction that is later aborted, the effects of the UPDATE command disappear when the transaction is rolled back. Once the surrounding transaction is committed, the effects will persist until the end of the session, unless overridden by another UPDATE or SET.

48.68. pg_shadow

The view `pg_shadow` exists for backwards compatibility: it emulates a catalog that existed in PostgreSQL before version 8.1. It shows properties of all roles that are marked as `rolcanlogin` in `pg_authid`.

The name stems from the fact that this table should not be readable by the public since it contains passwords. `pg_user` is a publicly readable view on `pg_shadow` that blanks out the password field.

Table 48-69. `pg_shadow` Columns

Name	Type	References	Description
usename	name	pg_authid.rolname	User name
usesysid	oid	pg_authid.oid	ID of this user
usecreatedb	bool		User can create databases
usesuper	bool		User is a superuser
usecatupd	bool		User can update system catalogs. (Even a superuser cannot do this unless this column is true.)

Name	Type	References	Description
userepl	bool		User can initiate streaming replication and put the system in and out of backup mode.
passwd	text		Password (possibly encrypted); null if none. See `pg_authid` for details of how encrypted passwords are stored.
valuntil	abstime		Password expiry time (only used for password authentication)
useconfig	text[]		Session defaults for run-time configuration variables

48.69. `pg_stats`

The view `pg_stats` provides access to the information stored in the `pg_statistic` catalog. This view allows access only to rows of `pg_statistic` that correspond to tables the user has permission to read, and therefore it is safe to allow public read access to this view.

`pg_stats` is also designed to present the information in a more readable format than the underlying catalog — at the cost that its schema must be extended whenever new slot types are defined for `pg_statistic`.

Table 48-70. `pg_stats` Columns

Name	Type	References	Description
schemaname	name	pg_namespace.nspname	Name of schema containing table
tablename	name	pg_class.relname	Name of table
attname	name	pg_attribute.attname	Name of the column described by this row
inherited	bool		If true, this row includes inheritance child columns, not just the values in the specified table
null_frac	real		Fraction of column entries that are null

Name	Type	References	Description
avg_width	integer		Average width in bytes of column's entries
n_distinct	real		If greater than zero, the estimated number of distinct values in the column. If less than zero, the negative of the number of distinct values divided by the number of rows. (The negated form is used when ANALYZE believes that the number of distinct values is likely to increase as the table grows; the positive form is used when the column seems to have a fixed number of possible values.) For example, -1 indicates a unique column in which the number of distinct values is the same as the number of rows.
most_common_vals	anyarray		A list of the most common values in the column. (Null if no values seem to be more common than any others.)
most_common_freqs	real[]		A list of the frequencies of the most common values, i.e., number of occurrences of each divided by total number of rows. (Null when most_common_vals is.)

Name	Type	References	Description
histogram_bounds	anyarray		A list of values that divide the column's values into groups of approximately equal population. The values in most_common_vals, if present, are omitted from this histogram calculation. (This column is null if the column data type does not have a < operator or if the most_common_vals list accounts for the entire population.)
correlation	real		Statistical correlation between physical row ordering and logical ordering of the column values. This ranges from -1 to +1. When the value is near -1 or +1, an index scan on the column will be estimated to be cheaper than when it is near zero, due to reduction of random access to the disk. (This column is null if the column data type does not have a < operator.)
most_common_elems	anyarray		A list of non-null element values most often appearing within values of the column. (Null for scalar types.)

Name	Type	References	Description
most_common_elem_freqs	real[]		A list of the frequencies of the most common element values, i.e., the fraction of rows containing at least one instance of the given value. Two or three additional values follow the per-element frequencies; these are the minimum and maximum of the preceding per-element frequencies, and optionally the frequency of null elements. (Null when most_common_elems is.)
elem_count_histogram	real[]		A histogram of the counts of distinct non-null element values within the values of the column, followed by the average number of distinct non-null elements. (Null for scalar types.)

The maximum number of entries in the array fields can be controlled on a column-by-column basis using the ALTER TABLE SET STATISTICS command, or globally by setting the default_statistics_target run-time parameter.

48.70. pg_tables

The view pg_tables provides access to useful information about each table in the database.

Table 48-71. pg_tables Columns

Name	Type	References	Description
schemaname	name	pg_namespace.nspname	Name of schema containing table
tablename	name	pg_class.relname	Name of table
tableowner	name	pg_authid.rolname	Name of table's owner

Name	Type	References	Description
tablespace	name	pg_tablespace.spcname	Name of tablespace containing table (null if default for database)
hasindexes	boolean	pg_class.relhasindex	True if table has (or recently had) any indexes
hasrules	boolean	pg_class.relhasrules	True if table has (or once had) rules
hastriggers	boolean	pg_class.relhastrigger	True if table has (or once had) triggers

48.71. `pg_timezone_abbrevs`

The view `pg_timezone_abbrevs` provides a list of time zone abbreviations that are currently recognized by the datetime input routines. The contents of this view change when the timezone_abbreviations run-time parameter is modified.

Table 48-72. `pg_timezone_abbrevs` Columns

Name	Type	Description
abbrev	text	Time zone abbreviation
utc_offset	interval	Offset from UTC (positive means east of Greenwich)
is_dst	boolean	True if this is a daylight-savings abbreviation

48.72. `pg_timezone_names`

The view `pg_timezone_names` provides a list of time zone names that are recognized by SET TIMEZONE, along with their associated abbreviations, UTC offsets, and daylight-savings status. (Technically, PostgreSQL uses UT1 rather than UTC because leap seconds are not handled.) Unlike the abbreviations shown in `pg_timezone_abbrevs`, many of these names imply a set of daylight-savings transition date rules. Therefore, the associated information changes across local DST boundaries. The displayed information is computed based on the current value of CURRENT_TIMESTAMP.

Table 48-73. `pg_timezone_names` Columns

Name	Type	Description
name	text	Time zone name
abbrev	text	Time zone abbreviation

Name	Type	Description
utc_offset	interval	Offset from UTC (positive means east of Greenwich)
is_dst	boolean	True if currently observing daylight savings

48.73. `pg_user`

The view `pg_user` provides access to information about database users. This is simply a publicly readable view of `pg_shadow` that blanks out the password field.

Table 48-74. `pg_user` Columns

Name	Type	Description
usename	name	User name
usesysid	oid	ID of this user
usecreatedb	bool	User can create databases
usesuper	bool	User is a superuser
usecatupd	bool	User can update system catalogs. (Even a superuser cannot do this unless this column is true.)
userepl	bool	User can initiate streaming replication and put the system in and out of backup mode.
passwd	text	Not the password (always reads as ********)
valuntil	abstime	Password expiry time (only used for password authentication)
useconfig	text[]	Session defaults for run-time configuration variables

48.74. `pg_user_mappings`

The view `pg_user_mappings` provides access to information about user mappings. This is essentially a publicly readable view of `pg_user_mapping` that leaves out the options field if the user has no rights to use it.

Table 48-75. `pg_user_mappings` Columns

Name	Type	References	Description

Name	Type	References	Description
umid	oid	pg_user_mapping.oid	OID of the user mapping
srvid	oid	pg_foreign_server.oid	The OID of the foreign server that contains this mapping
srvname	name	pg_foreign_server.srvname	Name of the foreign server
umuser	oid	pg_authid.oid	OID of the local role being mapped, 0 if the user mapping is public
usename	name		Name of the local user to be mapped
umoptions	text[]		User mapping specific options, as "keyword=value" strings, if the current user is the owner of the foreign server, else null

48.75. `pg_views`

The view `pg_views` provides access to useful information about each view in the database.

Table 48-76. `pg_views` Columns

Name	Type	References	Description
schemaname	name	pg_namespace.nspname	Name of schema containing view
viewname	name	pg_class.relname	Name of view
viewowner	name	pg_authid.rolname	Name of view's owner
definition	text		View definition (a reconstructed SELECT query)

Chapter 49. Frontend/Backend Protocol

PostgreSQL uses a message-based protocol for communication between frontends and backends (clients and servers). The protocol is supported over TCP/IP and also over Unix-domain sockets. Port number 5432 has been registered with IANA as the customary TCP port number for servers supporting this protocol, but in practice any non-privileged port number can be used.

This document describes version 3.0 of the protocol, implemented in PostgreSQL 7.4 and later. For descriptions of the earlier protocol versions, see previous releases of the PostgreSQL documentation. A single server can support multiple protocol versions. The initial startup-request message tells the server which protocol version the client is attempting to use, and then the server follows that protocol if it is able.

In order to serve multiple clients efficiently, the server launches a new "backend" process for each client. In the current implementation, a new child process is created immediately after an incoming connection is detected. This is transparent to the protocol, however. For purposes of the protocol, the terms "backend" and "server" are interchangeable; likewise "frontend" and "client" are interchangeable.

49.1. Overview

The protocol has separate phases for startup and normal operation. In the startup phase, the frontend opens a connection to the server and authenticates itself to the satisfaction of the server. (This might involve a single message, or multiple messages depending on the authentication method being used.) If all goes well, the server then sends status information to the frontend, and finally enters normal operation. Except for the initial startup-request message, this part of the protocol is driven by the server.

During normal operation, the frontend sends queries and other commands to the backend, and the backend sends back query results and other responses. There are a few cases (such as NOTIFY) wherein the backend will send unsolicited messages, but for the most part this portion of a session is driven by frontend requests.

Termination of the session is normally by frontend choice, but can be forced by the backend in certain cases. In any case, when the backend closes the connection, it will roll back any open (incomplete) transaction before exiting.

Within normal operation, SQL commands can be executed through either of two sub-protocols. In the "simple query" protocol, the frontend just sends a textual query string, which is parsed and immediately executed by the backend. In the "extended query" protocol, processing of queries is separated into multiple steps: parsing, binding of parameter values, and execution. This offers flexibility and performance benefits, at the cost of extra complexity.

Normal operation has additional sub-protocols for special operations such as COPY.

49.1.1. Messaging Overview

All communication is through a stream of messages. The first byte of a message identifies the message type, and the next four bytes specify the length of the rest of the message (this length count includes itself, but not the message-type byte). The remaining contents of the message are determined by the message type. For historical reasons, the very first message sent by the client (the startup message) has no initial message-type byte.

To avoid losing synchronization with the message stream, both servers and clients typically read an entire message into a buffer (using the byte count) before attempting to process its contents. This allows easy recovery if an error is detected while processing the contents. In extreme situations (such as not having enough memory to buffer the message), the receiver can use the byte count to determine how much input to skip before it resumes reading messages.

Conversely, both servers and clients must take care never to send an incomplete message. This is commonly done by marshaling the entire message in a buffer before beginning to send it. If a communications failure occurs partway through sending or receiving a message, the only sensible response is to abandon the connection, since there is little hope of recovering message-boundary synchronization.

49.1.2. Extended Query Overview

In the extended-query protocol, execution of SQL commands is divided into multiple steps. The state retained between steps is represented by two types of objects: *prepared statements* and *portals*. A prepared statement represents the result of parsing and semantic analysis of a textual query string. A prepared statement is not in itself ready to execute, because it might lack specific values for *parameters*. A portal represents a ready-to-execute or already-partially-executed statement, with any missing parameter values filled in. (For SELECT statements, a portal is equivalent to an open cursor, but we choose to use a different term since cursors don't handle non-SELECT statements.)

The overall execution cycle consists of a *parse* step, which creates a prepared statement from a textual query string; a *bind* step, which creates a portal given a prepared statement and values for any needed parameters; and an *execute* step that runs a portal's query. In the case of a query that returns rows (SELECT, SHOW, etc), the execute step can be told to fetch only a limited number of rows, so that multiple execute steps might be needed to complete the operation.

The backend can keep track of multiple prepared statements and portals (but note that these exist only within a session, and are never shared across sessions). Existing prepared statements and portals are referenced by names assigned when they were created. In addition, an "unnamed" prepared statement and portal exist. Although these behave largely the same as named objects, operations on them are optimized for the case of executing a query only once and then discarding it, whereas operations on named objects are optimized on the expectation of multiple uses.

49.1.3. Formats and Format Codes

Data of a particular data type might be transmitted in any of several different *formats*. As of PostgreSQL 7.4 the only supported formats are "text" and "binary", but the protocol makes provision for future extensions. The desired format for any value is specified by a *format code*. Clients can specify a format code for each transmitted parameter value and for each column of a query result. Text has format code zero, binary has format code one, and all other format codes are reserved for future definition.

The text representation of values is whatever strings are produced and accepted by the input/output conversion functions for the particular data type. In the transmitted representation, there is no trailing null character; the frontend must add one to received values if it wants to process them as C strings. (The text format does not allow embedded nulls, by the way.)

Binary representations for integers use network byte order (most significant byte first). For other data types consult the documentation or source code to learn about the binary representation. Keep in mind that binary representations for complex data types might change across server versions; the text format is usually the more portable choice.

49.2. Message Flow

This section describes the message flow and the semantics of each message type. (Details of the exact representation of each message appear in Section 49.5.) There are several different sub-protocols depending on the state of the connection: start-up, query, function call, COPY, and termination. There are also special provisions for asynchronous operations (including notification responses and command cancellation), which can occur at any time after the start-up phase.

49.2.1. Start-up

To begin a session, a frontend opens a connection to the server and sends a startup message. This message includes the names of the user and of the database the user wants to connect to; it also identifies the particular protocol version to be used. (Optionally, the startup message can include additional settings for run-time parameters.) The server then uses this information and the contents of its configuration files (such as pg_hba.conf) to determine whether the connection is provisionally acceptable, and what additional authentication is required (if any).

The server then sends an appropriate authentication request message, to which the frontend must reply with an appropriate authentication response message (such as a password). For all authentication methods except GSSAPI and SSPI, there is at most one request and one response. In some methods, no response at all is needed from the frontend, and so no authentication request occurs. For GSSAPI and SSPI, multiple exchanges of packets may be needed to complete the authentication.

The authentication cycle ends with the server either rejecting the connection attempt (ErrorResponse), or sending AuthenticationOk.

The possible messages from the server in this phase are:

ErrorResponse

The connection attempt has been rejected. The server then immediately closes the connection.

AuthenticationOk

The authentication exchange is successfully completed.

AuthenticationKerberosV5

The frontend must now take part in a Kerberos V5 authentication dialog (not described here, part of the Kerberos specification) with the server. If this is successful, the server responds with an AuthenticationOk, otherwise it responds with an ErrorResponse. This is no longer supported.

AuthenticationCleartextPassword

The frontend must now send a PasswordMessage containing the password in clear-text form. If this is the correct password, the server responds with an AuthenticationOk, otherwise it responds with an

ErrorResponse.

AuthenticationMD5Password

The frontend must now send a PasswordMessage containing the password (with username) encrypted via MD5, then encrypted again using the 4-byte random salt specified in the AuthenticationMD5Password message. If this is the correct password, the server responds with an AuthenticationOk, otherwise it responds with an ErrorResponse. The actual PasswordMessage can be computed in SQL as `concat('md5', md5(concat(md5(concat(password, username)), random-salt)))`. (Keep in mind the `md5()` function returns its result as a hex string.)

AuthenticationSCMCredential

This response is only possible for local Unix-domain connections on platforms that support SCM credential messages. The frontend must issue an SCM credential message and then send a single data byte. (The contents of the data byte are uninteresting; it's only used to ensure that the server waits long enough to receive the credential message.) If the credential is acceptable, the server responds with an AuthenticationOk, otherwise it responds with an ErrorResponse. (This message type is only issued by pre-9.1 servers. It may eventually be removed from the protocol specification.)

AuthenticationGSS

The frontend must now initiate a GSSAPI negotiation. The frontend will send a PasswordMessage with the first part of the GSSAPI data stream in response to this. If further messages are needed, the server will respond with AuthenticationGSSContinue.

AuthenticationSSPI

The frontend must now initiate a SSPI negotiation. The frontend will send a PasswordMessage with the first part of the SSPI data stream in response to this. If further messages are needed, the server will respond with AuthenticationGSSContinue.

AuthenticationGSSContinue

This message contains the response data from the previous step of GSSAPI or SSPI negotiation (AuthenticationGSS, AuthenticationSSPI or a previous AuthenticationGSSContinue). If the GSSAPI or SSPI data in this message indicates more data is needed to complete the authentication, the frontend must send that data as another PasswordMessage. If GSSAPI or SSPI authentication is completed by this message, the server will next send AuthenticationOk to indicate successful authentication or ErrorResponse to indicate failure.

If the frontend does not support the authentication method requested by the server, then it should immediately close the connection.

After having received AuthenticationOk, the frontend must wait for further messages from the server. In this phase a backend process is being started, and the frontend is just an interested bystander. It is still possible for the startup attempt to fail (ErrorResponse), but in the normal case the backend will send some ParameterStatus messages, BackendKeyData, and finally ReadyForQuery.

During this phase the backend will attempt to apply any additional run-time parameter settings that were given in the startup message. If successful, these values become session defaults. An error causes ErrorResponse and exit.

The possible messages from the backend in this phase are:

BackendKeyData

> This message provides secret-key data that the frontend must save if it wants to be able to issue cancel requests later. The frontend should not respond to this message, but should continue listening for a ReadyForQuery message.

ParameterStatus

> This message informs the frontend about the current (initial) setting of backend parameters, such as client_encoding or DateStyle. The frontend can ignore this message, or record the settings for its future use; see Section 49.2.6 for more details. The frontend should not respond to this message, but should continue listening for a ReadyForQuery message.

ReadyForQuery

> Start-up is completed. The frontend can now issue commands.

ErrorResponse

> Start-up failed. The connection is closed after sending this message.

NoticeResponse

> A warning message has been issued. The frontend should display the message but continue listening for ReadyForQuery or ErrorResponse.

The ReadyForQuery message is the same one that the backend will issue after each command cycle. Depending on the coding needs of the frontend, it is reasonable to consider ReadyForQuery as starting a command cycle, or to consider ReadyForQuery as ending the start-up phase and each subsequent command cycle.

49.2.2. Simple Query

A simple query cycle is initiated by the frontend sending a Query message to the backend. The message includes an SQL command (or commands) expressed as a text string. The backend then sends one or more response messages depending on the contents of the query command string, and finally a ReadyForQuery response message. ReadyForQuery informs the frontend that it can safely send a new command. (It is not actually necessary for the frontend to wait for ReadyForQuery before issuing another command, but the frontend must then take responsibility for figuring out what happens if the earlier command fails and already-issued later commands succeed.)

The possible response messages from the backend are:

CommandComplete

> An SQL command completed normally.

CopyInResponse

> The backend is ready to copy data from the frontend to a table; see Section 49.2.5.

CopyOutResponse

> The backend is ready to copy data from a table to the frontend; see Section 49.2.5.

RowDescription

> Indicates that rows are about to be returned in response to a SELECT, FETCH, etc query. The contents of this message describe the column layout of the rows. This will be followed by a DataRow message for each row being returned to the frontend.

DataRow

> One of the set of rows returned by a SELECT, FETCH, etc query.

EmptyQueryResponse

> An empty query string was recognized.

ErrorResponse

> An error has occurred.

ReadyForQuery

> Processing of the query string is complete. A separate message is sent to indicate this because the query string might contain multiple SQL commands. (CommandComplete marks the end of processing one SQL command, not the whole string.) ReadyForQuery will always be sent, whether processing terminates successfully or with an error.

NoticeResponse

> A warning message has been issued in relation to the query. Notices are in addition to other responses, i.e., the backend will continue processing the command.

The response to a SELECT query (or other queries that return row sets, such as EXPLAIN or SHOW) normally consists of RowDescription, zero or more DataRow messages, and then CommandComplete. COPY to or from the frontend invokes special protocol as described in Section 49.2.5. All other query types normally produce only a CommandComplete message.

Since a query string could contain several queries (separated by semicolons), there might be several such response sequences before the backend finishes processing the query string. ReadyForQuery is issued when the entire string has been processed and the backend is ready to accept a new query string.

If a completely empty (no contents other than whitespace) query string is received, the response is EmptyQueryResponse followed by ReadyForQuery.

In the event of an error, ErrorResponse is issued followed by ReadyForQuery. All further processing of the query string is aborted by ErrorResponse (even if more queries remained in it). Note that this might occur partway through the sequence of messages generated by an individual query.

In simple Query mode, the format of retrieved values is always text, except when the given command is a FETCH from a cursor declared with the BINARY option. In that case, the retrieved values are in binary format. The format codes given in the RowDescription message tell which format is being used.

A frontend must be prepared to accept ErrorResponse and NoticeResponse messages whenever it is expecting any other type of message. See also Section 49.2.6 concerning messages that the backend might generate due to outside events.

Recommended practice is to code frontends in a state-machine style that will accept any message type at any time that it could make sense, rather than wiring in assumptions about the exact sequence of messages.

49.2.3. Extended Query

The extended query protocol breaks down the above-described simple query protocol into multiple steps. The results of preparatory steps can be re-used multiple times for improved efficiency. Furthermore, additional features are available, such as the possibility of supplying data values as separate parameters instead of having to insert them directly into a query string.

In the extended protocol, the frontend first sends a Parse message, which contains a textual query string, optionally some information about data types of parameter placeholders, and the name of a destination prepared-statement object (an empty string selects the unnamed prepared statement). The response is either ParseComplete or ErrorResponse. Parameter data types can be specified by OID; if not given, the parser attempts to infer the data types in the same way as it would do for untyped literal string constants.

> **Note:** A parameter data type can be left unspecified by setting it to zero, or by making the array of parameter type OIDs shorter than the number of parameter symbols ($n) used in the query string. Another special case is that a parameter's type can be specified as void (that is, the OID of the void pseudotype). This is meant to allow parameter symbols to be used for function parameters that are actually OUT parameters. Ordinarily there is no context in which a void parameter could be used, but if such a parameter symbol appears in a function's parameter list, it is effectively ignored. For example, a function call such as foo($1,$2,$3,$4) could match a function with two IN and two OUT arguments, if $3 and $4 are specified as having type void.

> **Note:** The query string contained in a Parse message cannot include more than one SQL statement; else a syntax error is reported. This restriction does not exist in the simple-query protocol, but it does exist in the extended protocol, because allowing prepared statements or portals to contain multiple commands would complicate the protocol unduly.

If successfully created, a named prepared-statement object lasts till the end of the current session, unless explicitly destroyed. An unnamed prepared statement lasts only until the next Parse statement specifying the unnamed statement as destination is issued. (Note that a simple Query message also destroys the unnamed statement.) Named prepared statements must be explicitly closed before they can be redefined by another Parse message, but this is not required for the unnamed statement. Named prepared statements can also be created and accessed at the SQL command level, using PREPARE and EXECUTE.

Once a prepared statement exists, it can be readied for execution using a Bind message. The Bind message gives the name of the source prepared statement (empty string denotes the unnamed prepared statement), the name of the destination portal (empty string denotes the unnamed portal), and the values to use for any parameter placeholders present in the prepared statement. The supplied parameter set must match those needed by the prepared statement. (If you declared any void parameters in the Parse message, pass NULL values for them in the Bind message.) Bind also specifies the format to use for any data returned by the query; the format can be specified overall, or per-column. The response is either BindComplete or ErrorResponse.

> **Note:** The choice between text and binary output is determined by the format codes given in Bind, regardless of the SQL command involved. The BINARY attribute in cursor declarations is irrelevant when using extended query protocol.

Query planning typically occurs when the Bind message is processed. If the prepared statement has no parameters, or is executed repeatedly, the server might save the created plan and re-use it during subsequent Bind messages for the same prepared statement. However, it will do so only if it finds that a generic plan can be created that is not much less efficient than a plan that depends on the specific parameter values supplied. This happens transparently so far as the protocol is concerned.

If successfully created, a named portal object lasts till the end of the current transaction, unless explicitly destroyed. An unnamed portal is destroyed at the end of the transaction, or as soon as the next Bind statement specifying the unnamed portal as destination is issued. (Note that a simple Query message also destroys the unnamed portal.) Named portals must be explicitly closed before they can be redefined by another Bind message, but this is not required for the unnamed portal. Named portals can also be created and accessed at the SQL command level, using `DECLARE CURSOR` and `FETCH`.

Once a portal exists, it can be executed using an Execute message. The Execute message specifies the portal name (empty string denotes the unnamed portal) and a maximum result-row count (zero meaning "fetch all rows"). The result-row count is only meaningful for portals containing commands that return row sets; in other cases the command is always executed to completion, and the row count is ignored. The possible responses to Execute are the same as those described above for queries issued via simple query protocol, except that Execute doesn't cause ReadyForQuery or RowDescription to be issued.

If Execute terminates before completing the execution of a portal (due to reaching a nonzero result-row count), it will send a PortalSuspended message; the appearance of this message tells the frontend that another Execute should be issued against the same portal to complete the operation. The CommandComplete message indicating completion of the source SQL command is not sent until the portal's execution is completed. Therefore, an Execute phase is always terminated by the appearance of exactly one of these messages: CommandComplete, EmptyQueryResponse (if the portal was created from an empty query string), ErrorResponse, or PortalSuspended.

At completion of each series of extended-query messages, the frontend should issue a Sync message. This parameterless message causes the backend to close the current transaction if it's not inside a `BEGIN`/`COMMIT` transaction block ("close" meaning to commit if no error, or roll back if error). Then a ReadyForQuery response is issued. The purpose of Sync is to provide a resynchronization point for error recovery. When an error is detected while processing any extended-query message, the backend issues ErrorResponse, then reads and discards messages until a Sync is reached, then issues ReadyForQuery and returns to normal message processing. (But note that no skipping occurs if an error is detected *while* processing Sync — this ensures that there is one and only one ReadyForQuery sent for each Sync.)

> **Note:** Sync does not cause a transaction block opened with `BEGIN` to be closed. It is possible to detect this situation since the ReadyForQuery message includes transaction status information.

In addition to these fundamental, required operations, there are several optional operations that can be used with extended-query protocol.

The Describe message (portal variant) specifies the name of an existing portal (or an empty string for the unnamed portal). The response is a RowDescription message describing the rows that will be returned by executing the portal; or a NoData message if the portal does not contain a query that will return rows; or ErrorResponse if there is no such portal.

The Describe message (statement variant) specifies the name of an existing prepared statement (or an empty string for the unnamed prepared statement). The response is a ParameterDescription message describing the parameters needed by the statement, followed by a RowDescription message describing the rows that will be returned when the statement is eventually executed (or a NoData message if the statement will not return rows). ErrorResponse is issued if there is no such prepared statement. Note that since Bind has not yet been issued, the formats to be used for returned columns are not yet known to the backend; the format code fields in the RowDescription message will be zeroes in this case.

> **Tip:** In most scenarios the frontend should issue one or the other variant of Describe before issuing Execute, to ensure that it knows how to interpret the results it will get back.

The Close message closes an existing prepared statement or portal and releases resources. It is not an error to issue Close against a nonexistent statement or portal name. The response is normally CloseComplete, but could be ErrorResponse if some difficulty is encountered while releasing resources. Note that closing a prepared statement implicitly closes any open portals that were constructed from that statement.

The Flush message does not cause any specific output to be generated, but forces the backend to deliver any data pending in its output buffers. A Flush must be sent after any extended-query command except Sync, if the frontend wishes to examine the results of that command before issuing more commands. Without Flush, messages returned by the backend will be combined into the minimum possible number of packets to minimize network overhead.

> **Note:** The simple Query message is approximately equivalent to the series Parse, Bind, portal Describe, Execute, Close, Sync, using the unnamed prepared statement and portal objects and no parameters. One difference is that it will accept multiple SQL statements in the query string, automatically performing the bind/describe/execute sequence for each one in succession. Another difference is that it will not return ParseComplete, BindComplete, CloseComplete, or NoData messages.

49.2.4. Function Call

The Function Call sub-protocol allows the client to request a direct call of any function that exists in the database's `pg_proc` system catalog. The client must have execute permission for the function.

> **Note:** The Function Call sub-protocol is a legacy feature that is probably best avoided in new code. Similar results can be accomplished by setting up a prepared statement that does `SELECT function($1, ...)`. The Function Call cycle can then be replaced with Bind/Execute.

A Function Call cycle is initiated by the frontend sending a FunctionCall message to the backend. The backend then sends one or more response messages depending on the results of the function call, and finally a ReadyForQuery response message. ReadyForQuery informs the frontend that it can safely send a new query or function call.

The possible response messages from the backend are:

ErrorResponse

An error has occurred.

FunctionCallResponse

The function call was completed and returned the result given in the message. (Note that the Function Call protocol can only handle a single scalar result, not a row type or set of results.)

ReadyForQuery

Processing of the function call is complete. ReadyForQuery will always be sent, whether processing terminates successfully or with an error.

NoticeResponse

A warning message has been issued in relation to the function call. Notices are in addition to other responses, i.e., the backend will continue processing the command.

49.2.5. COPY Operations

The COPY command allows high-speed bulk data transfer to or from the server. Copy-in and copy-out operations each switch the connection into a distinct sub-protocol, which lasts until the operation is completed.

Copy-in mode (data transfer to the server) is initiated when the backend executes a COPY FROM STDIN SQL statement. The backend sends a CopyInResponse message to the frontend. The frontend should then send zero or more CopyData messages, forming a stream of input data. (The message boundaries are not required to have anything to do with row boundaries, although that is often a reasonable choice.) The frontend can terminate the copy-in mode by sending either a CopyDone message (allowing successful termination) or a CopyFail message (which will cause the COPY SQL statement to fail with an error). The backend then reverts to the command-processing mode it was in before the COPY started, which will be either simple or extended query protocol. It will next send either CommandComplete (if successful) or ErrorResponse (if not).

In the event of a backend-detected error during copy-in mode (including receipt of a CopyFail message), the backend will issue an ErrorResponse message. If the COPY command was issued via an extended-query message, the backend will now discard frontend messages until a Sync message is received, then it will issue ReadyForQuery and return to normal processing. If the COPY command was issued in a simple Query message, the rest of that message is discarded and ReadyForQuery is issued. In either case, any subsequent CopyData, CopyDone, or CopyFail messages issued by the frontend will simply be dropped.

The backend will ignore Flush and Sync messages received during copy-in mode. Receipt of any other non-copy message type constitutes an error that will abort the copy-in state as described above. (The exception for Flush and Sync is for the convenience of client libraries that always send Flush or Sync after an Execute message, without checking whether the command to be executed is a COPY FROM STDIN.)

Copy-out mode (data transfer from the server) is initiated when the backend executes a COPY TO STDOUT SQL statement. The backend sends a CopyOutResponse message to the frontend, followed by zero or more CopyData messages (always one per row), followed by CopyDone. The backend then reverts to the command-processing mode it was in before the COPY started, and sends CommandComplete. The frontend cannot abort the transfer (except by closing the connection or issuing a Cancel request), but it can discard unwanted CopyData and CopyDone messages.

In the event of a backend-detected error during copy-out mode, the backend will issue an ErrorResponse message and revert to normal processing. The frontend should treat receipt of ErrorResponse as terminating the copy-out mode.

It is possible for NoticeResponse and ParameterStatus messages to be interspersed between CopyData messages; frontends must handle these cases, and should be prepared for other asynchronous message types as well (see Section 49.2.6). Otherwise, any message type other than CopyData or CopyDone may be treated as terminating copy-out mode.

There is another Copy-related mode called copy-both, which allows high-speed bulk data transfer to *and* from the server. Copy-both mode is initiated when a backend in walsender mode executes a START_REPLICATION statement. The backend sends a CopyBothResponse message to the frontend. Both the backend and the frontend may then send CopyData messages until either end sends a CopyDone message. After the client sends a CopyDone message, the connection goes from copy-both mode to copy-out mode, and the client may not send any more CopyData messages. Similarly, when the server sends a CopyDone message, the connection goes into copy-in mode, and the server may not send any more CopyData messages. After both sides have sent a CopyDone message, the copy mode is terminated, and the backend reverts to the command-processing mode. In the event of a backend-detected error during copy-both mode, the backend will issue an ErrorResponse message, discard frontend messages until a Sync message is received, and then issue ReadyForQuery and return to normal processing. The frontend should treat receipt of ErrorResponse as terminating the copy in both directions; no CopyDone should be sent in this case. See Section 49.3 for more information on the subprotocol transmitted over copy-both mode.

The CopyInResponse, CopyOutResponse and CopyBothResponse messages include fields that inform the frontend of the number of columns per row and the format codes being used for each column. (As of the present implementation, all columns in a given COPY operation will use the same format, but the message design does not assume this.)

49.2.6. Asynchronous Operations

There are several cases in which the backend will send messages that are not specifically prompted by the frontend's command stream. Frontends must be prepared to deal with these messages at any time, even when not engaged in a query. At minimum, one should check for these cases before beginning to read a query response.

It is possible for NoticeResponse messages to be generated due to outside activity; for example, if the database administrator commands a "fast" database shutdown, the backend will send a NoticeResponse indicating this fact before closing the connection. Accordingly, frontends should always be prepared to accept and display NoticeResponse messages, even when the connection is nominally idle.

ParameterStatus messages will be generated whenever the active value changes for any of the parameters the backend believes the frontend should know about. Most commonly this occurs in response to a SET SQL command executed by the frontend, and this case is effectively synchronous — but it is also possible for parameter status changes to occur because the administrator changed a configuration file and then sent the SIGHUP signal to the server. Also, if a SET command is rolled back, an appropriate ParameterStatus message will be generated to report the current effective value.

At present there is a hard-wired set of parameters for which ParameterStatus will be generated: they are server_version, server_encoding, client_encoding, application_name, is_superuser, session_authorization, DateStyle, IntervalStyle, TimeZone, integer_datetimes, and standard_conforming_strings. (server_encoding, TimeZone, and integer_datetimes were not reported by releases before 8.0; standard_conforming_strings was not reported by releases before 8.1; IntervalStyle was not reported by releases before 8.4; application_name was not reported by releases before 9.0.) Note that server_version, server_encoding and integer_datetimes are pseudo-parameters that cannot change after startup. This set might change in the future, or even become configurable. Accordingly, a frontend should simply ignore ParameterStatus for parameters that it does not understand or care about.

If a frontend issues a LISTEN command, then the backend will send a NotificationResponse message (not to be confused with NoticeResponse!) whenever a NOTIFY command is executed for the same channel name.

> **Note:** At present, NotificationResponse can only be sent outside a transaction, and thus it will not occur in the middle of a command-response series, though it might occur just before ReadyForQuery. It is unwise to design frontend logic that assumes that, however. Good practice is to be able to accept NotificationResponse at any point in the protocol.

49.2.7. Canceling Requests in Progress

During the processing of a query, the frontend might request cancellation of the query. The cancel request is not sent directly on the open connection to the backend for reasons of implementation efficiency: we don't want to have the backend constantly checking for new input from the frontend during query processing. Cancel requests should be relatively infrequent, so we make them slightly cumbersome in order to avoid a penalty in the normal case.

To issue a cancel request, the frontend opens a new connection to the server and sends a CancelRequest message, rather than the StartupMessage message that would ordinarily be sent across a new connection. The server will process this request and then close the connection. For security reasons, no direct reply is made to the cancel request message.

A CancelRequest message will be ignored unless it contains the same key data (PID and secret key) passed to the frontend during connection start-up. If the request matches the PID and secret key for a currently executing backend, the processing of the current query is aborted. (In the existing implementation, this is done by sending a special signal to the backend process that is processing the query.)

The cancellation signal might or might not have any effect — for example, if it arrives after the backend has finished processing the query, then it will have no effect. If the cancellation is effective, it results in the current command being terminated early with an error message.

The upshot of all this is that for reasons of both security and efficiency, the frontend has no direct way to tell whether a cancel request has succeeded. It must continue to wait for the backend to respond to the query. Issuing a cancel simply improves the odds that the current query will finish soon, and improves the odds that it will fail with an error message instead of succeeding.

Since the cancel request is sent across a new connection to the server and not across the regular frontend/backend communication link, it is possible for the cancel request to be issued by any process, not just the frontend whose query is to be canceled. This might provide additional flexibility when building multiple-process applications. It also introduces a security risk, in that unauthorized persons might try to cancel queries. The security risk is addressed by requiring a dynamically generated secret key to be supplied in cancel requests.

49.2.8. Termination

The normal, graceful termination procedure is that the frontend sends a Terminate message and immediately closes the connection. On receipt of this message, the backend closes the connection and terminates.

In rare cases (such as an administrator-commanded database shutdown) the backend might disconnect without any frontend request to do so. In such cases the backend will attempt to send an error or notice message giving the reason for the disconnection before it closes the connection.

Other termination scenarios arise from various failure cases, such as core dump at one end or the other, loss of the communications link, loss of message-boundary synchronization, etc. If either frontend or backend sees an unexpected closure of the connection, it should clean up and terminate. The frontend has the option of launching a new backend by recontacting the server if it doesn't want to terminate itself. Closing the connection is also advisable if an unrecognizable message type is received, since this probably indicates loss of message-boundary sync.

For either normal or abnormal termination, any open transaction is rolled back, not committed. One should note however that if a frontend disconnects while a non-SELECT query is being processed, the backend will probably finish the query before noticing the disconnection. If the query is outside any transaction block (BEGIN ... COMMIT sequence) then its results might be committed before the disconnection is recognized.

49.2.9. SSL Session Encryption

If PostgreSQL was built with SSL support, frontend/backend communications can be encrypted using SSL. This provides communication security in environments where attackers might be able to capture the session traffic. For more information on encrypting PostgreSQL sessions with SSL, see Section 17.9.

To initiate an SSL-encrypted connection, the frontend initially sends an SSLRequest message rather than a StartupMessage. The server then responds with a single byte containing S or N, indicating that it is willing or unwilling to perform SSL, respectively. The frontend might close the connection at this point if it is dissatisfied with the response. To continue after S, perform an SSL startup handshake (not described here, part of the SSL specification) with the server. If this is successful, continue with sending the usual StartupMessage. In this case the StartupMessage and all subsequent data will be SSL-encrypted. To continue after N, send the usual StartupMessage and proceed without encryption.

The frontend should also be prepared to handle an ErrorMessage response to SSLRequest from the server. This would only occur if the server predates the addition of SSL support to PostgreSQL. (Such servers are now very ancient, and likely do not exist in the wild anymore.) In this case the connection must be closed, but the frontend might choose to open a fresh connection and proceed without requesting SSL.

An initial SSLRequest can also be used in a connection that is being opened to send a CancelRequest message.

While the protocol itself does not provide a way for the server to force SSL encryption, the administrator can configure the server to reject unencrypted sessions as a byproduct of authentication checking.

49.3. Streaming Replication Protocol

To initiate streaming replication, the frontend sends the `replication` parameter in the startup message. A Boolean value of `true` tells the backend to go into walsender mode, wherein a small set of replication commands can be issued instead of SQL statements. Only the simple query protocol can be used in walsender mode. Passing `database` as the value instructs walsender to connect to the database specified in the `dbname` parameter, which will allow the connection to be used for logical replication from that database.

For the purpose of testing replication commands, you can make a replication connection via psql or any other `libpq`-using tool with a connection string including the `replication` option, e.g.:

```
psql "dbname=postgres replication=database" -c "IDENTIFY_SYSTEM;"
```

However it is often more useful to use pg_receivexlog (for physical replication) or pg_recvlogical (for logical replication).

The commands accepted in walsender mode are:

IDENTIFY_SYSTEM

> Requests the server to identify itself. Server replies with a result set of a single row, containing four fields:

> systemid

>> The unique system identifier identifying the cluster. This can be used to check that the base backup used to initialize the standby came from the same cluster.

> timeline

>> Current TimelineID. Also useful to check that the standby is consistent with the master.

> xlogpos

>> Current xlog flush location. Useful to get a known location in the transaction log where streaming can start.

> dbname

>> Database connected to or NULL.

TIMELINE_HISTORY *tli*

> Requests the server to send over the timeline history file for timeline *tli*. Server replies with a result set of a single row, containing two fields:

> filename

>> Filename of the timeline history file, e.g `00000002.history`.

> content

>> Contents of the timeline history file.

CREATE_REPLICATION_SLOT *slot_name* { PHYSICAL | LOGICAL *output_plugin* }

>   Create a physical or logical replication slot. See Section 25.2.6 for more about replication slots.

>   *slot_name*

>>   The name of the slot to create. Must be a valid replication slot name (see Section 25.2.6.1).

>   *output_plugin*

>>   The name of the output plugin used for logical decoding (see Section 46.6).

START_REPLICATION [SLOT *slot_name*] [PHYSICAL] *XXX/XXX* [TIMELINE *tli*]

>   Instructs server to start streaming WAL, starting at WAL position *XXX/XXX*. If TIMELINE option is specified, streaming starts on timeline *tli*; otherwise, the server's current timeline is selected. The server can reply with an error, e.g. if the requested section of WAL has already been recycled. On success, server responds with a CopyBothResponse message, and then starts to stream WAL to the frontend.

>   If a slot's name is provided via *slot_name*, it will be updated as replication progresses so that the server knows which WAL segments, and if hot_standby_feedback is on which transactions, are still needed by the standby.

>   If the client requests a timeline that's not the latest, but is part of the history of the server, the server will stream all the WAL on that timeline starting from the requested startpoint, up to the point where the server switched to another timeline. If the client requests streaming at exactly the end of an old timeline, the server responds immediately with CommandComplete without entering COPY mode.

>   After streaming all the WAL on a timeline that is not the latest one, the server will end streaming by exiting the COPY mode. When the client acknowledges this by also exiting COPY mode, the server sends a result set with one row and two columns, indicating the next timeline in this server's history. The first column is the next timeline's ID, and the second column is the XLOG position where the switch happened. Usually, the switch position is the end of the WAL that was streamed, but there are corner cases where the server can send some WAL from the old timeline that it has not itself replayed before promoting. Finally, the server sends CommandComplete message, and is ready to accept a new command.

>   WAL data is sent as a series of CopyData messages. (This allows other information to be intermixed; in particular the server can send an ErrorResponse message if it encounters a failure after beginning to stream.) The payload of each CopyData message from server to the client contains a message of one of the following formats:

>   XLogData (B)

>>   Byte1('w')

>>>   Identifies the message as WAL data.

>>   Int64

>>>   The starting point of the WAL data in this message.

>>   Int64

>>>   The current end of WAL on the server.

Int64

> The server's system clock at the time of transmission, as microseconds since midnight on 2000-01-01.

Byte*n*

> A section of the WAL data stream.

> A single WAL record is never split across two XLogData messages. When a WAL record crosses a WAL page boundary, and is therefore already split using continuation records, it can be split at the page boundary. In other words, the first main WAL record and its continuation records can be sent in different XLogData messages.

Primary keepalive message (B)

Byte1('k')

> Identifies the message as a sender keepalive.

Int64

> The current end of WAL on the server.

Int64

> The server's system clock at the time of transmission, as microseconds since midnight on 2000-01-01.

Byte1

> 1 means that the client should reply to this message as soon as possible, to avoid a timeout disconnect. 0 otherwise.

The receiving process can send replies back to the sender at any time, using one of the following message formats (also in the payload of a CopyData message):

Standby status update (F)

Byte1('r')

> Identifies the message as a receiver status update.

Int64

> The location of the last WAL byte + 1 received and written to disk in the standby.

Int64

> The location of the last WAL byte + 1 flushed to disk in the standby.

Int64

> The location of the last WAL byte + 1 applied in the standby.

Int64

The client's system clock at the time of transmission, as microseconds since midnight on 2000-01-01.

Byte1

If 1, the client requests the server to reply to this message immediately. This can be used to ping the server, to test if the connection is still healthy.

Hot Standby feedback message (F)

Byte1('h')

Identifies the message as a Hot Standby feedback message.

Int64

The client's system clock at the time of transmission, as microseconds since midnight on 2000-01-01.

Int32

The standby's current xmin. This may be 0, if the standby is sending notification that Hot Standby feedback will no longer be sent on this connection. Later non-zero messages may reinitiate the feedback mechanism.

Int32

The standby's current epoch.

START_REPLICATION SLOT `slot_name` LOGICAL *XXX/XXX* [(`option_name` [`option_value`] [, ...])]

Instructs server to start streaming WAL for logical replication, starting at WAL position *XXX/XXX*. The server can reply with an error, e.g. if the requested section of WAL has already been recycled. On success, server responds with a CopyBothResponse message, and then starts to stream WAL to the frontend.

The messages inside the CopyBothResponse messages are of the same format documented for START_REPLICATION ... PHYSICAL.

The output plugin associated with the selected slot is used to process the output for streaming.

SLOT `slot_name`

The name of the slot to stream changes from. This parameter is required, and must correspond to an existing logical replication slot created with CREATE_REPLICATION_SLOT in LOGICAL mode.

XXX/XXX

The WAL position to begin streaming at.

option_name

> The name of an option passed to the slot's logical decoding plugin.

option_value

> Optional value, in the form of a string constant, associated with the specified option.

DROP_REPLICATION_SLOT *slot_name*

> Drops a replication slot, freeing any reserved server-side resources. If the slot is currently in use by an active connection, this command fails.

slot_name

> The name of the slot to drop.

BASE_BACKUP [LABEL *'label'*] [PROGRESS] [FAST] [WAL] [NOWAIT] [MAX_RATE *rate*]

> Instructs the server to start streaming a base backup. The system will automatically be put in backup mode before the backup is started, and taken out of it when the backup is complete. The following options are accepted:

LABEL *'label'*

> Sets the label of the backup. If none is specified, a backup label of base backup will be used. The quoting rules for the label are the same as a standard SQL string with standard_conforming_strings turned on.

PROGRESS

> Request information required to generate a progress report. This will send back an approximate size in the header of each tablespace, which can be used to calculate how far along the stream is done. This is calculated by enumerating all the file sizes once before the transfer is even started, and may as such have a negative impact on the performance - in particular it may take longer before the first data is streamed. Since the database files can change during the backup, the size is only approximate and may both grow and shrink between the time of approximation and the sending of the actual files.

FAST

> Request a fast checkpoint.

WAL

> Include the necessary WAL segments in the backup. This will include all the files between start and stop backup in the pg_xlog directory of the base directory tar file.

NOWAIT

> By default, the backup will wait until the last required xlog segment has been archived, or emit a warning if log archiving is not enabled. Specifying NOWAIT disables both the waiting and the warning, leaving the client responsible for ensuring the required log is available.

MAX_RATE *rate*

> Limit (throttle) the maximum amount of data transferred from server to client per unit of time. The expected unit is kilobytes per second. If this option is specified, the value must either be equal to zero or it must fall within the range from 32 kB through 1 GB (inclusive). If zero is passed or the option is not specified, no restriction is imposed on the transfer.

When the backup is started, the server will first send two ordinary result sets, followed by one or more CopyResponse results.

The first ordinary result set contains the starting position of the backup, in a single row with two columns. The first column contains the start position given in XLogRecPtr format, and the second column contains the corresponding timeline ID.

The second ordinary result set has one row for each tablespace. The fields in this row are:

spcoid

> The oid of the tablespace, or NULL if it's the base directory.

spclocation

> The full path of the tablespace directory, or NULL if it's the base directory.

size

> The approximate size of the tablespace, if progress report has been requested; otherwise it's NULL.

After the second regular result set, one or more CopyResponse results will be sent, one for PGDATA and one for each additional tablespace other than `pg_default` and `pg_global`. The data in the CopyResponse results will be a tar format (following the "ustar interchange format" specified in the POSIX 1003.1-2008 standard) dump of the tablespace contents, except that the two trailing blocks of zeroes specified in the standard are omitted. After the tar data is complete, a final ordinary result set will be sent, containing the WAL end position of the backup, in the same format as the start position.

The tar archive for the data directory and each tablespace will contain all files in the directories, regardless of whether they are PostgreSQL files or other files added to the same directory. The only excluded files are:

- `postmaster.pid`
- `postmaster.opts`
- various temporary files created during the operation of the PostgreSQL server
- `pg_xlog`, including subdirectories. If the backup is run with WAL files included, a synthesized version of `pg_xlog` will be included, but it will only contain the files necessary for the backup to work, not the rest of the contents.
- `pg_replslot` is copied as an empty directory.
- Files other than regular files and directories, such as symbolic links and special device files, are skipped. (Symbolic links in `pg_tblspc` are maintained.)

Owner, group and file mode are set if the underlying file system on the server supports it.

Once all tablespaces have been sent, a final regular result set will be sent. This result set contains the end position of the backup, given in XLogRecPtr format as a single column in a single row.

49.4. Message Data Types

This section describes the base data types used in messages.

Int*n*(i)

> An *n*-bit integer in network byte order (most significant byte first). If i is specified it is the exact value that will appear, otherwise the value is variable. Eg. Int16, Int32(42).

Int*n*[k]

> An array of k *n*-bit integers, each in network byte order. The array length k is always determined by an earlier field in the message. Eg. Int16[M].

String(s)

> A null-terminated string (C-style string). There is no specific length limitation on strings. If s is specified it is the exact value that will appear, otherwise the value is variable. Eg. String, String("user").

> > **Note:** *There is no predefined limit* on the length of a string that can be returned by the backend. Good coding strategy for a frontend is to use an expandable buffer so that anything that fits in memory can be accepted. If that's not feasible, read the full string and discard trailing characters that don't fit into your fixed-size buffer.

Byte*n*(c)

> Exactly *n* bytes. If the field width *n* is not a constant, it is always determinable from an earlier field in the message. If c is specified it is the exact value. Eg. Byte2, Byte1('\n').

49.5. Message Formats

This section describes the detailed format of each message. Each is marked to indicate that it can be sent by a frontend (F), a backend (B), or both (F & B). Notice that although each message includes a byte count at the beginning, the message format is defined so that the message end can be found without reference to the byte count. This aids validity checking. (The CopyData message is an exception, because it forms part of a data stream; the contents of any individual CopyData message cannot be interpretable on their own.)

AuthenticationOk (B)

> Byte1('R')

> > Identifies the message as an authentication request.

> Int32(8)

> > Length of message contents in bytes, including self.

Int32(0)

> Specifies that the authentication was successful.

AuthenticationKerberosV5 (B)

> Byte1('R')
>
> > Identifies the message as an authentication request.
>
> Int32(8)
>
> > Length of message contents in bytes, including self.
>
> Int32(2)
>
> > Specifies that Kerberos V5 authentication is required.

AuthenticationCleartextPassword (B)

> Byte1('R')
>
> > Identifies the message as an authentication request.
>
> Int32(8)
>
> > Length of message contents in bytes, including self.
>
> Int32(3)
>
> > Specifies that a clear-text password is required.

AuthenticationMD5Password (B)

> Byte1('R')
>
> > Identifies the message as an authentication request.
>
> Int32(12)
>
> > Length of message contents in bytes, including self.
>
> Int32(5)
>
> > Specifies that an MD5-encrypted password is required.
>
> Byte4
>
> > The salt to use when encrypting the password.

AuthenticationSCMCredential (B)

> Byte1('R')
>
> > Identifies the message as an authentication request.

Int32(8)

Length of message contents in bytes, including self.

Int32(6)

Specifies that an SCM credentials message is required.

AuthenticationGSS (B)

Byte1('R')

Identifies the message as an authentication request.

Int32(8)

Length of message contents in bytes, including self.

Int32(7)

Specifies that GSSAPI authentication is required.

AuthenticationSSPI (B)

Byte1('R')

Identifies the message as an authentication request.

Int32(8)

Length of message contents in bytes, including self.

Int32(9)

Specifies that SSPI authentication is required.

AuthenticationGSSContinue (B)

Byte1('R')

Identifies the message as an authentication request.

Int32

Length of message contents in bytes, including self.

Int32(8)

Specifies that this message contains GSSAPI or SSPI data.

Byte*n*

GSSAPI or SSPI authentication data.

BackendKeyData (B)

Byte1('K')

Identifies the message as cancellation key data. The frontend must save these values if it wishes to be able to issue CancelRequest messages later.

Int32(12)

Length of message contents in bytes, including self.

Int32

The process ID of this backend.

Int32

The secret key of this backend.

Bind (F)

Byte1('B')

Identifies the message as a Bind command.

Int32

Length of message contents in bytes, including self.

String

The name of the destination portal (an empty string selects the unnamed portal).

String

The name of the source prepared statement (an empty string selects the unnamed prepared statement).

Int16

The number of parameter format codes that follow (denoted c below). This can be zero to indicate that there are no parameters or that the parameters all use the default format (text); or one, in which case the specified format code is applied to all parameters; or it can equal the actual number of parameters.

Int16[c]

The parameter format codes. Each must presently be zero (text) or one (binary).

Int16

The number of parameter values that follow (possibly zero). This must match the number of parameters needed by the query.

Next, the following pair of fields appear for each parameter:

Int32

The length of the parameter value, in bytes (this count does not include itself). Can be zero. As a special case, -1 indicates a NULL parameter value. No value bytes follow in the NULL case.

Byte*n*

> The value of the parameter, in the format indicated by the associated format code. *n* is the above length.

After the last parameter, the following fields appear:

Int16

> The number of result-column format codes that follow (denoted *R* below). This can be zero to indicate that there are no result columns or that the result columns should all use the default format (text); or one, in which case the specified format code is applied to all result columns (if any); or it can equal the actual number of result columns of the query.

Int16[*R*]

> The result-column format codes. Each must presently be zero (text) or one (binary).

BindComplete (B)

Byte1('2')

> Identifies the message as a Bind-complete indicator.

Int32(4)

> Length of message contents in bytes, including self.

CancelRequest (F)

Int32(16)

> Length of message contents in bytes, including self.

Int32(80877102)

> The cancel request code. The value is chosen to contain 1234 in the most significant 16 bits, and 5678 in the least 16 significant bits. (To avoid confusion, this code must not be the same as any protocol version number.)

Int32

> The process ID of the target backend.

Int32

> The secret key for the target backend.

Close (F)

Byte1('C')

> Identifies the message as a Close command.

Int32

Length of message contents in bytes, including self.

Byte1

'S' to close a prepared statement; or 'P' to close a portal.

String

The name of the prepared statement or portal to close (an empty string selects the unnamed prepared statement or portal).

CloseComplete (B)

Byte1('3')

Identifies the message as a Close-complete indicator.

Int32(4)

Length of message contents in bytes, including self.

CommandComplete (B)

Byte1('C')

Identifies the message as a command-completed response.

Int32

Length of message contents in bytes, including self.

String

The command tag. This is usually a single word that identifies which SQL command was completed.

For an INSERT command, the tag is INSERT *oid rows*, where *rows* is the number of rows inserted. *oid* is the object ID of the inserted row if *rows* is 1 and the target table has OIDs; otherwise *oid* is 0.

For a DELETE command, the tag is DELETE *rows* where *rows* is the number of rows deleted.

For an UPDATE command, the tag is UPDATE *rows* where *rows* is the number of rows updated.

For a SELECT or CREATE TABLE AS command, the tag is SELECT *rows* where *rows* is the number of rows retrieved.

For a MOVE command, the tag is MOVE *rows* where *rows* is the number of rows the cursor's position has been changed by.

For a FETCH command, the tag is FETCH *rows* where *rows* is the number of rows that have been retrieved from the cursor.

For a COPY command, the tag is COPY *rows* where *rows* is the number of rows copied. (Note: the row count appears only in PostgreSQL 8.2 and later.)

CopyData (F & B)

Byte1('d')

Identifies the message as COPY data.

Int32

Length of message contents in bytes, including self.

Byte*n*

Data that forms part of a COPY data stream. Messages sent from the backend will always correspond to single data rows, but messages sent by frontends might divide the data stream arbitrarily.

CopyDone (F & B)

Byte1('c')

Identifies the message as a COPY-complete indicator.

Int32(4)

Length of message contents in bytes, including self.

CopyFail (F)

Byte1('f')

Identifies the message as a COPY-failure indicator.

Int32

Length of message contents in bytes, including self.

String

An error message to report as the cause of failure.

CopyInResponse (B)

Byte1('G')

Identifies the message as a Start Copy In response. The frontend must now send copy-in data (if not prepared to do so, send a CopyFail message).

Int32

Length of message contents in bytes, including self.

Int8

0 indicates the overall COPY format is textual (rows separated by newlines, columns separated by separator characters, etc). 1 indicates the overall copy format is binary (similar to DataRow format). See COPY for more information.

Int16

>The number of columns in the data to be copied (denoted N below).

Int16[N]

>The format codes to be used for each column. Each must presently be zero (text) or one (binary). All must be zero if the overall copy format is textual.

CopyOutResponse (B)

Byte1('H')

>Identifies the message as a Start Copy Out response. This message will be followed by copy-out data.

Int32

>Length of message contents in bytes, including self.

Int8

>0 indicates the overall COPY format is textual (rows separated by newlines, columns separated by separator characters, etc). 1 indicates the overall copy format is binary (similar to DataRow format). See COPY for more information.

Int16

>The number of columns in the data to be copied (denoted N below).

Int16[N]

>The format codes to be used for each column. Each must presently be zero (text) or one (binary). All must be zero if the overall copy format is textual.

CopyBothResponse (B)

Byte1('W')

>Identifies the message as a Start Copy Both response. This message is used only for Streaming Replication.

Int32

>Length of message contents in bytes, including self.

Int8

>0 indicates the overall COPY format is textual (rows separated by newlines, columns separated by separator characters, etc). 1 indicates the overall copy format is binary (similar to DataRow format). See COPY for more information.

Int16

>The number of columns in the data to be copied (denoted N below).

Int16[*N*]

> The format codes to be used for each column. Each must presently be zero (text) or one (binary). All must be zero if the overall copy format is textual.

DataRow (B)

> Byte1('D')
>
> > Identifies the message as a data row.
>
> Int32
>
> > Length of message contents in bytes, including self.
>
> Int16
>
> > The number of column values that follow (possibly zero).
>
> Next, the following pair of fields appear for each column:
>
> Int32
>
> > The length of the column value, in bytes (this count does not include itself). Can be zero. As a special case, -1 indicates a NULL column value. No value bytes follow in the NULL case.
>
> Byte*n*
>
> > The value of the column, in the format indicated by the associated format code. *n* is the above length.

Describe (F)

> Byte1('D')
>
> > Identifies the message as a Describe command.
>
> Int32
>
> > Length of message contents in bytes, including self.
>
> Byte1
>
> > 'S' to describe a prepared statement; or 'P' to describe a portal.
>
> String
>
> > The name of the prepared statement or portal to describe (an empty string selects the unnamed prepared statement or portal).

EmptyQueryResponse (B)

> Byte1('I')
>
> > Identifies the message as a response to an empty query string. (This substitutes for Command-Complete.)

Int32(4)

>Length of message contents in bytes, including self.

ErrorResponse (B)

Byte1('E')

>Identifies the message as an error.

Int32

>Length of message contents in bytes, including self.

The message body consists of one or more identified fields, followed by a zero byte as a terminator. Fields can appear in any order. For each field there is the following:

Byte1

>A code identifying the field type; if zero, this is the message terminator and no string follows. The presently defined field types are listed in Section 49.6. Since more field types might be added in future, frontends should silently ignore fields of unrecognized type.

String

>The field value.

Execute (F)

Byte1('E')

>Identifies the message as an Execute command.

Int32

>Length of message contents in bytes, including self.

String

>The name of the portal to execute (an empty string selects the unnamed portal).

Int32

>Maximum number of rows to return, if portal contains a query that returns rows (ignored otherwise). Zero denotes "no limit".

Flush (F)

Byte1('H')

>Identifies the message as a Flush command.

Int32(4)

>Length of message contents in bytes, including self.

FunctionCall (F)

Byte1('F')

Identifies the message as a function call.

Int32

Length of message contents in bytes, including self.

Int32

Specifies the object ID of the function to call.

Int16

The number of argument format codes that follow (denoted c below). This can be zero to indicate that there are no arguments or that the arguments all use the default format (text); or one, in which case the specified format code is applied to all arguments; or it can equal the actual number of arguments.

Int16[c]

The argument format codes. Each must presently be zero (text) or one (binary).

Int16

Specifies the number of arguments being supplied to the function.

Next, the following pair of fields appear for each argument:

Int32

The length of the argument value, in bytes (this count does not include itself). Can be zero. As a special case, -1 indicates a NULL argument value. No value bytes follow in the NULL case.

Byte$n$

The value of the argument, in the format indicated by the associated format code. n is the above length.

After the last argument, the following field appears:

Int16

The format code for the function result. Must presently be zero (text) or one (binary).

FunctionCallResponse (B)

Byte1('V')

Identifies the message as a function call result.

Int32

Length of message contents in bytes, including self.

Int32

The length of the function result value, in bytes (this count does not include itself). Can be zero. As a special case, -1 indicates a NULL function result. No value bytes follow in the NULL case.

Byte*n*

> The value of the function result, in the format indicated by the associated format code. *n* is the above length.

NoData (B)

Byte1('n')

> Identifies the message as a no-data indicator.

Int32(4)

> Length of message contents in bytes, including self.

NoticeResponse (B)

Byte1('N')

> Identifies the message as a notice.

Int32

> Length of message contents in bytes, including self.

The message body consists of one or more identified fields, followed by a zero byte as a terminator. Fields can appear in any order. For each field there is the following:

Byte1

> A code identifying the field type; if zero, this is the message terminator and no string follows. The presently defined field types are listed in Section 49.6. Since more field types might be added in future, frontends should silently ignore fields of unrecognized type.

String

> The field value.

NotificationResponse (B)

Byte1('A')

> Identifies the message as a notification response.

Int32

> Length of message contents in bytes, including self.

Int32

> The process ID of the notifying backend process.

String

> The name of the channel that the notify has been raised on.

String

> The "payload" string passed from the notifying process.

ParameterDescription (B)

Byte1('t')

> Identifies the message as a parameter description.

Int32

> Length of message contents in bytes, including self.

Int16

> The number of parameters used by the statement (can be zero).

Then, for each parameter, there is the following:

Int32

> Specifies the object ID of the parameter data type.

ParameterStatus (B)

Byte1('S')

> Identifies the message as a run-time parameter status report.

Int32

> Length of message contents in bytes, including self.

String

> The name of the run-time parameter being reported.

String

> The current value of the parameter.

Parse (F)

Byte1('P')

> Identifies the message as a Parse command.

Int32

> Length of message contents in bytes, including self.

String

> The name of the destination prepared statement (an empty string selects the unnamed prepared statement).

String

> The query string to be parsed.

Int16

> The number of parameter data types specified (can be zero). Note that this is not an indication of the number of parameters that might appear in the query string, only the number that the frontend wants to prespecify types for.

Then, for each parameter, there is the following:

Int32

> Specifies the object ID of the parameter data type. Placing a zero here is equivalent to leaving the type unspecified.

ParseComplete (B)

Byte1('1')

> Identifies the message as a Parse-complete indicator.

Int32(4)

> Length of message contents in bytes, including self.

PasswordMessage (F)

Byte1('p')

> Identifies the message as a password response. Note that this is also used for GSSAPI and SSPI response messages (which is really a design error, since the contained data is not a null-terminated string in that case, but can be arbitrary binary data).

Int32

> Length of message contents in bytes, including self.

String

> The password (encrypted, if requested).

PortalSuspended (B)

Byte1('s')

> Identifies the message as a portal-suspended indicator. Note this only appears if an Execute message's row-count limit was reached.

Int32(4)

> Length of message contents in bytes, including self.

Query (F)

Byte1('Q')

Identifies the message as a simple query.

Int32

Length of message contents in bytes, including self.

String

The query string itself.

ReadyForQuery (B)

Byte1('Z')

Identifies the message type. ReadyForQuery is sent whenever the backend is ready for a new query cycle.

Int32(5)

Length of message contents in bytes, including self.

Byte1

Current backend transaction status indicator. Possible values are 'I' if idle (not in a transaction block); 'T' if in a transaction block; or 'E' if in a failed transaction block (queries will be rejected until block is ended).

RowDescription (B)

Byte1('T')

Identifies the message as a row description.

Int32

Length of message contents in bytes, including self.

Int16

Specifies the number of fields in a row (can be zero).

Then, for each field, there is the following:

String

The field name.

Int32

If the field can be identified as a column of a specific table, the object ID of the table; otherwise zero.

Int16

> If the field can be identified as a column of a specific table, the attribute number of the column; otherwise zero.

Int32

> The object ID of the field's data type.

Int16

> The data type size (see `pg_type.typlen`). Note that negative values denote variable-width types.

Int32

> The type modifier (see `pg_attribute.atttypmod`). The meaning of the modifier is type-specific.

Int16

> The format code being used for the field. Currently will be zero (text) or one (binary). In a RowDescription returned from the statement variant of Describe, the format code is not yet known and will always be zero.

SSLRequest (F)

Int32(8)

> Length of message contents in bytes, including self.

Int32(80877103)

> The SSL request code. The value is chosen to contain 1234 in the most significant 16 bits, and 5679 in the least 16 significant bits. (To avoid confusion, this code must not be the same as any protocol version number.)

StartupMessage (F)

Int32

> Length of message contents in bytes, including self.

Int32(196608)

> The protocol version number. The most significant 16 bits are the major version number (3 for the protocol described here). The least significant 16 bits are the minor version number (0 for the protocol described here).

The protocol version number is followed by one or more pairs of parameter name and value strings. A zero byte is required as a terminator after the last name/value pair. Parameters can appear in any order. user is required, others are optional. Each parameter is specified as:

String

The parameter name. Currently recognized names are:

`user`

The database user name to connect as. Required; there is no default.

`database`

The database to connect to. Defaults to the user name.

`options`

Command-line arguments for the backend. (This is deprecated in favor of setting individual run-time parameters.)

In addition to the above, any run-time parameter that can be set at backend start time might be listed. Such settings will be applied during backend start (after parsing the command-line options if any). The values will act as session defaults.

String

The parameter value.

Sync (F)

Byte1('S')

Identifies the message as a Sync command.

Int32(4)

Length of message contents in bytes, including self.

Terminate (F)

Byte1('X')

Identifies the message as a termination.

Int32(4)

Length of message contents in bytes, including self.

49.6. Error and Notice Message Fields

This section describes the fields that can appear in ErrorResponse and NoticeResponse messages. Each field type has a single-byte identification token. Note that any given field type should appear at most once per message.

S

Severity: the field contents are ERROR, FATAL, or PANIC (in an error message), or WARNING, NOTICE, DEBUG, INFO, or LOG (in a notice message), or a localized translation of one of these. Always present.

C

Code: the SQLSTATE code for the error (see Appendix A). Not localizable. Always present.

M

Message: the primary human-readable error message. This should be accurate but terse (typically one line). Always present.

D

Detail: an optional secondary error message carrying more detail about the problem. Might run to multiple lines.

H

Hint: an optional suggestion what to do about the problem. This is intended to differ from Detail in that it offers advice (potentially inappropriate) rather than hard facts. Might run to multiple lines.

P

Position: the field value is a decimal ASCII integer, indicating an error cursor position as an index into the original query string. The first character has index 1, and positions are measured in characters not bytes.

p

Internal position: this is defined the same as the P field, but it is used when the cursor position refers to an internally generated command rather than the one submitted by the client. The q field will always appear when this field appears.

q

Internal query: the text of a failed internally-generated command. This could be, for example, a SQL query issued by a PL/pgSQL function.

W

Where: an indication of the context in which the error occurred. Presently this includes a call stack traceback of active procedural language functions and internally-generated queries. The trace is one entry per line, most recent first.

s

Schema name: if the error was associated with a specific database object, the name of the schema containing that object, if any.

t

Table name: if the error was associated with a specific table, the name of the table. (Refer to the schema name field for the name of the table's schema.)

c

Column name: if the error was associated with a specific table column, the name of the column. (Refer to the schema and table name fields to identify the table.)

d

Data type name: if the error was associated with a specific data type, the name of the data type. (Refer to the schema name field for the name of the data type's schema.)

n

Constraint name: if the error was associated with a specific constraint, the name of the constraint. Refer to fields listed above for the associated table or domain. (For this purpose, indexes are treated as constraints, even if they weren't created with constraint syntax.)

F

File: the file name of the source-code location where the error was reported.

L

Line: the line number of the source-code location where the error was reported.

R

Routine: the name of the source-code routine reporting the error.

Note: The fields for schema name, table name, column name, data type name, and constraint name are supplied only for a limited number of error types; see Appendix A. Frontends should not assume that the presence of any of these fields guarantees the presence of another field. Core error sources observe the interrelationships noted above, but user-defined functions may use these fields in other ways. In the same vein, clients should not assume that these fields denote contemporary objects in the current database.

The client is responsible for formatting displayed information to meet its needs; in particular it should break long lines as needed. Newline characters appearing in the error message fields should be treated as paragraph breaks, not line breaks.

49.7. Summary of Changes since Protocol 2.0

This section provides a quick checklist of changes, for the benefit of developers trying to update existing client libraries to protocol 3.0.

The initial startup packet uses a flexible list-of-strings format instead of a fixed format. Notice that session default values for run-time parameters can now be specified directly in the startup packet. (Actually, you could do that before using the `options` field, but given the limited width of `options` and the lack of any way to quote whitespace in the values, it wasn't a very safe technique.)

All messages now have a length count immediately following the message type byte (except for startup packets, which have no type byte). Also note that PasswordMessage now has a type byte.

ErrorResponse and NoticeResponse ('E' and 'N') messages now contain multiple fields, from which the client code can assemble an error message of the desired level of verbosity. Note that individual fields will typically not end with a newline, whereas the single string sent in the older protocol always did.

The ReadyForQuery ('Z') message includes a transaction status indicator.

The distinction between BinaryRow and DataRow message types is gone; the single DataRow message type serves for returning data in all formats. Note that the layout of DataRow has changed to make it easier to parse. Also, the representation of binary values has changed: it is no longer directly tied to the server's internal representation.

There is a new "extended query" sub-protocol, which adds the frontend message types Parse, Bind, Execute, Describe, Close, Flush, and Sync, and the backend message types ParseComplete, BindComplete, PortalSuspended, ParameterDescription, NoData, and CloseComplete. Existing clients do not have to concern themselves with this sub-protocol, but making use of it might allow improvements in performance or functionality.

COPY data is now encapsulated into CopyData and CopyDone messages. There is a well-defined way to recover from errors during COPY. The special "\." last line is not needed anymore, and is not sent during COPY OUT. (It is still recognized as a terminator during COPY IN, but its use is deprecated and will eventually be removed.) Binary COPY is supported. The CopyInResponse and CopyOutResponse messages include fields indicating the number of columns and the format of each column.

The layout of FunctionCall and FunctionCallResponse messages has changed. FunctionCall can now support passing NULL arguments to functions. It also can handle passing parameters and retrieving results in either text or binary format. There is no longer any reason to consider FunctionCall a potential security hole, since it does not offer direct access to internal server data representations.

The backend sends ParameterStatus ('S') messages during connection startup for all parameters it considers interesting to the client library. Subsequently, a ParameterStatus message is sent whenever the active value changes for any of these parameters.

The RowDescription ('T') message carries new table OID and column number fields for each column of the described row. It also shows the format code for each column.

The CursorResponse ('P') message is no longer generated by the backend.

The NotificationResponse ('A') message has an additional string field, which can carry a "payload" string passed from the NOTIFY event sender.

The EmptyQueryResponse ('I') message used to include an empty string parameter; this has been removed.

Chapter 50. PostgreSQL Coding Conventions

50.1. Formatting

Source code formatting uses 4 column tab spacing, with tabs preserved (i.e., tabs are not expanded to spaces). Each logical indentation level is one additional tab stop.

Layout rules (brace positioning, etc) follow BSD conventions. In particular, curly braces for the controlled blocks of `if`, `while`, `switch`, etc go on their own lines.

Limit line lengths so that the code is readable in an 80-column window. (This doesn't mean that you must never go past 80 columns. For instance, breaking a long error message string in arbitrary places just to keep the code within 80 columns is probably not a net gain in readability.)

Do not use C++ style comments (`//` comments). Strict ANSI C compilers do not accept them. For the same reason, do not use C++ extensions such as declaring new variables mid-block.

The preferred style for multi-line comment blocks is

```
/*
 * comment text begins here
 * and continues here
 */
```

Note that comment blocks that begin in column 1 will be preserved as-is by pgindent, but it will re-flow indented comment blocks as though they were plain text. If you want to preserve the line breaks in an indented block, add dashes like this:

```
    /*----------
     * comment text begins here
     * and continues here
     *----------
     */
```

While submitted patches do not absolutely have to follow these formatting rules, it's a good idea to do so. Your code will get run through pgindent before the next release, so there's no point in making it look nice under some other set of formatting conventions. A good rule of thumb for patches is "make the new code look like the existing code around it".

The `src/tools` directory contains sample settings files that can be used with the emacs, xemacs or vim editors to help ensure that they format code according to these conventions.

The text browsing tools more and less can be invoked as:

```
more -x4
less -x4
```

to make them show tabs appropriately.

50.2. Reporting Errors Within the Server

Error, warning, and log messages generated within the server code should be created using ereport, or its older cousin elog. The use of this function is complex enough to require some explanation.

There are two required elements for every message: a severity level (ranging from DEBUG to PANIC) and a primary message text. In addition there are optional elements, the most common of which is an error identifier code that follows the SQL spec's SQLSTATE conventions. ereport itself is just a shell function, that exists mainly for the syntactic convenience of making message generation look like a function call in the C source code. The only parameter accepted directly by ereport is the severity level. The primary message text and any optional message elements are generated by calling auxiliary functions, such as errmsg, within the ereport call.

A typical call to ereport might look like this:

```
ereport(ERROR,
        (errcode(ERRCODE_DIVISION_BY_ZERO),
         errmsg("division by zero")));
```

This specifies error severity level ERROR (a run-of-the-mill error). The errcode call specifies the SQL-STATE error code using a macro defined in src/include/utils/errcodes.h. The errmsg call provides the primary message text. Notice the extra set of parentheses surrounding the auxiliary function calls — these are annoying but syntactically necessary.

Here is a more complex example:

```
ereport(ERROR,
        (errcode(ERRCODE_AMBIGUOUS_FUNCTION),
         errmsg("function %s is not unique",
                func_signature_string(funcname, nargs,
                                      NIL, actual_arg_types)),
         errhint("Unable to choose a best candidate function. "
                 "You might need to add explicit typecasts.")));
```

This illustrates the use of format codes to embed run-time values into a message text. Also, an optional "hint" message is provided.

If the severity level is ERROR or higher, ereport aborts the execution of the user-defined function and does not return to the caller. If the severity level is lower than ERROR, ereport returns normally.

The available auxiliary routines for ereport are:

* errcode(sqlerrcode) specifies the SQLSTATE error identifier code for the condition. If this routine is not called, the error identifier defaults to ERRCODE_INTERNAL_ERROR when the error severity level is ERROR or higher, ERRCODE_WARNING when the error level is WARNING, otherwise (for NOTICE and below) ERRCODE_SUCCESSFUL_COMPLETION. While these defaults are often convenient, always think whether they are appropriate before omitting the errcode() call.

* errmsg(const char *msg, ...) specifies the primary error message text, and possibly run-time values to insert into it. Insertions are specified by sprintf-style format codes. In addition to the standard format codes accepted by sprintf, the format code %m can be used to insert the error message

returned by `strerror` for the current value of `errno`. [1] `%m` does not require any corresponding entry in the parameter list for `errmsg`. Note that the message string will be run through `gettext` for possible localization before format codes are processed.

- `errmsg_internal(const char *msg, ...)` is the same as `errmsg`, except that the message string will not be translated nor included in the internationalization message dictionary. This should be used for "cannot happen" cases that are probably not worth expending translation effort on.

- `errmsg_plural(const char *fmt_singular, const char *fmt_plural, unsigned long n, ...)` is like `errmsg`, but with support for various plural forms of the message. *fmt_singular* is the English singular format, *fmt_plural* is the English plural format, *n* is the integer value that determines which plural form is needed, and the remaining arguments are formatted according to the selected format string. For more information see Section 51.2.2.

- `errdetail(const char *msg, ...)` supplies an optional "detail" message; this is to be used when there is additional information that seems inappropriate to put in the primary message. The message string is processed in just the same way as for `errmsg`.

- `errdetail_internal(const char *msg, ...)` is the same as `errdetail`, except that the message string will not be translated nor included in the internationalization message dictionary. This should be used for detail messages that are not worth expending translation effort on, for instance because they are too technical to be useful to most users.

- `errdetail_plural(const char *fmt_singular, const char *fmt_plural, unsigned long n, ...)` is like `errdetail`, but with support for various plural forms of the message. For more information see Section 51.2.2.

- `errdetail_log(const char *msg, ...)` is the same as `errdetail` except that this string goes only to the server log, never to the client. If both `errdetail` (or one of its equivalents above) and `errdetail_log` are used then one string goes to the client and the other to the log. This is useful for error details that are too security-sensitive or too bulky to include in the report sent to the client.

- `errdetail_log_plural(const char *fmt_singuar, const char *fmt_plural, unsigned long n, ...)` is like `errdetail_log`, but with support for various plural forms of the message. For more information see Section 51.2.2.

- `errhint(const char *msg, ...)` supplies an optional "hint" message; this is to be used when offering suggestions about how to fix the problem, as opposed to factual details about what went wrong. The message string is processed in just the same way as for `errmsg`.

- `errcontext(const char *msg, ...)` is not normally called directly from an `ereport` message site; rather it is used in `error_context_stack` callback functions to provide information about the context in which an error occurred, such as the current location in a PL function. The message string is processed in just the same way as for `errmsg`. Unlike the other auxiliary functions, this can be called more than once per `ereport` call; the successive strings thus supplied are concatenated with separating newlines.

- `errposition(int cursorpos)` specifies the textual location of an error within a query string. Currently it is only useful for errors detected in the lexical and syntactic analysis phases of query processing.

---

1. That is, the value that was current when the `ereport` call was reached; changes of `errno` within the auxiliary reporting routines will not affect it. That would not be true if you were to write `strerror(errno)` explicitly in `errmsg`'s parameter list; accordingly, do not do so.

- `errtable(Relation rel)` specifies a relation whose name and schema name should be included as auxiliary fields in the error report.

- `errtablecol(Relation rel, int attnum)` specifies a column whose name, table name, and schema name should be included as auxiliary fields in the error report.

- `errtableconstraint(Relation rel, const char *conname)` specifies a table constraint whose name, table name, and schema name should be included as auxiliary fields in the error report. Indexes should be considered to be constraints for this purpose, whether or not they have an associated `pg_constraint` entry. Be careful to pass the underlying heap relation, not the index itself, as `rel`.

- `errdatatype(Oid datatypeOid)` specifies a data type whose name and schema name should be included as auxiliary fields in the error report.

- `errdomainconstraint(Oid datatypeOid, const char *conname)` specifies a domain constraint whose name, domain name, and schema name should be included as auxiliary fields in the error report.

- `errcode_for_file_access()` is a convenience function that selects an appropriate SQLSTATE error identifier for a failure in a file-access-related system call. It uses the saved `errno` to determine which error code to generate. Usually this should be used in combination with `%m` in the primary error message text.

- `errcode_for_socket_access()` is a convenience function that selects an appropriate SQLSTATE error identifier for a failure in a socket-related system call.

- `errhidestmt(bool hide_stmt)` can be called to specify suppression of the `STATEMENT:` portion of a message in the postmaster log. Generally this is appropriate if the message text includes the current statement already.

> **Note:** At most one of the functions `errtable`, `errtablecol`, `errtableconstraint`, `errdatatype`, or `errdomainconstraint` should be used in an `ereport` call. These functions exist to allow applications to extract the name of a database object associated with the error condition without having to examine the potentially-localized error message text. These functions should be used in error reports for which it's likely that applications would wish to have automatic error handling. As of PostgreSQL 9.3, complete coverage exists only for errors in SQLSTATE class 23 (integrity constraint violation), but this is likely to be expanded in future.

There is an older function `elog` that is still heavily used. An `elog` call:

```
elog(level, "format string", ...);
```

is exactly equivalent to:

```
ereport(level, (errmsg_internal("format string", ...)));
```

Notice that the SQLSTATE error code is always defaulted, and the message string is not subject to translation. Therefore, `elog` should be used only for internal errors and low-level debug logging. Any message that is likely to be of interest to ordinary users should go through `ereport`. Nonetheless, there are enough internal "cannot happen" error checks in the system that `elog` is still widely used; it is preferred for those messages for its notational simplicity.

Advice about writing good error messages can be found in Section 50.3.

50.3. Error Message Style Guide

This style guide is offered in the hope of maintaining a consistent, user-friendly style throughout all the messages generated by PostgreSQL.

50.3.1. What Goes Where

The primary message should be short, factual, and avoid reference to implementation details such as specific function names. "Short" means "should fit on one line under normal conditions". Use a detail message if needed to keep the primary message short, or if you feel a need to mention implementation details such as the particular system call that failed. Both primary and detail messages should be factual. Use a hint message for suggestions about what to do to fix the problem, especially if the suggestion might not always be applicable.

For example, instead of:

```
IpcMemoryCreate: shmget(key=%d, size=%u, 0%o) failed: %m
(plus a long addendum that is basically a hint)
```

write:

```
Primary:    could not create shared memory segment: %m
Detail:     Failed syscall was shmget(key=%d, size=%u, 0%o).
Hint:       the addendum
```

Rationale: keeping the primary message short helps keep it to the point, and lets clients lay out screen space on the assumption that one line is enough for error messages. Detail and hint messages can be relegated to a verbose mode, or perhaps a pop-up error-details window. Also, details and hints would normally be suppressed from the server log to save space. Reference to implementation details is best avoided since users don't know the details anyway.

50.3.2. Formatting

Don't put any specific assumptions about formatting into the message texts. Expect clients and the server log to wrap lines to fit their own needs. In long messages, newline characters (\n) can be used to indicate suggested paragraph breaks. Don't end a message with a newline. Don't use tabs or other formatting characters. (In error context displays, newlines are automatically added to separate levels of context such as function calls.)

Rationale: Messages are not necessarily displayed on terminal-type displays. In GUI displays or browsers these formatting instructions are at best ignored.

50.3.3. Quotation Marks

English text should use double quotes when quoting is appropriate. Text in other languages should consistently use one kind of quotes that is consistent with publishing customs and computer output of other programs.

Rationale: The choice of double quotes over single quotes is somewhat arbitrary, but tends to be the preferred use. Some have suggested choosing the kind of quotes depending on the type of object according to SQL conventions (namely, strings single quoted, identifiers double quoted). But this is a language-internal technical issue that many users aren't even familiar with, it won't scale to other kinds of quoted terms, it doesn't translate to other languages, and it's pretty pointless, too.

50.3.4. Use of Quotes

Use quotes always to delimit file names, user-supplied identifiers, and other variables that might contain words. Do not use them to mark up variables that will not contain words (for example, operator names).

There are functions in the backend that will double-quote their own output at need (for example, `format_type_be()`). Do not put additional quotes around the output of such functions.

Rationale: Objects can have names that create ambiguity when embedded in a message. Be consistent about denoting where a plugged-in name starts and ends. But don't clutter messages with unnecessary or duplicate quote marks.

50.3.5. Grammar and Punctuation

The rules are different for primary error messages and for detail/hint messages:

Primary error messages: Do not capitalize the first letter. Do not end a message with a period. Do not even think about ending a message with an exclamation point.

Detail and hint messages: Use complete sentences, and end each with a period. Capitalize the first word of sentences. Put two spaces after the period if another sentence follows (for English text; might be inappropriate in other languages).

Error context strings: Do not capitalize the first letter and do not end the string with a period. Context strings should normally not be complete sentences.

Rationale: Avoiding punctuation makes it easier for client applications to embed the message into a variety of grammatical contexts. Often, primary messages are not grammatically complete sentences anyway. (And if they're long enough to be more than one sentence, they should be split into primary and detail parts.) However, detail and hint messages are longer and might need to include multiple sentences. For consistency, they should follow complete-sentence style even when there's only one sentence.

50.3.6. Upper Case vs. Lower Case

Use lower case for message wording, including the first letter of a primary error message. Use upper case for SQL commands and key words if they appear in the message.

Rationale: It's easier to make everything look more consistent this way, since some messages are complete sentences and some not.

50.3.7. Avoid Passive Voice

Use the active voice. Use complete sentences when there is an acting subject ("A could not do B"). Use telegram style without subject if the subject would be the program itself; do not use "I" for the program.

Rationale: The program is not human. Don't pretend otherwise.

50.3.8. Present vs. Past Tense

Use past tense if an attempt to do something failed, but could perhaps succeed next time (perhaps after fixing some problem). Use present tense if the failure is certainly permanent.

There is a nontrivial semantic difference between sentences of the form:

```
could not open file "%s": %m
```

and:

```
cannot open file "%s"
```

The first one means that the attempt to open the file failed. The message should give a reason, such as "disk full" or "file doesn't exist". The past tense is appropriate because next time the disk might not be full anymore or the file in question might exist.

The second form indicates that the functionality of opening the named file does not exist at all in the program, or that it's conceptually impossible. The present tense is appropriate because the condition will persist indefinitely.

Rationale: Granted, the average user will not be able to draw great conclusions merely from the tense of the message, but since the language provides us with a grammar we should use it correctly.

50.3.9. Type of the Object

When citing the name of an object, state what kind of object it is.

Rationale: Otherwise no one will know what "foo.bar.baz" refers to.

50.3.10. Brackets

Square brackets are only to be used (1) in command synopses to denote optional arguments, or (2) to denote an array subscript.

Rationale: Anything else does not correspond to widely-known customary usage and will confuse people.

50.3.11. Assembling Error Messages

When a message includes text that is generated elsewhere, embed it in this style:

```
could not open file %s: %m
```

Rationale: It would be difficult to account for all possible error codes to paste this into a single smooth sentence, so some sort of punctuation is needed. Putting the embedded text in parentheses has also been suggested, but it's unnatural if the embedded text is likely to be the most important part of the message, as is often the case.

50.3.12. Reasons for Errors

Messages should always state the reason why an error occurred. For example:

```
BAD:     could not open file %s
BETTER:  could not open file %s (I/O failure)
```

If no reason is known you better fix the code.

50.3.13. Function Names

Don't include the name of the reporting routine in the error text. We have other mechanisms for finding that out when needed, and for most users it's not helpful information. If the error text doesn't make as much sense without the function name, reword it.

```
BAD:     pg_atoi: error in "z": cannot parse "z"
BETTER:  invalid input syntax for integer: "z"
```

Avoid mentioning called function names, either; instead say what the code was trying to do:

```
BAD:     open() failed: %m
BETTER:  could not open file %s: %m
```

If it really seems necessary, mention the system call in the detail message. (In some cases, providing the actual values passed to the system call might be appropriate information for the detail message.)

Rationale: Users don't know what all those functions do.

50.3.14. Tricky Words to Avoid

Unable. "Unable" is nearly the passive voice. Better use "cannot" or "could not", as appropriate.

Bad. Error messages like "bad result" are really hard to interpret intelligently. It's better to write why the result is "bad", e.g., "invalid format".

Illegal. "Illegal" stands for a violation of the law, the rest is "invalid". Better yet, say why it's invalid.

Unknown. Try to avoid "unknown". Consider "error: unknown response". If you don't know what the response is, how do you know it's erroneous? "Unrecognized" is often a better choice. Also, be sure to include the value being complained of.

```
BAD:    unknown node type
BETTER: unrecognized node type: 42
```

Find vs. Exists. If the program uses a nontrivial algorithm to locate a resource (e.g., a path search) and that algorithm fails, it is fair to say that the program couldn't "find" the resource. If, on the other hand, the expected location of the resource is known but the program cannot access it there then say that the resource doesn't "exist". Using "find" in this case sounds weak and confuses the issue.

May vs. Can vs. Might. "May" suggests permission (e.g., "You may borrow my rake."), and has little use in documentation or error messages. "Can" suggests ability (e.g., "I can lift that log."), and "might" suggests possibility (e.g., "It might rain today."). Using the proper word clarifies meaning and assists translation.

Contractions. Avoid contractions, like "can't"; use "cannot" instead.

50.3.15. Proper Spelling

Spell out words in full. For instance, avoid:

- spec
- stats
- parens
- auth
- xact

Rationale: This will improve consistency.

50.3.16. Localization

Keep in mind that error message texts need to be translated into other languages. Follow the guidelines in Section 51.2.2 to avoid making life difficult for translators.

Chapter 51. Native Language Support

51.1. For the Translator

PostgreSQL programs (server and client) can issue their messages in your favorite language — if the messages have been translated. Creating and maintaining translated message sets needs the help of people who speak their own language well and want to contribute to the PostgreSQL effort. You do not have to be a programmer at all to do this. This section explains how to help.

51.1.1. Requirements

We won't judge your language skills — this section is about software tools. Theoretically, you only need a text editor. But this is only in the unlikely event that you do not want to try out your translated messages. When you configure your source tree, be sure to use the `--enable-nls` option. This will also check for the libintl library and the `msgfmt` program, which all end users will need anyway. To try out your work, follow the applicable portions of the installation instructions.

If you want to start a new translation effort or want to do a message catalog merge (described later), you will need the programs `xgettext` and `msgmerge`, respectively, in a GNU-compatible implementation. Later, we will try to arrange it so that if you use a packaged source distribution, you won't need `xgettext`. (If working from Git, you will still need it.) GNU Gettext 0.10.36 or later is currently recommended.

Your local gettext implementation should come with its own documentation. Some of that is probably duplicated in what follows, but for additional details you should look there.

51.1.2. Concepts

The pairs of original (English) messages and their (possibly) translated equivalents are kept in *message catalogs*, one for each program (although related programs can share a message catalog) and for each target language. There are two file formats for message catalogs: The first is the "PO" file (for Portable Object), which is a plain text file with special syntax that translators edit. The second is the "MO" file (for Machine Object), which is a binary file generated from the respective PO file and is used while the internationalized program is run. Translators do not deal with MO files; in fact hardly anyone does.

The extension of the message catalog file is to no surprise either `.po` or `.mo`. The base name is either the name of the program it accompanies, or the language the file is for, depending on the situation. This is a bit confusing. Examples are `psql.po` (PO file for psql) or `fr.mo` (MO file in French).

The file format of the PO files is illustrated here:

```
# comment

msgid "original string"
msgstr "translated string"
```

```
msgid "more original"
msgstr "another translated"
"string can be broken up like this"

...
```

The msgid's are extracted from the program source. (They need not be, but this is the most common way.) The msgstr lines are initially empty and are filled in with useful strings by the translator. The strings can contain C-style escape characters and can be continued across lines as illustrated. (The next line must start at the beginning of the line.)

The # character introduces a comment. If whitespace immediately follows the # character, then this is a comment maintained by the translator. There can also be automatic comments, which have a non-whitespace character immediately following the #. These are maintained by the various tools that operate on the PO files and are intended to aid the translator.

```
#. automatic comment
#: filename.c:1023
#, flags, flags
```

The #. style comments are extracted from the source file where the message is used. Possibly the programmer has inserted information for the translator, such as about expected alignment. The #: comment indicates the exact location(s) where the message is used in the source. The translator need not look at the program source, but he can if there is doubt about the correct translation. The #, comments contain flags that describe the message in some way. There are currently two flags: `fuzzy` is set if the message has possibly been outdated because of changes in the program source. The translator can then verify this and possibly remove the fuzzy flag. Note that fuzzy messages are not made available to the end user. The other flag is `c-format`, which indicates that the message is a `printf`-style format template. This means that the translation should also be a format string with the same number and type of placeholders. There are tools that can verify this, which key off the c-format flag.

51.1.3. Creating and Maintaining Message Catalogs

OK, so how does one create a "blank" message catalog? First, go into the directory that contains the program whose messages you want to translate. If there is a file `nls.mk`, then this program has been prepared for translation.

If there are already some `.po` files, then someone has already done some translation work. The files are named *language*`.po`, where *language* is the ISO 639-1 two-letter language code (in lower case)[1], e.g., `fr.po` for French. If there is really a need for more than one translation effort per language then the files can also be named *language_region*`.po` where *region* is the ISO 3166-1 two-letter country code (in upper case)[2], e.g., `pt_BR.po` for Portuguese in Brazil. If you find the language you wanted you can just start working on that file.

If you need to start a new translation effort, then first run the command:

```
make init-po
```

---

1. http://www.loc.gov/standards/iso639-2/php/English_list.php
2. http://www.iso.org/iso/country_names_and_code_elements

This will create a file `progname.pot`. (`.pot` to distinguish it from PO files that are "in production". The `T` stands for "template".) Copy this file to `language.po` and edit it. To make it known that the new language is available, also edit the file `nls.mk` and add the language (or language and country) code to the line that looks like:

```
AVAIL_LANGUAGES := de fr
```

(Other languages can appear, of course.)

As the underlying program or library changes, messages might be changed or added by the programmers. In this case you do not need to start from scratch. Instead, run the command:

```
make update-po
```

which will create a new blank message catalog file (the pot file you started with) and will merge it with the existing PO files. If the merge algorithm is not sure about a particular message it marks it "fuzzy" as explained above. The new PO file is saved with a `.po.new` extension.

51.1.4. Editing the PO Files

The PO files can be edited with a regular text editor. The translator should only change the area between the quotes after the msgstr directive, add comments, and alter the fuzzy flag. There is (unsurprisingly) a PO mode for Emacs, which I find quite useful.

The PO files need not be completely filled in. The software will automatically fall back to the original string if no translation (or an empty translation) is available. It is no problem to submit incomplete translations for inclusions in the source tree; that gives room for other people to pick up your work. However, you are encouraged to give priority to removing fuzzy entries after doing a merge. Remember that fuzzy entries will not be installed; they only serve as reference for what might be the right translation.

Here are some things to keep in mind while editing the translations:

- Make sure that if the original ends with a newline, the translation does, too. Similarly for tabs, etc.

- If the original is a `printf` format string, the translation also needs to be. The translation also needs to have the same format specifiers in the same order. Sometimes the natural rules of the language make this impossible or at least awkward. In that case you can modify the format specifiers like this:
  ```
  msgstr "Die Datei %2$s hat %1$u Zeichen."
  ```
  Then the first placeholder will actually use the second argument from the list. The *digits*$ needs to follow the % immediately, before any other format manipulators. (This feature really exists in the `printf` family of functions. You might not have heard of it before because there is little use for it outside of message internationalization.)

- If the original string contains a linguistic mistake, report that (or fix it yourself in the program source) and translate normally. The corrected string can be merged in when the program sources have been updated. If the original string contains a factual mistake, report that (or fix it yourself) and do not translate it. Instead, you can mark the string with a comment in the PO file.

- Maintain the style and tone of the original string. Specifically, messages that are not sentences (`cannot open file %s`) should probably not start with a capital letter (if your language distinguishes letter case) or end with a period (if your language uses punctuation marks). It might help to read Section 50.3.

- If you don't know what a message means, or if it is ambiguous, ask on the developers' mailing list. Chances are that English speaking end users might also not understand it or find it ambiguous, so it's best to improve the message.

51.2. For the Programmer

51.2.1. Mechanics

This section describes how to implement native language support in a program or library that is part of the PostgreSQL distribution. Currently, it only applies to C programs.

Adding NLS Support to a Program

1. Insert this code into the start-up sequence of the program:

    ```
    #ifdef ENABLE_NLS
    #include <locale.h>
    #endif
    ```

    ```
    ...
    ```

    ```
    #ifdef ENABLE_NLS
    setlocale(LC_ALL, "");
    bindtextdomain("progname", LOCALEDIR);
    textdomain("progname");
    #endif
    ```
    (The *progname* can actually be chosen freely.)

2. Wherever a message that is a candidate for translation is found, a call to `gettext()` needs to be inserted. E.g.:

    ```
    fprintf(stderr, "panic level %d\n", lvl);
    ```
    would be changed to:

    ```
    fprintf(stderr, gettext("panic level %d\n"), lvl);
    ```
    (`gettext` is defined as a no-op if NLS support is not configured.)

    This tends to add a lot of clutter. One common shortcut is to use:

    ```
    #define _(x) gettext(x)
    ```
    Another solution is feasible if the program does much of its communication through one or a few functions, such as `ereport()` in the backend. Then you make this function call `gettext` internally on all input strings.

3. Add a file `nls.mk` in the directory with the program sources. This file will be read as a makefile. The following variable assignments need to be made here:

CATALOG_NAME

> The program name, as provided in the `textdomain()` call.

AVAIL_LANGUAGES

> List of provided translations — initially empty.

GETTEXT_FILES

> List of files that contain translatable strings, i.e., those marked with `gettext` or an alternative solution. Eventually, this will include nearly all source files of the program. If this list gets too long you can make the first "file" be a + and the second word be a file that contains one file name per line.

GETTEXT_TRIGGERS

> The tools that generate message catalogs for the translators to work on need to know what function calls contain translatable strings. By default, only `gettext()` calls are known. If you used _ or other identifiers you need to list them here. If the translatable string is not the first argument, the item needs to be of the form `func:2` (for the second argument). If you have a function that supports pluralized messages, the item should look like `func:1,2` (identifying the singular and plural message arguments).

The build system will automatically take care of building and installing the message catalogs.

51.2.2. Message-writing Guidelines

Here are some guidelines for writing messages that are easily translatable.

- Do not construct sentences at run-time, like:

```
printf("Files were %s.\n", flag ? "copied" : "removed");
```

The word order within the sentence might be different in other languages. Also, even if you remember to call `gettext()` on each fragment, the fragments might not translate well separately. It's better to duplicate a little code so that each message to be translated is a coherent whole. Only numbers, file names, and such-like run-time variables should be inserted at run time into a message text.

- For similar reasons, this won't work:

```
printf("copied %d file%s", n, n!=1 ? "s" : "");
```

because it assumes how the plural is formed. If you figured you could solve it like this:

```
if (n==1)
    printf("copied 1 file");
else
    printf("copied %d files", n):
```

then be disappointed. Some languages have more than two forms, with some peculiar rules. It's often best to design the message to avoid the issue altogether, for instance like this:

```
printf("number of copied files: %d", n);
```

If you really want to construct a properly pluralized message, there is support for this, but it's a bit awkward. When generating a primary or detail error message in `ereport()`, you can write something like this:

```
errmsg_plural("copied %d file",
              "copied %d files",
              n,
              n)
```

The first argument is the format string appropriate for English singular form, the second is the format string appropriate for English plural form, and the third is the integer control value that determines which plural form to use. Subsequent arguments are formatted per the format string as usual. (Normally, the pluralization control value will also be one of the values to be formatted, so it has to be written twice.) In English it only matters whether n is 1 or not 1, but in other languages there can be many different plural forms. The translator sees the two English forms as a group and has the opportunity to supply multiple substitute strings, with the appropriate one being selected based on the run-time value of n.

If you need to pluralize a message that isn't going directly to an `errmsg` or `errdetail` report, you have to use the underlying function `ngettext`. See the gettext documentation.

- If you want to communicate something to the translator, such as about how a message is intended to line up with other output, precede the occurrence of the string with a comment that starts with `translator`, e.g.:

```
/* translator: This message is not what it seems to be. */
```

These comments are copied to the message catalog files so that the translators can see them.

Chapter 52. Writing A Procedural Language Handler

All calls to functions that are written in a language other than the current "version 1" interface for compiled languages (this includes functions in user-defined procedural languages, functions written in SQL, and functions using the version 0 compiled language interface) go through a *call handler* function for the specific language. It is the responsibility of the call handler to execute the function in a meaningful way, such as by interpreting the supplied source text. This chapter outlines how a new procedural language's call handler can be written.

The call handler for a procedural language is a "normal" function that must be written in a compiled language such as C, using the version-1 interface, and registered with PostgreSQL as taking no arguments and returning the type `language_handler`. This special pseudotype identifies the function as a call handler and prevents it from being called directly in SQL commands. For more details on C language calling conventions and dynamic loading, see Section 35.9.

The call handler is called in the same way as any other function: It receives a pointer to a `FunctionCallInfoData struct` containing argument values and information about the called function, and it is expected to return a `Datum` result (and possibly set the `isnull` field of the `FunctionCallInfoData` structure, if it wishes to return an SQL null result). The difference between a call handler and an ordinary callee function is that the `flinfo->fn_oid` field of the `FunctionCallInfoData` structure will contain the OID of the actual function to be called, not of the call handler itself. The call handler must use this field to determine which function to execute. Also, the passed argument list has been set up according to the declaration of the target function, not of the call handler.

It's up to the call handler to fetch the entry of the function from the `pg_proc` system catalog and to analyze the argument and return types of the called function. The `AS` clause from the `CREATE FUNCTION` command for the function will be found in the `prosrc` column of the `pg_proc` row. This is commonly source text in the procedural language, but in theory it could be something else, such as a path name to a file, or anything else that tells the call handler what to do in detail.

Often, the same function is called many times per SQL statement. A call handler can avoid repeated lookups of information about the called function by using the `flinfo->fn_extra` field. This will initially be `NULL`, but can be set by the call handler to point at information about the called function. On subsequent calls, if `flinfo->fn_extra` is already non-`NULL` then it can be used and the information lookup step skipped. The call handler must make sure that `flinfo->fn_extra` is made to point at memory that will live at least until the end of the current query, since an `FmgrInfo` data structure could be kept that long. One way to do this is to allocate the extra data in the memory context specified by `flinfo->fn_mcxt`; such data will normally have the same lifespan as the `FmgrInfo` itself. But the handler could also choose to use a longer-lived memory context so that it can cache function definition information across queries.

When a procedural-language function is invoked as a trigger, no arguments are passed in the usual way, but the `FunctionCallInfoData`'s `context` field points at a `TriggerData` structure, rather than being `NULL` as it is in a plain function call. A language handler should provide mechanisms for procedural-language functions to get at the trigger information.

This is a template for a procedural-language handler written in C:

```c
#include "postgres.h"
#include "executor/spi.h"
#include "commands/trigger.h"
#include "fmgr.h"
#include "access/heapam.h"
#include "utils/syscache.h"
#include "catalog/pg_proc.h"
#include "catalog/pg_type.h"

#ifdef PG_MODULE_MAGIC
PG_MODULE_MAGIC;
#endif


PG_FUNCTION_INFO_V1(plsample_call_handler);


Datum
plsample_call_handler(PG_FUNCTION_ARGS)
{
    Datum          retval;

    if (CALLED_AS_TRIGGER(fcinfo))
    {
        /*
         * Called as a trigger procedure
         */
        TriggerData    *trigdata = (TriggerData *) fcinfo->context;

        retval = ...
    }
    else
    {
        /*
         * Called as a function
         */

        retval = ...
    }

    return retval;
}
```

Only a few thousand lines of code have to be added instead of the dots to complete the call handler.

After having compiled the handler function into a loadable module (see Section 35.9.6), the following commands then register the sample procedural language:

```sql
CREATE FUNCTION plsample_call_handler() RETURNS language_handler
    AS 'filename'
    LANGUAGE C;
CREATE LANGUAGE plsample
```

```
HANDLER plsample_call_handler;
```

Although providing a call handler is sufficient to create a minimal procedural language, there are two other functions that can optionally be provided to make the language more convenient to use. These are a *validator* and an *inline handler*. A validator can be provided to allow language-specific checking to be done during CREATE FUNCTION. An inline handler can be provided to allow the language to support anonymous code blocks executed via the DO command.

If a validator is provided by a procedural language, it must be declared as a function taking a single parameter of type `oid`. The validator's result is ignored, so it is customarily declared to return `void`. The validator will be called at the end of a CREATE FUNCTION command that has created or updated a function written in the procedural language. The passed-in OID is the OID of the function's `pg_proc` row. The validator must fetch this row in the usual way, and do whatever checking is appropriate. First, call `CheckFunctionValidatorAccess()` to diagnose explicit calls to the validator that the user could not achieve through CREATE FUNCTION. Typical checks then include verifying that the function's argument and result types are supported by the language, and that the function's body is syntactically correct in the language. If the validator finds the function to be okay, it should just return. If it finds an error, it should report that via the normal `ereport()` error reporting mechanism. Throwing an error will force a transaction rollback and thus prevent the incorrect function definition from being committed.

Validator functions should typically honor the check_function_bodies parameter: if it is turned off then any expensive or context-sensitive checking should be skipped. If the language provides for code execution at compilation time, the validator must suppress checks that would induce such execution. In particular, this parameter is turned off by pg_dump so that it can load procedural language functions without worrying about side effects or dependencies of the function bodies on other database objects. (Because of this requirement, the call handler should avoid assuming that the validator has fully checked the function. The point of having a validator is not to let the call handler omit checks, but to notify the user immediately if there are obvious errors in a CREATE FUNCTION command.) While the choice of exactly what to check is mostly left to the discretion of the validator function, note that the core CREATE FUNCTION code only executes SET clauses attached to a function when `check_function_bodies` is on. Therefore, checks whose results might be affected by GUC parameters definitely should be skipped when `check_function_bodies` is off, to avoid false failures when reloading a dump.

If an inline handler is provided by a procedural language, it must be declared as a function taking a single parameter of type `internal`. The inline handler's result is ignored, so it is customarily declared to return `void`. The inline handler will be called when a DO statement is executed specifying the procedural language. The parameter actually passed is a pointer to an `InlineCodeBlock` struct, which contains information about the DO statement's parameters, in particular the text of the anonymous code block to be executed. The inline handler should execute this code and return.

It's recommended that you wrap all these function declarations, as well as the CREATE LANGUAGE command itself, into an *extension* so that a simple CREATE EXTENSION command is sufficient to install the language. See Section 35.15 for information about writing extensions.

The procedural languages included in the standard distribution are good references when trying to write your own language handler. Look into the `src/pl` subdirectory of the source tree. The CREATE LANGUAGE reference page also has some useful details.

Chapter 53. Writing A Foreign Data Wrapper

All operations on a foreign table are handled through its foreign data wrapper, which consists of a set of functions that the core server calls. The foreign data wrapper is responsible for fetching data from the remote data source and returning it to the PostgreSQL executor. If updating foreign tables is to be supported, the wrapper must handle that, too. This chapter outlines how to write a new foreign data wrapper.

The foreign data wrappers included in the standard distribution are good references when trying to write your own. Look into the `contrib` subdirectory of the source tree. The CREATE FOREIGN DATA WRAPPER reference page also has some useful details.

> **Note:** The SQL standard specifies an interface for writing foreign data wrappers. However, PostgreSQL does not implement that API, because the effort to accommodate it into PostgreSQL would be large, and the standard API hasn't gained wide adoption anyway.

53.1. Foreign Data Wrapper Functions

The FDW author needs to implement a handler function, and optionally a validator function. Both functions must be written in a compiled language such as C, using the version-1 interface. For details on C language calling conventions and dynamic loading, see Section 35.9.

The handler function simply returns a struct of function pointers to callback functions that will be called by the planner, executor, and various maintenance commands. Most of the effort in writing an FDW is in implementing these callback functions. The handler function must be registered with PostgreSQL as taking no arguments and returning the special pseudo-type `fdw_handler`. The callback functions are plain C functions and are not visible or callable at the SQL level. The callback functions are described in Section 53.2.

The validator function is responsible for validating options given in CREATE and ALTER commands for its foreign data wrapper, as well as foreign servers, user mappings, and foreign tables using the wrapper. The validator function must be registered as taking two arguments, a text array containing the options to be validated, and an OID representing the type of object the options are associated with (in the form of the OID of the system catalog the object would be stored in, either `ForeignDataWrapperRelationId`, `ForeignServerRelationId`, `UserMappingRelationId`, or `ForeignTableRelationId`). If no validator function is supplied, options are not checked at object creation time or object alteration time.

53.2. Foreign Data Wrapper Callback Routines

The FDW handler function returns a palloc'd `FdwRoutine` struct containing pointers to the callback functions described below. The scan-related functions are required, the rest are optional.

The `FdwRoutine` struct type is declared in `src/include/foreign/fdwapi.h`, which see for additional details.

53.2.1. FDW Routines For Scanning Foreign Tables

```
void
GetForeignRelSize (PlannerInfo *root,
                   RelOptInfo *baserel,
                   Oid foreigntableid);
```

Obtain relation size estimates for a foreign table. This is called at the beginning of planning for a query that scans a foreign table. `root` is the planner's global information about the query; `baserel` is the planner's information about this table; and `foreigntableid` is the `pg_class` OID of the foreign table. (`foreigntableid` could be obtained from the planner data structures, but it's passed explicitly to save effort.)

This function should update `baserel->rows` to be the expected number of rows returned by the table scan, after accounting for the filtering done by the restriction quals. The initial value of `baserel->rows` is just a constant default estimate, which should be replaced if at all possible. The function may also choose to update `baserel->width` if it can compute a better estimate of the average result row width.

See Section 53.4 for additional information.

```
void
GetForeignPaths (PlannerInfo *root,
                 RelOptInfo *baserel,
                 Oid foreigntableid);
```

Create possible access paths for a scan on a foreign table. This is called during query planning. The parameters are the same as for `GetForeignRelSize`, which has already been called.

This function must generate at least one access path (`ForeignPath` node) for a scan on the foreign table and must call `add_path` to add each such path to `baserel->pathlist`. It's recommended to use `create_foreignscan_path` to build the `ForeignPath` nodes. The function can generate multiple access paths, e.g., a path which has valid `pathkeys` to represent a pre-sorted result. Each access path must contain cost estimates, and can contain any FDW-private information that is needed to identify the specific scan method intended.

See Section 53.4 for additional information.

```
ForeignScan *
GetForeignPlan (PlannerInfo *root,
                RelOptInfo *baserel,
                Oid foreigntableid,
                ForeignPath *best_path,
                List *tlist,
                List *scan_clauses);
```

Create a `ForeignScan` plan node from the selected foreign access path. This is called at the end of query planning. The parameters are as for `GetForeignRelSize`, plus the selected `ForeignPath` (previously produced by `GetForeignPaths`), the target list to be emitted by the plan node, and the restriction clauses to be enforced by the plan node.

This function must create and return a `ForeignScan` plan node; it's recommended to use `make_foreignscan` to build the `ForeignScan` node.

See Section 53.4 for additional information.

```
void
BeginForeignScan (ForeignScanState *node,
                  int eflags);
```

Begin executing a foreign scan. This is called during executor startup. It should perform any initialization needed before the scan can start, but not start executing the actual scan (that should be done upon the first call to `IterateForeignScan`). The `ForeignScanState` node has already been created, but its `fdw_state` field is still NULL. Information about the table to scan is accessible through the `ForeignScanState` node (in particular, from the underlying `ForeignScan` plan node, which contains any FDW-private information provided by `GetForeignPlan`). `eflags` contains flag bits describing the executor's operating mode for this plan node.

Note that when `(eflags & EXEC_FLAG_EXPLAIN_ONLY)` is true, this function should not perform any externally-visible actions; it should only do the minimum required to make the node state valid for `ExplainForeignScan` and `EndForeignScan`.

```
TupleTableSlot *
IterateForeignScan (ForeignScanState *node);
```

Fetch one row from the foreign source, returning it in a tuple table slot (the node's `ScanTupleSlot` should be used for this purpose). Return NULL if no more rows are available. The tuple table slot infrastructure allows either a physical or virtual tuple to be returned; in most cases the latter choice is preferable from a performance standpoint. Note that this is called in a short-lived memory context that will be reset between invocations. Create a memory context in `BeginForeignScan` if you need longer-lived storage, or use the `es_query_cxt` of the node's `EState`.

The rows returned must match the column signature of the foreign table being scanned. If you choose to optimize away fetching columns that are not needed, you should insert nulls in those column positions.

Note that PostgreSQL's executor doesn't care whether the rows returned violate any NOT NULL constraints that were defined on the foreign table columns — but the planner does care, and may optimize queries incorrectly if NULL values are present in a column declared not to contain them. If a NULL value is encountered when the user has declared that none should be present, it may be appropriate to raise an error (just as you would need to do in the case of a data type mismatch).

```
void
ReScanForeignScan (ForeignScanState *node);
```

Restart the scan from the beginning. Note that any parameters the scan depends on may have changed value, so the new scan does not necessarily return exactly the same rows.

```
void
EndForeignScan (ForeignScanState *node);
```

End the scan and release resources. It is normally not important to release palloc'd memory, but for example open files and connections to remote servers should be cleaned up.

53.2.2. FDW Routines For Updating Foreign Tables

If an FDW supports writable foreign tables, it should provide some or all of the following callback functions depending on the needs and capabilities of the FDW:

```
void
AddForeignUpdateTargets (Query *parsetree,
                         RangeTblEntry *target_rte,
                         Relation target_relation);
```

UPDATE and DELETE operations are performed against rows previously fetched by the table-scanning functions. The FDW may need extra information, such as a row ID or the values of primary-key columns, to ensure that it can identify the exact row to update or delete. To support that, this function can add extra hidden, or "junk", target columns to the list of columns that are to be retrieved from the foreign table during an UPDATE or DELETE.

To do that, add TargetEntry items to parsetree->targetList, containing expressions for the extra values to be fetched. Each such entry must be marked resjunk = true, and must have a distinct resname that will identify it at execution time. Avoid using names matching ctid*N*, wholerow, or wholerow*N*, as the core system can generate junk columns of these names.

This function is called in the rewriter, not the planner, so the information available is a bit different from that available to the planning routines. parsetree is the parse tree for the UPDATE or DELETE command, while target_rte and target_relation describe the target foreign table.

If the AddForeignUpdateTargets pointer is set to NULL, no extra target expressions are added. (This will make it impossible to implement DELETE operations, though UPDATE may still be feasible if the FDW relies on an unchanging primary key to identify rows.)

```
List *
PlanForeignModify (PlannerInfo *root,
                   ModifyTable *plan,
                   Index resultRelation,
                   int subplan_index);
```

Perform any additional planning actions needed for an insert, update, or delete on a foreign table. This function generates the FDW-private information that will be attached to the ModifyTable plan node that performs the update action. This private information must have the form of a List, and will be delivered to BeginForeignModify during the execution stage.

root is the planner's global information about the query. plan is the ModifyTable plan node, which is complete except for the fdwPrivLists field. resultRelation identifies the target foreign table by its range table index. subplan_index identifies which target of the ModifyTable plan node this is, counting from zero; use this if you want to index into plan->plans or other substructure of the plan node.

See Section 53.4 for additional information.

If the `PlanForeignModify` pointer is set to `NULL`, no additional plan-time actions are taken, and the `fdw_private` list delivered to `BeginForeignModify` will be NIL.

```
void
BeginForeignModify (ModifyTableState *mtstate,
                    ResultRelInfo *rinfo,
                    List *fdw_private,
                    int subplan_index,
                    int eflags);
```

Begin executing a foreign table modification operation. This routine is called during executor startup. It should perform any initialization needed prior to the actual table modifications. Subsequently, `ExecForeignInsert`, `ExecForeignUpdate` or `ExecForeignDelete` will be called for each tuple to be inserted, updated, or deleted.

`mtstate` is the overall state of the `ModifyTable` plan node being executed; global data about the plan and execution state is available via this structure. `rinfo` is the `ResultRelInfo` struct describing the target foreign table. (The `ri_FdwState` field of `ResultRelInfo` is available for the FDW to store any private state it needs for this operation.) `fdw_private` contains the private data generated by `PlanForeignModify`, if any. `subplan_index` identifies which target of the `ModifyTable` plan node this is. `eflags` contains flag bits describing the executor's operating mode for this plan node.

Note that when `(eflags & EXEC_FLAG_EXPLAIN_ONLY)` is true, this function should not perform any externally-visible actions; it should only do the minimum required to make the node state valid for `ExplainForeignModify` and `EndForeignModify`.

If the `BeginForeignModify` pointer is set to `NULL`, no action is taken during executor startup.

```
TupleTableSlot *
ExecForeignInsert (EState *estate,
                   ResultRelInfo *rinfo,
                   TupleTableSlot *slot,
                   TupleTableSlot *planSlot);
```

Insert one tuple into the foreign table. `estate` is global execution state for the query. `rinfo` is the `ResultRelInfo` struct describing the target foreign table. `slot` contains the tuple to be inserted; it will match the row-type definition of the foreign table. `planSlot` contains the tuple that was generated by the `ModifyTable` plan node's subplan; it differs from `slot` in possibly containing additional "junk" columns. (The `planSlot` is typically of little interest for INSERT cases, but is provided for completeness.)

The return value is either a slot containing the data that was actually inserted (this might differ from the data supplied, for example as a result of trigger actions), or NULL if no row was actually inserted (again, typically as a result of triggers). The passed-in `slot` can be re-used for this purpose.

The data in the returned slot is used only if the INSERT query has a RETURNING clause or the foreign table has an AFTER ROW trigger. Triggers require all columns, but the FDW could choose to optimize away returning some or all columns depending on the contents of the RETURNING clause. Regardless, some slot must be returned to indicate success, or the query's reported row count will be wrong.

If the `ExecForeignInsert` pointer is set to `NULL`, attempts to insert into the foreign table will fail with an error message.

```
TupleTableSlot *
```

```
ExecForeignUpdate (EState *estate,
                   ResultRelInfo *rinfo,
                   TupleTableSlot *slot,
                   TupleTableSlot *planSlot);
```

Update one tuple in the foreign table. `estate` is global execution state for the query. `rinfo` is the `ResultRelInfo` struct describing the target foreign table. `slot` contains the new data for the tuple; it will match the row-type definition of the foreign table. `planSlot` contains the tuple that was generated by the `ModifyTable` plan node's subplan; it differs from `slot` in possibly containing additional "junk" columns. In particular, any junk columns that were requested by `AddForeignUpdateTargets` will be available from this slot.

The return value is either a slot containing the row as it was actually updated (this might differ from the data supplied, for example as a result of trigger actions), or NULL if no row was actually updated (again, typically as a result of triggers). The passed-in `slot` can be re-used for this purpose.

The data in the returned slot is used only if the UPDATE query has a RETURNING clause or the foreign table has an AFTER ROW trigger. Triggers require all columns, but the FDW could choose to optimize away returning some or all columns depending on the contents of the RETURNING clause. Regardless, some slot must be returned to indicate success, or the query's reported row count will be wrong.

If the `ExecForeignUpdate` pointer is set to NULL, attempts to update the foreign table will fail with an error message.

```
TupleTableSlot *
ExecForeignDelete (EState *estate,
                   ResultRelInfo *rinfo,
                   TupleTableSlot *slot,
                   TupleTableSlot *planSlot);
```

Delete one tuple from the foreign table. `estate` is global execution state for the query. `rinfo` is the `ResultRelInfo` struct describing the target foreign table. `slot` contains nothing useful upon call, but can be used to hold the returned tuple. `planSlot` contains the tuple that was generated by the `ModifyTable` plan node's subplan; in particular, it will carry any junk columns that were requested by `AddForeignUpdateTargets`. The junk column(s) must be used to identify the tuple to be deleted.

The return value is either a slot containing the row that was deleted, or NULL if no row was deleted (typically as a result of triggers). The passed-in `slot` can be used to hold the tuple to be returned.

The data in the returned slot is used only if the DELETE query has a RETURNING clause or the foreign table has an AFTER ROW trigger. Triggers require all columns, but the FDW could choose to optimize away returning some or all columns depending on the contents of the RETURNING clause. Regardless, some slot must be returned to indicate success, or the query's reported row count will be wrong.

If the `ExecForeignDelete` pointer is set to NULL, attempts to delete from the foreign table will fail with an error message.

```
void
EndForeignModify (EState *estate,
                  ResultRelInfo *rinfo);
```

End the table update and release resources. It is normally not important to release palloc'd memory, but for example open files and connections to remote servers should be cleaned up.

If the `EndForeignModify` pointer is set to `NULL`, no action is taken during executor shutdown.

```
int
IsForeignRelUpdatable (Relation rel);
```

Report which update operations the specified foreign table supports. The return value should be a bit mask of rule event numbers indicating which operations are supported by the foreign table, using the `CmdType` enumeration; that is, `(1 << CMD_UPDATE) = 4` for UPDATE, `(1 << CMD_INSERT) = 8` for INSERT, and `(1 << CMD_DELETE) = 16` for DELETE.

If the `IsForeignRelUpdatable` pointer is set to `NULL`, foreign tables are assumed to be insertable, updatable, or deletable if the FDW provides `ExecForeignInsert`, `ExecForeignUpdate`, or `ExecForeignDelete` respectively. This function is only needed if the FDW supports some tables that are updatable and some that are not. (Even then, it's permissible to throw an error in the execution routine instead of checking in this function. However, this function is used to determine updatability for display in the `information_schema` views.)

53.2.3. FDW Routines for EXPLAIN

```
void
ExplainForeignScan (ForeignScanState *node,
                    ExplainState *es);
```

Print additional EXPLAIN output for a foreign table scan. This function can call `ExplainPropertyText` and related functions to add fields to the EXPLAIN output. The flag fields in `es` can be used to determine what to print, and the state of the `ForeignScanState` node can be inspected to provide run-time statistics in the EXPLAIN ANALYZE case.

If the `ExplainForeignScan` pointer is set to `NULL`, no additional information is printed during EXPLAIN.

```
void
ExplainForeignModify (ModifyTableState *mtstate,
                      ResultRelInfo *rinfo,
                      List *fdw_private,
                      int subplan_index,
                      struct ExplainState *es);
```

Print additional EXPLAIN output for a foreign table update. This function can call `ExplainPropertyText` and related functions to add fields to the EXPLAIN output. The flag fields in `es` can be used to determine what to print, and the state of the `ModifyTableState` node can be inspected to provide run-time statistics in the EXPLAIN ANALYZE case. The first four arguments are the same as for `BeginForeignModify`.

If the `ExplainForeignModify` pointer is set to `NULL`, no additional information is printed during EXPLAIN.

53.2.4. FDW Routines for ANALYZE

```
bool
AnalyzeForeignTable (Relation relation,
                     AcquireSampleRowsFunc *func,
                     BlockNumber *totalpages);
```

This function is called when ANALYZE is executed on a foreign table. If the FDW can collect statistics for this foreign table, it should return `true`, and provide a pointer to a function that will collect sample rows from the table in `func`, plus the estimated size of the table in pages in `totalpages`. Otherwise, return `false`.

If the FDW does not support collecting statistics for any tables, the `AnalyzeForeignTable` pointer can be set to `NULL`.

If provided, the sample collection function must have the signature

```
int
AcquireSampleRowsFunc (Relation relation, int elevel,
                       HeapTuple *rows, int targrows,
                       double *totalrows,
                       double *totaldeadrows);
```

A random sample of up to `targrows` rows should be collected from the table and stored into the caller-provided `rows` array. The actual number of rows collected must be returned. In addition, store estimates of the total numbers of live and dead rows in the table into the output parameters `totalrows` and `totaldeadrows`. (Set `totaldeadrows` to zero if the FDW does not have any concept of dead rows.)

53.3. Foreign Data Wrapper Helper Functions

Several helper functions are exported from the core server so that authors of foreign data wrappers can get easy access to attributes of FDW-related objects, such as FDW options. To use any of these functions, you need to include the header file `foreign/foreign.h` in your source file. That header also defines the struct types that are returned by these functions.

```
ForeignDataWrapper *
GetForeignDataWrapper (Oid fdwid);
```

This function returns a `ForeignDataWrapper` object for the foreign-data wrapper with the given OID. A `ForeignDataWrapper` object contains properties of the FDW (see `foreign/foreign.h` for details).

```
ForeignServer *
GetForeignServer (Oid serverid);
```

This function returns a `ForeignServer` object for the foreign server with the given OID. A `ForeignServer` object contains properties of the server (see `foreign/foreign.h` for details).

```
UserMapping *
```

```
GetUserMapping(Oid userid, Oid serverid);
```

This function returns a `UserMapping` object for the user mapping of the given role on the given server. (If there is no mapping for the specific user, it will return the mapping for `PUBLIC`, or throw error if there is none.) A `UserMapping` object contains properties of the user mapping (see `foreign/foreign.h` for details).

```
ForeignTable *
GetForeignTable(Oid relid);
```

This function returns a `ForeignTable` object for the foreign table with the given OID. A `ForeignTable` object contains properties of the foreign table (see `foreign/foreign.h` for details).

```
List *
GetForeignColumnOptions(Oid relid, AttrNumber attnum);
```

This function returns the per-column FDW options for the column with the given foreign table OID and attribute number, in the form of a list of `DefElem`. NIL is returned if the column has no options.

Some object types have name-based lookup functions in addition to the OID-based ones:

```
ForeignDataWrapper *
GetForeignDataWrapperByName(const char *name, bool missing_ok);
```

This function returns a `ForeignDataWrapper` object for the foreign-data wrapper with the given name. If the wrapper is not found, return NULL if missing_ok is true, otherwise raise an error.

```
ForeignServer *
GetForeignServerByName(const char *name, bool missing_ok);
```

This function returns a `ForeignServer` object for the foreign server with the given name. If the server is not found, return NULL if missing_ok is true, otherwise raise an error.

53.4. Foreign Data Wrapper Query Planning

The FDW callback functions `GetForeignRelSize`, `GetForeignPaths`, `GetForeignPlan`, and `PlanForeignModify` must fit into the workings of the PostgreSQL planner. Here are some notes about what they must do.

The information in `root` and `baserel` can be used to reduce the amount of information that has to be fetched from the foreign table (and therefore reduce the cost). `baserel->baserestrictinfo` is particularly interesting, as it contains restriction quals (`WHERE` clauses) that should be used to filter the rows to be fetched. (The FDW itself is not required to enforce these quals, as the core executor can check them instead.) `baserel->reltargetlist` can be used to determine which columns need to be fetched; but note that it only lists columns that have to be emitted by the `ForeignScan` plan node, not columns that are used in qual evaluation but not output by the query.

Various private fields are available for the FDW planning functions to keep information in. Generally, whatever you store in FDW private fields should be palloc'd, so that it will be reclaimed at the end of planning.

baserel->fdw_private is a void pointer that is available for FDW planning functions to store information relevant to the particular foreign table. The core planner does not touch it except to initialize it to NULL when the baserel node is created. It is useful for passing information forward from GetForeignRelSize to GetForeignPaths and/or GetForeignPaths to GetForeignPlan, thereby avoiding recalculation.

GetForeignPaths can identify the meaning of different access paths by storing private information in the fdw_private field of ForeignPath nodes. fdw_private is declared as a List pointer, but could actually contain anything since the core planner does not touch it. However, best practice is to use a representation that's dumpable by nodeToString, for use with debugging support available in the backend.

GetForeignPlan can examine the fdw_private field of the selected ForeignPath node, and can generate fdw_exprs and fdw_private lists to be placed in the ForeignScan plan node, where they will be available at execution time. Both of these lists must be represented in a form that copyObject knows how to copy. The fdw_private list has no other restrictions and is not interpreted by the core backend in any way. The fdw_exprs list, if not NIL, is expected to contain expression trees that are intended to be executed at run time. These trees will undergo post-processing by the planner to make them fully executable.

In GetForeignPlan, generally the passed-in target list can be copied into the plan node as-is. The passed scan_clauses list contains the same clauses as baserel->baserestrictinfo, but may be re-ordered for better execution efficiency. In simple cases the FDW can just strip RestrictInfo nodes from the scan_clauses list (using extract_actual_clauses) and put all the clauses into the plan node's qual list, which means that all the clauses will be checked by the executor at run time. More complex FDWs may be able to check some of the clauses internally, in which case those clauses can be removed from the plan node's qual list so that the executor doesn't waste time rechecking them.

As an example, the FDW might identify some restriction clauses of the form *foreign_variable = sub_expression*, which it determines can be executed on the remote server given the locally-evaluated value of the *sub_expression*. The actual identification of such a clause should happen during GetForeignPaths, since it would affect the cost estimate for the path. The path's fdw_private field would probably include a pointer to the identified clause's RestrictInfo node. Then GetForeignPlan would remove that clause from scan_clauses, but add the *sub_expression* to fdw_exprs to ensure that it gets massaged into executable form. It would probably also put control information into the plan node's fdw_private field to tell the execution functions what to do at run time. The query transmitted to the remote server would involve something like WHERE *foreign_variable* = $1, with the parameter value obtained at run time from evaluation of the fdw_exprs expression tree.

The FDW should always construct at least one path that depends only on the table's restriction clauses. In join queries, it might also choose to construct path(s) that depend on join clauses, for example *foreign_variable = local_variable*. Such clauses will not be found in baserel->baserestrictinfo but must be sought in the relation's join lists. A path using such a clause is called a "parameterized path". It must identify the other relations used in the selected join clause(s) with a suitable value of param_info; use get_baserel_parampathinfo to compute that value. In GetForeignPlan, the *local_variable* portion of the join clause would be added to fdw_exprs, and then at run time the case works the same as for an ordinary restriction clause.

When planning an UPDATE or DELETE, PlanForeignModify can look up the RelOptInfo struct for the foreign table and make use of the baserel->fdw_private data previously created by the scan-planning functions. However, in INSERT the target table is not scanned so there is no RelOptInfo for it. The List returned by PlanForeignModify has the same restrictions as the fdw_private list of a ForeignScan plan node, that is it must contain only structures that copyObject knows how to copy.

For an UPDATE or DELETE against an external data source that supports concurrent updates, it is recommended that the ForeignScan operation lock the rows that it fetches, perhaps via the equivalent of SELECT FOR UPDATE. The FDW may also choose to lock rows at fetch time when the foreign table is referenced in a SELECT FOR UPDATE/SHARE; if it does not, the FOR UPDATE or FOR SHARE option is essentially a no-op so far as the foreign table is concerned. This behavior may yield semantics slightly different from operations on local tables, where row locking is customarily delayed as long as possible: remote rows may get locked even though they subsequently fail locally-applied restriction or join conditions. However, matching the local semantics exactly would require an additional remote access for every row, and might be impossible anyway depending on what locking semantics the external data source provides.

Chapter 54. Genetic Query Optimizer

Author: Written by Martin Utesch (<utesch@aut.tu-freiberg.de>) for the Institute of Automatic Control at the University of Mining and Technology in Freiberg, Germany.

54.1. Query Handling as a Complex Optimization Problem

Among all relational operators the most difficult one to process and optimize is the *join*. The number of possible query plans grows exponentially with the number of joins in the query. Further optimization effort is caused by the support of a variety of *join methods* (e.g., nested loop, hash join, merge join in PostgreSQL) to process individual joins and a diversity of *indexes* (e.g., B-tree, hash, GiST and GIN in PostgreSQL) as access paths for relations.

The normal PostgreSQL query optimizer performs a *near-exhaustive search* over the space of alternative strategies. This algorithm, first introduced in IBM's System R database, produces a near-optimal join order, but can take an enormous amount of time and memory space when the number of joins in the query grows large. This makes the ordinary PostgreSQL query optimizer inappropriate for queries that join a large number of tables.

The Institute of Automatic Control at the University of Mining and Technology, in Freiberg, Germany, encountered some problems when it wanted to use PostgreSQL as the backend for a decision support knowledge based system for the maintenance of an electrical power grid. The DBMS needed to handle large join queries for the inference machine of the knowledge based system. The number of joins in these queries made using the normal query optimizer infeasible.

In the following we describe the implementation of a *genetic algorithm* to solve the join ordering problem in a manner that is efficient for queries involving large numbers of joins.

54.2. Genetic Algorithms

The genetic algorithm (GA) is a heuristic optimization method which operates through randomized search. The set of possible solutions for the optimization problem is considered as a *population* of *individuals*. The degree of adaptation of an individual to its environment is specified by its *fitness*.

The coordinates of an individual in the search space are represented by *chromosomes*, in essence a set of character strings. A *gene* is a subsection of a chromosome which encodes the value of a single parameter being optimized. Typical encodings for a gene could be *binary* or *integer*.

Through simulation of the evolutionary operations *recombination*, *mutation*, and *selection* new generations of search points are found that show a higher average fitness than their ancestors.

According to the comp.ai.genetic FAQ it cannot be stressed too strongly that a GA is not a pure random search for a solution to a problem. A GA uses stochastic processes, but the result is distinctly non-random (better than random).

Figure 54-1. Structured Diagram of a Genetic Algorithm

P(t)   generation of ancestors at a time t

P"(t)   generation of descendants at a time t

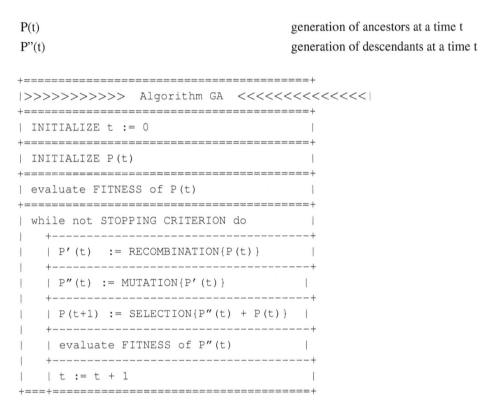

54.3. Genetic Query Optimization (GEQO) in PostgreSQL

The GEQO module approaches the query optimization problem as though it were the well-known traveling salesman problem (TSP). Possible query plans are encoded as integer strings. Each string represents the join order from one relation of the query to the next. For example, the join tree

```
  /\
 /\ 2
/\ 3
4  1
```

is encoded by the integer string '4-1-3-2', which means, first join relation '4' and '1', then '3', and then '2', where 1, 2, 3, 4 are relation IDs within the PostgreSQL optimizer.

Specific characteristics of the GEQO implementation in PostgreSQL are:

- Usage of a *steady state* GA (replacement of the least fit individuals in a population, not whole-generational replacement) allows fast convergence towards improved query plans. This is essential for query handling with reasonable time;
- Usage of *edge recombination crossover* which is especially suited to keep edge losses low for the solution of the TSP by means of a GA;
- Mutation as genetic operator is deprecated so that no repair mechanisms are needed to generate legal TSP tours.

Parts of the GEQO module are adapted from D. Whitley's Genitor algorithm.

The GEQO module allows the PostgreSQL query optimizer to support large join queries effectively through non-exhaustive search.

54.3.1. Generating Possible Plans with GEQO

The GEQO planning process uses the standard planner code to generate plans for scans of individual relations. Then join plans are developed using the genetic approach. As shown above, each candidate join plan is represented by a sequence in which to join the base relations. In the initial stage, the GEQO code simply generates some possible join sequences at random. For each join sequence considered, the standard planner code is invoked to estimate the cost of performing the query using that join sequence. (For each step of the join sequence, all three possible join strategies are considered; and all the initially-determined relation scan plans are available. The estimated cost is the cheapest of these possibilities.) Join sequences with lower estimated cost are considered "more fit" than those with higher cost. The genetic algorithm discards the least fit candidates. Then new candidates are generated by combining genes of more-fit candidates — that is, by using randomly-chosen portions of known low-cost join sequences to create new sequences for consideration. This process is repeated until a preset number of join sequences have been considered; then the best one found at any time during the search is used to generate the finished plan.

This process is inherently nondeterministic, because of the randomized choices made during both the initial population selection and subsequent "mutation" of the best candidates. To avoid surprising changes of the selected plan, each run of the GEQO algorithm restarts its random number generator with the current geqo_seed parameter setting. As long as `geqo_seed` and the other GEQO parameters are kept fixed, the same plan will be generated for a given query (and other planner inputs such as statistics). To experiment with different search paths, try changing `geqo_seed`.

54.3.2. Future Implementation Tasks for PostgreSQL GEQO

Work is still needed to improve the genetic algorithm parameter settings. In file `src/backend/optimizer/geqo/geqo_main.c`, routines `gimme_pool_size` and `gimme_number_generations`, we have to find a compromise for the parameter settings to satisfy two competing demands:

- Optimality of the query plan
- Computing time

In the current implementation, the fitness of each candidate join sequence is estimated by running the standard planner's join selection and cost estimation code from scratch. To the extent that different candidates use similar sub-sequences of joins, a great deal of work will be repeated. This could be made significantly faster by retaining cost estimates for sub-joins. The problem is to avoid expending unreasonable amounts of memory on retaining that state.

At a more basic level, it is not clear that solving query optimization with a GA algorithm designed for TSP is appropriate. In the TSP case, the cost associated with any substring (partial tour) is independent of the rest of the tour, but this is certainly not true for query optimization. Thus it is questionable whether edge recombination crossover is the most effective mutation procedure.

54.4. Further Reading

The following resources contain additional information about genetic algorithms:

- The Hitch-Hiker's Guide to Evolutionary Computation[1], (FAQ for news://comp.ai.genetic)
- Evolutionary Computation and its application to art and design[2], by Craig Reynolds
- *Fundamentals of Database Systems*
- *The design and implementation of the POSTGRES query optimizer*

---

1. http://www.aip.de/~ast/EvolCompFAQ/
2. http://www.red3d.com/cwr/evolve.html

Chapter 55. Index Access Method Interface Definition

This chapter defines the interface between the core PostgreSQL system and *index access methods*, which manage individual index types. The core system knows nothing about indexes beyond what is specified here, so it is possible to develop entirely new index types by writing add-on code.

All indexes in PostgreSQL are what are known technically as *secondary indexes*; that is, the index is physically separate from the table file that it describes. Each index is stored as its own physical *relation* and so is described by an entry in the `pg_class` catalog. The contents of an index are entirely under the control of its index access method. In practice, all index access methods divide indexes into standard-size pages so that they can use the regular storage manager and buffer manager to access the index contents. (All the existing index access methods furthermore use the standard page layout described in Section 59.6, and they all use the same format for index tuple headers; but these decisions are not forced on an access method.)

An index is effectively a mapping from some data key values to *tuple identifiers*, or TIDs, of row versions (tuples) in the index's parent table. A TID consists of a block number and an item number within that block (see Section 59.6). This is sufficient information to fetch a particular row version from the table. Indexes are not directly aware that under MVCC, there might be multiple extant versions of the same logical row; to an index, each tuple is an independent object that needs its own index entry. Thus, an update of a row always creates all-new index entries for the row, even if the key values did not change. (HOT tuples are an exception to this statement; but indexes do not deal with those, either.) Index entries for dead tuples are reclaimed (by vacuuming) when the dead tuples themselves are reclaimed.

55.1. Catalog Entries for Indexes

Each index access method is described by a row in the `pg_am` system catalog (see Section 48.3). The principal contents of a `pg_am` row are references to `pg_proc` entries that identify the index access functions supplied by the access method. The APIs for these functions are defined later in this chapter. In addition, the `pg_am` row specifies a few fixed properties of the access method, such as whether it can support multi-column indexes. There is not currently any special support for creating or deleting `pg_am` entries; anyone able to write a new access method is expected to be competent to insert an appropriate row for themselves.

To be useful, an index access method must also have one or more *operator families* and *operator classes* defined in `pg_opfamily`, `pg_opclass`, `pg_amop`, and `pg_amproc`. These entries allow the planner to determine what kinds of query qualifications can be used with indexes of this access method. Operator families and classes are described in Section 35.14, which is prerequisite material for reading this chapter.

An individual index is defined by a `pg_class` entry that describes it as a physical relation, plus a `pg_index` entry that shows the logical content of the index — that is, the set of index columns it has and the semantics of those columns, as captured by the associated operator classes. The index columns (key values) can be either simple columns of the underlying table or expressions over the table rows. The index access method normally has no interest in where the index key values come from (it is always handed precomputed key values) but it will be very interested in the operator class information in `pg_index`. Both of these catalog entries can be accessed as part of the `Relation` data structure that is passed to all operations on the index.

Some of the flag columns of `pg_am` have nonobvious implications. The requirements of `amcanunique` are discussed in Section 55.5. The `amcanmulticol` flag asserts that the access method supports multicolumn indexes, while `amoptionalkey` asserts that it allows scans where no indexable restriction clause is given for the first index column. When `amcanmulticol` is false, `amoptionalkey` essentially says whether the access method supports full-index scans without any restriction clause. Access methods that support multiple index columns *must* support scans that omit restrictions on any or all of the columns after the first; however they are permitted to require some restriction to appear for the first index column, and this is signaled by setting `amoptionalkey` false. One reason that an index AM might set `amoptionalkey` false is if it doesn't index null values. Since most indexable operators are strict and hence cannot return true for null inputs, it is at first sight attractive to not store index entries for null values: they could never be returned by an index scan anyway. However, this argument fails when an index scan has no restriction clause for a given index column. In practice this means that indexes that have `amoptionalkey` true must index nulls, since the planner might decide to use such an index with no scan keys at all. A related restriction is that an index access method that supports multiple index columns *must* support indexing null values in columns after the first, because the planner will assume the index can be used for queries that do not restrict these columns. For example, consider an index on (a,b) and a query with `WHERE a = 4`. The system will assume the index can be used to scan for rows with `a = 4`, which is wrong if the index omits rows where `b` is null. It is, however, OK to omit rows where the first indexed column is null. An index access method that does index nulls may also set `amsearchnulls`, indicating that it supports `IS NULL` and `IS NOT NULL` clauses as search conditions.

55.2. Index Access Method Functions

The index construction and maintenance functions that an index access method must provide are:

```
IndexBuildResult *
ambuild (Relation heapRelation,
         Relation indexRelation,
         IndexInfo *indexInfo);
```

Build a new index. The index relation has been physically created, but is empty. It must be filled in with whatever fixed data the access method requires, plus entries for all tuples already existing in the table. Ordinarily the `ambuild` function will call `IndexBuildHeapScan()` to scan the table for existing tuples and compute the keys that need to be inserted into the index. The function must return a palloc'd struct containing statistics about the new index.

```
void
ambuildempty (Relation indexRelation);
```

Build an empty index, and write it to the initialization fork (`INIT_FORKNUM`) of the given relation. This method is called only for unlogged tables; the empty index written to the initialization fork will be copied over the main relation fork on each server restart.

```
bool
```

```
aminsert (Relation indexRelation,
          Datum *values,
          bool *isnull,
          ItemPointer heap_tid,
          Relation heapRelation,
          IndexUniqueCheck checkUnique);
```

Insert a new tuple into an existing index. The `values` and `isnull` arrays give the key values to be indexed, and `heap_tid` is the TID to be indexed. If the access method supports unique indexes (its `pg_am.amcanunique` flag is true) then `checkUnique` indicates the type of uniqueness check to perform. This varies depending on whether the unique constraint is deferrable; see Section 55.5 for details. Normally the access method only needs the `heapRelation` parameter when performing uniqueness checking (since then it will have to look into the heap to verify tuple liveness).

The function's Boolean result value is significant only when `checkUnique` is `UNIQUE_CHECK_PARTIAL`. In this case a TRUE result means the new entry is known unique, whereas FALSE means it might be non-unique (and a deferred uniqueness check must be scheduled). For other cases a constant FALSE result is recommended.

Some indexes might not index all tuples. If the tuple is not to be indexed, `aminsert` should just return without doing anything.

```
IndexBulkDeleteResult *
ambulkdelete (IndexVacuumInfo *info,
              IndexBulkDeleteResult *stats,
              IndexBulkDeleteCallback callback,
              void *callback_state);
```

Delete tuple(s) from the index. This is a "bulk delete" operation that is intended to be implemented by scanning the whole index and checking each entry to see if it should be deleted. The passed-in `callback` function must be called, in the style `callback(`*TID*`, callback_state) returns bool`, to determine whether any particular index entry, as identified by its referenced TID, is to be deleted. Must return either NULL or a palloc'd struct containing statistics about the effects of the deletion operation. It is OK to return NULL if no information needs to be passed on to `amvacuumcleanup`.

Because of limited `maintenance_work_mem`, `ambulkdelete` might need to be called more than once when many tuples are to be deleted. The `stats` argument is the result of the previous call for this index (it is NULL for the first call within a VACUUM operation). This allows the AM to accumulate statistics across the whole operation. Typically, `ambulkdelete` will modify and return the same struct if the passed `stats` is not null.

```
IndexBulkDeleteResult *
amvacuumcleanup (IndexVacuumInfo *info,
                 IndexBulkDeleteResult *stats);
```

Clean up after a VACUUM operation (zero or more `ambulkdelete` calls). This does not have to do anything beyond returning index statistics, but it might perform bulk cleanup such as reclaiming empty index pages. `stats` is whatever the last `ambulkdelete` call returned, or NULL if `ambulkdelete` was not called because no tuples needed to be deleted. If the result is not NULL it must be a palloc'd struct. The statistics it contains will be used to update `pg_class`, and will be reported by VACUUM if VERBOSE is given. It is

OK to return NULL if the index was not changed at all during the VACUUM operation, but otherwise correct stats should be returned.

As of PostgreSQL 8.4, amvacuumcleanup will also be called at completion of an ANALYZE operation. In this case stats is always NULL and any return value will be ignored. This case can be distinguished by checking info->analyze_only. It is recommended that the access method do nothing except post-insert cleanup in such a call, and that only in an autovacuum worker process.

```
bool
amcanreturn (Relation indexRelation);
```

Check whether the index can support *index-only scans* by returning the indexed column values for an index entry in the form of an IndexTuple. Return TRUE if so, else FALSE. If the index AM can never support index-only scans (an example is hash, which stores only the hash values not the original data), it is sufficient to set its amcanreturn field to zero in pg_am.

```
void
amcostestimate (PlannerInfo *root,
                IndexPath *path,
                double loop_count,
                Cost *indexStartupCost,
                Cost *indexTotalCost,
                Selectivity *indexSelectivity,
                double *indexCorrelation);
```

Estimate the costs of an index scan. This function is described fully in Section 55.6, below.

```
bytea *
amoptions (ArrayType *reloptions,
           bool validate);
```

Parse and validate the reloptions array for an index. This is called only when a non-null reloptions array exists for the index. reloptions is a text array containing entries of the form *name=value*. The function should construct a bytea value, which will be copied into the rd_options field of the index's relcache entry. The data contents of the bytea value are open for the access method to define; most of the standard access methods use struct StdRdOptions. When validate is true, the function should report a suitable error message if any of the options are unrecognized or have invalid values; when validate is false, invalid entries should be silently ignored. (validate is false when loading options already stored in pg_catalog; an invalid entry could only be found if the access method has changed its rules for options, and in that case ignoring obsolete entries is appropriate.) It is OK to return NULL if default behavior is wanted.

The purpose of an index, of course, is to support scans for tuples matching an indexable WHERE condition, often called a *qualifier* or *scan key*. The semantics of index scanning are described more fully in Section 55.3, below. An index access method can support "plain" index scans, "bitmap" index scans, or both. The scan-related functions that an index access method must or may provide are:

```
IndexScanDesc
ambeginscan (Relation indexRelation,
             int nkeys,
             int norderbys);
```

Prepare for an index scan. The `nkeys` and `norderbys` parameters indicate the number of quals and ordering operators that will be used in the scan; these may be useful for space allocation purposes. Note that the actual values of the scan keys aren't provided yet. The result must be a palloc'd struct. For implementation reasons the index access method *must* create this struct by calling `RelationGetIndexScan()`. In most cases `ambeginscan` does little beyond making that call and perhaps acquiring locks; the interesting parts of index-scan startup are in `amrescan`.

```
void
amrescan (IndexScanDesc scan,
          ScanKey keys,
          int nkeys,
          ScanKey orderbys,
          int norderbys);
```

Start or restart an index scan, possibly with new scan keys. (To restart using previously-passed keys, NULL is passed for `keys` and/or `orderbys`.) Note that it is not allowed for the number of keys or order-by operators to be larger than what was passed to `ambeginscan`. In practice the restart feature is used when a new outer tuple is selected by a nested-loop join and so a new key comparison value is needed, but the scan key structure remains the same.

```
boolean
amgettuple (IndexScanDesc scan,
            ScanDirection direction);
```

Fetch the next tuple in the given scan, moving in the given direction (forward or backward in the index). Returns TRUE if a tuple was obtained, FALSE if no matching tuples remain. In the TRUE case the tuple TID is stored into the `scan` structure. Note that "success" means only that the index contains an entry that matches the scan keys, not that the tuple necessarily still exists in the heap or will pass the caller's snapshot test. On success, `amgettuple` must also set `scan->xs_recheck` to TRUE or FALSE. FALSE means it is certain that the index entry matches the scan keys. TRUE means this is not certain, and the conditions represented by the scan keys must be rechecked against the heap tuple after fetching it. This provision supports "lossy" index operators. Note that rechecking will extend only to the scan conditions; a partial index predicate (if any) is never rechecked by `amgettuple` callers.

If the index supports index-only scans (i.e., `amcanreturn` returns TRUE for it), then on success the AM must also check `scan->xs_want_itup`, and if that is true it must return the original indexed data for the index entry, in the form of an `IndexTuple` pointer stored at `scan->xs_itup`, with tuple descriptor `scan->xs_itupdesc`. (Management of the data referenced by the pointer is the access method's responsibility. The data must remain good at least until the next `amgettuple`, `amrescan`, or `amendscan` call for the scan.)

The `amgettuple` function need only be provided if the access method supports "plain" index scans. If it doesn't, the `amgettuple` field in its `pg_am` row must be set to zero.

```
int64
amgetbitmap (IndexScanDesc scan,
             TIDBitmap *tbm);
```

Fetch all tuples in the given scan and add them to the caller-supplied `TIDBitmap` (that is, OR the set of tuple IDs into whatever set is already in the bitmap). The number of tuples fetched is returned (this might be just an approximate count, for instance some AMs do not detect duplicates). While inserting tuple IDs into the bitmap, `amgetbitmap` can indicate that rechecking of the scan conditions is required for specific tuple IDs. This is analogous to the `xs_recheck` output parameter of `amgettuple`. Note: in the current implementation, support for this feature is conflated with support for lossy storage of the bitmap itself, and therefore callers recheck both the scan conditions and the partial index predicate (if any) for recheckable tuples. That might not always be true, however. `amgetbitmap` and `amgettuple` cannot be used in the same index scan; there are other restrictions too when using `amgetbitmap`, as explained in Section 55.3.

The `amgetbitmap` function need only be provided if the access method supports "bitmap" index scans. If it doesn't, the `amgetbitmap` field in its `pg_am` row must be set to zero.

```
void
amendscan (IndexScanDesc scan);
```

End a scan and release resources. The `scan` struct itself should not be freed, but any locks or pins taken internally by the access method must be released.

```
void
ammarkpos (IndexScanDesc scan);
```

Mark current scan position. The access method need only support one remembered scan position per scan.

```
void
amrestrpos (IndexScanDesc scan);
```

Restore the scan to the most recently marked position.

By convention, the `pg_proc` entry for an index access method function should show the correct number of arguments, but declare them all as type `internal` (since most of the arguments have types that are not known to SQL, and we don't want users calling the functions directly anyway). The return type is declared as `void`, `internal`, or `boolean` as appropriate. The only exception is `amoptions`, which should be correctly declared as taking `text[]` and `bool` and returning `bytea`. This provision allows client code to execute `amoptions` to test validity of options settings.

55.3. Index Scanning

In an index scan, the index access method is responsible for regurgitating the TIDs of all the tuples it has been told about that match the *scan keys*. The access method is *not* involved in actually fetching those tuples from the index's parent table, nor in determining whether they pass the scan's time qualification test or other conditions.

A scan key is the internal representation of a `WHERE` clause of the form *index_key operator constant*, where the index key is one of the columns of the index and the operator is one of the members of the operator family associated with that index column. An index scan has zero or more scan keys, which are implicitly ANDed — the returned tuples are expected to satisfy all the indicated conditions.

The access method can report that the index is *lossy*, or requires rechecks, for a particular query. This implies that the index scan will return all the entries that pass the scan key, plus possibly additional entries that do not. The core system's index-scan machinery will then apply the index conditions again to the heap tuple to verify whether or not it really should be selected. If the recheck option is not specified, the index scan must return exactly the set of matching entries.

Note that it is entirely up to the access method to ensure that it correctly finds all and only the entries passing all the given scan keys. Also, the core system will simply hand off all the WHERE clauses that match the index keys and operator families, without any semantic analysis to determine whether they are redundant or contradictory. As an example, given WHERE x > 4 AND x > 14 where x is a b-tree indexed column, it is left to the b-tree amrescan function to realize that the first scan key is redundant and can be discarded. The extent of preprocessing needed during amrescan will depend on the extent to which the index access method needs to reduce the scan keys to a "normalized" form.

Some access methods return index entries in a well-defined order, others do not. There are actually two different ways that an access method can support sorted output:

- Access methods that always return entries in the natural ordering of their data (such as btree) should set pg_am.amcanorder to true. Currently, such access methods must use btree-compatible strategy numbers for their equality and ordering operators.

- Access methods that support ordering operators should set pg_am.amcanorderbyop to true. This indicates that the index is capable of returning entries in an order satisfying ORDER BY *index_key operator constant*. Scan modifiers of that form can be passed to amrescan as described previously.

The amgettuple function has a direction argument, which can be either ForwardScanDirection (the normal case) or BackwardScanDirection. If the first call after amrescan specifies BackwardScanDirection, then the set of matching index entries is to be scanned back-to-front rather than in the normal front-to-back direction, so amgettuple must return the last matching tuple in the index, rather than the first one as it normally would. (This will only occur for access methods that set amcanorder to true.) After the first call, amgettuple must be prepared to advance the scan in either direction from the most recently returned entry. (But if pg_am.amcanbackward is false, all subsequent calls will have the same direction as the first one.)

Access methods that support ordered scans must support "marking" a position in a scan and later returning to the marked position. The same position might be restored multiple times. However, only one position need be remembered per scan; a new ammarkpos call overrides the previously marked position. An access method that does not support ordered scans should still provide mark and restore functions in pg_am, but it is sufficient to have them throw errors if called.

Both the scan position and the mark position (if any) must be maintained consistently in the face of concurrent insertions or deletions in the index. It is OK if a freshly-inserted entry is not returned by a scan that would have found the entry if it had existed when the scan started, or for the scan to return such an entry upon rescanning or backing up even though it had not been returned the first time through. Similarly, a concurrent delete might or might not be reflected in the results of a scan. What is important is that insertions or deletions not cause the scan to miss or multiply return entries that were not themselves being inserted or deleted.

If the index stores the original indexed data values (and not some lossy representation of them), it is useful to support index-only scans, in which the index returns the actual data not just the TID of the heap tuple. This will only work if the visibility map shows that the TID is on an all-visible page; else the heap tuple must be visited anyway to check MVCC visibility. But that is no concern of the access method's.

Instead of using `amgettuple`, an index scan can be done with `amgetbitmap` to fetch all tuples in one call. This can be noticeably more efficient than `amgettuple` because it allows avoiding lock/unlock cycles within the access method. In principle `amgetbitmap` should have the same effects as repeated `amgettuple` calls, but we impose several restrictions to simplify matters. First of all, `amgetbitmap` returns all tuples at once and marking or restoring scan positions isn't supported. Secondly, the tuples are returned in a bitmap which doesn't have any specific ordering, which is why `amgetbitmap` doesn't take a `direction` argument. (Ordering operators will never be supplied for such a scan, either.) Also, there is no provision for index-only scans with `amgetbitmap`, since there is no way to return the contents of index tuples. Finally, `amgetbitmap` does not guarantee any locking of the returned tuples, with implications spelled out in Section 55.4.

Note that it is permitted for an access method to implement only `amgetbitmap` and not `amgettuple`, or vice versa, if its internal implementation is unsuited to one API or the other.

55.4. Index Locking Considerations

Index access methods must handle concurrent updates of the index by multiple processes. The core PostgreSQL system obtains `AccessShareLock` on the index during an index scan, and `RowExclusiveLock` when updating the index (including plain `VACUUM`). Since these lock types do not conflict, the access method is responsible for handling any fine-grained locking it might need. An exclusive lock on the index as a whole will be taken only during index creation, destruction, or `REINDEX`.

Building an index type that supports concurrent updates usually requires extensive and subtle analysis of the required behavior. For the b-tree and hash index types, you can read about the design decisions involved in `src/backend/access/nbtree/README` and `src/backend/access/hash/README`.

Aside from the index's own internal consistency requirements, concurrent updates create issues about consistency between the parent table (the *heap*) and the index. Because PostgreSQL separates accesses and updates of the heap from those of the index, there are windows in which the index might be inconsistent with the heap. We handle this problem with the following rules:

- A new heap entry is made before making its index entries. (Therefore a concurrent index scan is likely to fail to see the heap entry. This is okay because the index reader would be uninterested in an uncommitted row anyway. But see Section 55.5.)

- When a heap entry is to be deleted (by `VACUUM`), all its index entries must be removed first.

- An index scan must maintain a pin on the index page holding the item last returned by `amgettuple`, and `ambulkdelete` cannot delete entries from pages that are pinned by other backends. The need for this rule is explained below.

Without the third rule, it is possible for an index reader to see an index entry just before it is removed by `VACUUM`, and then to arrive at the corresponding heap entry after that was removed by `VACUUM`. This creates no serious problems if that item number is still unused when the reader reaches it, since an empty item slot will be ignored by `heap_fetch()`. But what if a third backend has already re-used the item slot for something else? When using an MVCC-compliant snapshot, there is no problem because the new occupant of the slot is certain to be too new to pass the snapshot test. However, with a non-MVCC-compliant snapshot (such as `SnapshotAny`), it would be possible to accept and return a row that does not in fact match the scan keys. We could defend against this scenario by requiring the scan keys to be rechecked against the heap row in all cases, but that is too expensive. Instead, we use a pin on an index page as a proxy to indicate that the reader might still be "in flight" from the index entry to the matching heap entry. Making `ambulkdelete` block on such a pin ensures that VACUUM cannot delete the heap entry before the reader is done with it. This solution costs little in run time, and adds blocking overhead only in the rare cases where there actually is a conflict.

This solution requires that index scans be "synchronous": we have to fetch each heap tuple immediately after scanning the corresponding index entry. This is expensive for a number of reasons. An "asynchronous" scan in which we collect many TIDs from the index, and only visit the heap tuples sometime later, requires much less index locking overhead and can allow a more efficient heap access pattern. Per the above analysis, we must use the synchronous approach for non-MVCC-compliant snapshots, but an asynchronous scan is workable for a query using an MVCC snapshot.

In an `amgetbitmap` index scan, the access method does not keep an index pin on any of the returned tuples. Therefore it is only safe to use such scans with MVCC-compliant snapshots.

When the `ampredlocks` flag is not set, any scan using that index access method within a serializable transaction will acquire a nonblocking predicate lock on the full index. This will generate a read-write conflict with the insert of any tuple into that index by a concurrent serializable transaction. If certain patterns of read-write conflicts are detected among a set of concurrent serializable transactions, one of those transactions may be canceled to protect data integrity. When the flag is set, it indicates that the index access method implements finer-grained predicate locking, which will tend to reduce the frequency of such transaction cancellations.

55.5. Index Uniqueness Checks

PostgreSQL enforces SQL uniqueness constraints using *unique indexes*, which are indexes that disallow multiple entries with identical keys. An access method that supports this feature sets `pg_am.amcanunique` true. (At present, only b-tree supports it.)

Because of MVCC, it is always necessary to allow duplicate entries to exist physically in an index: the entries might refer to successive versions of a single logical row. The behavior we actually want to enforce is that no MVCC snapshot could include two rows with equal index keys. This breaks down into the following cases that must be checked when inserting a new row into a unique index:

- If a conflicting valid row has been deleted by the current transaction, it's okay. (In particular, since an UPDATE always deletes the old row version before inserting the new version, this will allow an UPDATE on a row without changing the key.)

- If a conflicting row has been inserted by an as-yet-uncommitted transaction, the would-be inserter must wait to see if that transaction commits. If it rolls back then there is no conflict. If it commits without deleting the conflicting row again, there is a uniqueness violation. (In practice we just wait for the other transaction to end and then redo the visibility check in toto.)

- Similarly, if a conflicting valid row has been deleted by an as-yet-uncommitted transaction, the would-be inserter must wait for that transaction to commit or abort, and then repeat the test.

Furthermore, immediately before reporting a uniqueness violation according to the above rules, the access method must recheck the liveness of the row being inserted. If it is committed dead then no violation should be reported. (This case cannot occur during the ordinary scenario of inserting a row that's just been created by the current transaction. It can happen during CREATE UNIQUE INDEX CONCURRENTLY, however.)

We require the index access method to apply these tests itself, which means that it must reach into the heap to check the commit status of any row that is shown to have a duplicate key according to the index contents. This is without a doubt ugly and non-modular, but it saves redundant work: if we did a separate probe then the index lookup for a conflicting row would be essentially repeated while finding the place to insert the new row's index entry. What's more, there is no obvious way to avoid race conditions unless the conflict check is an integral part of insertion of the new index entry.

If the unique constraint is deferrable, there is additional complexity: we need to be able to insert an index entry for a new row, but defer any uniqueness-violation error until end of statement or even later. To avoid unnecessary repeat searches of the index, the index access method should do a preliminary uniqueness check during the initial insertion. If this shows that there is definitely no conflicting live tuple, we are done. Otherwise, we schedule a recheck to occur when it is time to enforce the constraint. If, at the time of the recheck, both the inserted tuple and some other tuple with the same key are live, then the error must be reported. (Note that for this purpose, "live" actually means "any tuple in the index entry's HOT chain is live".) To implement this, the aminsert function is passed a checkUnique parameter having one of the following values:

- UNIQUE_CHECK_NO indicates that no uniqueness checking should be done (this is not a unique index).

- UNIQUE_CHECK_YES indicates that this is a non-deferrable unique index, and the uniqueness check must be done immediately, as described above.

- UNIQUE_CHECK_PARTIAL indicates that the unique constraint is deferrable. PostgreSQL will use this mode to insert each row's index entry. The access method must allow duplicate entries into the index, and report any potential duplicates by returning FALSE from aminsert. For each row for which FALSE is returned, a deferred recheck will be scheduled.

  The access method must identify any rows which might violate the unique constraint, but it is not an error for it to report false positives. This allows the check to be done without waiting for other transactions to finish; conflicts reported here are not treated as errors and will be rechecked later, by which time they may no longer be conflicts.

- UNIQUE_CHECK_EXISTING indicates that this is a deferred recheck of a row that was reported as a potential uniqueness violation. Although this is implemented by calling aminsert, the access method must *not* insert a new index entry in this case. The index entry is already present. Rather, the access method must check to see if there is another live index entry. If so, and if the target row is also still live, report error.

  It is recommended that in a UNIQUE_CHECK_EXISTING call, the access method further verify that the target row actually does have an existing entry in the index, and report error if not. This is a good idea because the index tuple values passed to aminsert will have been recomputed. If the index definition involves functions that are not really immutable, we might be checking the wrong area of the index. Checking that the target row is found in the recheck verifies that we are scanning for the same tuple values as were used in the original insertion.

55.6. Index Cost Estimation Functions

The `amcostestimate` function is given information describing a possible index scan, including lists of WHERE and ORDER BY clauses that have been determined to be usable with the index. It must return estimates of the cost of accessing the index and the selectivity of the WHERE clauses (that is, the fraction of parent-table rows that will be retrieved during the index scan). For simple cases, nearly all the work of the cost estimator can be done by calling standard routines in the optimizer; the point of having an `amcostestimate` function is to allow index access methods to provide index-type-specific knowledge, in case it is possible to improve on the standard estimates.

Each `amcostestimate` function must have the signature:

```
void
amcostestimate (PlannerInfo *root,
                IndexPath *path,
                double loop_count,
                Cost *indexStartupCost,
                Cost *indexTotalCost,
                Selectivity *indexSelectivity,
                double *indexCorrelation);
```

The first three parameters are inputs:

root

    The planner's information about the query being processed.

path

    The index access path being considered. All fields except cost and selectivity values are valid.

loop_count

    The number of repetitions of the index scan that should be factored into the cost estimates. This will typically be greater than one when considering a parameterized scan for use in the inside of a nestloop join. Note that the cost estimates should still be for just one scan; a larger `loop_count` means that it may be appropriate to allow for some caching effects across multiple scans.

The last four parameters are pass-by-reference outputs:

*indexStartupCost

    Set to cost of index start-up processing

*indexTotalCost

    Set to total cost of index processing

*indexSelectivity

    Set to index selectivity

*indexCorrelation

    Set to correlation coefficient between index scan order and underlying table's order

Note that cost estimate functions must be written in C, not in SQL or any available procedural language, because they must access internal data structures of the planner/optimizer.

The index access costs should be computed using the parameters used by `src/backend/optimizer/path/costsize.c`: a sequential disk block fetch has cost `seq_page_cost`, a nonsequential fetch has cost `random_page_cost`, and the cost of processing one index row should usually be taken as `cpu_index_tuple_cost`. In addition, an appropriate multiple of `cpu_operator_cost` should be charged for any comparison operators invoked during index processing (especially evaluation of the indexquals themselves).

The access costs should include all disk and CPU costs associated with scanning the index itself, but *not* the costs of retrieving or processing the parent-table rows that are identified by the index.

The "start-up cost" is the part of the total scan cost that must be expended before we can begin to fetch the first row. For most indexes this can be taken as zero, but an index type with a high start-up cost might want to set it nonzero.

The `indexSelectivity` should be set to the estimated fraction of the parent table rows that will be retrieved during the index scan. In the case of a lossy query, this will typically be higher than the fraction of rows that actually pass the given qual conditions.

The `indexCorrelation` should be set to the correlation (ranging between -1.0 and 1.0) between the index order and the table order. This is used to adjust the estimate for the cost of fetching rows from the parent table.

When `loop_count` is greater than one, the returned numbers should be averages expected for any one scan of the index.

Cost Estimation

A typical cost estimator will proceed as follows:

1. Estimate and return the fraction of parent-table rows that will be visited based on the given qual conditions. In the absence of any index-type-specific knowledge, use the standard optimizer function `clauselist_selectivity()`:

    ```
    *indexSelectivity = clauselist_selectivity(root, path->indexquals,
                                                path->indexinfo->rel->relid,
                                                JOIN_INNER, NULL);
    ```

2. Estimate the number of index rows that will be visited during the scan. For many index types this is the same as `indexSelectivity` times the number of rows in the index, but it might be more. (Note that the index's size in pages and rows is available from the `path->indexinfo` struct.)

3. Estimate the number of index pages that will be retrieved during the scan. This might be just `indexSelectivity` times the index's size in pages.

4. Compute the index access cost. A generic estimator might do this:

    ```
    /*
     * Our generic assumption is that the index pages will be read
     * sequentially, so they cost seq_page_cost each, not random_page_cost.
     * Also, we charge for evaluation of the indexquals at each index row.
     * All the costs are assumed to be paid incrementally during the scan.
     */
    cost_qual_eval(&index_qual_cost, path->indexquals, root);
    ```

```
*indexStartupCost = index_qual_cost.startup;
*indexTotalCost = seq_page_cost * numIndexPages +
    (cpu_index_tuple_cost + index_qual_cost.per_tuple) * numIndexTuples;
```
However, the above does not account for amortization of index reads across repeated index scans.

5. Estimate the index correlation. For a simple ordered index on a single field, this can be retrieved from pg_statistic. If the correlation is not known, the conservative estimate is zero (no correlation).

Examples of cost estimator functions can be found in `src/backend/utils/adt/selfuncs.c`.

Chapter 56. GiST Indexes

56.1. Introduction

GiST stands for Generalized Search Tree. It is a balanced, tree-structured access method, that acts as a base template in which to implement arbitrary indexing schemes. B-trees, R-trees and many other indexing schemes can be implemented in GiST.

One advantage of GiST is that it allows the development of custom data types with the appropriate access methods, by an expert in the domain of the data type, rather than a database expert.

Some of the information here is derived from the University of California at Berkeley's GiST Indexing Project web site[1] and Marcel Kornacker's thesis, Access Methods for Next-Generation Database Systems[2]. The GiST implementation in PostgreSQL is primarily maintained by Teodor Sigaev and Oleg Bartunov, and there is more information on their web site[3].

56.2. Built-in Operator Classes

The core PostgreSQL distribution includes the GiST operator classes shown in Table 56-1. (Some of the optional modules described in Appendix F provide additional GiST operator classes.)

Table 56-1. Built-in GiST Operator Classes

Name	Indexed Data Type	Indexable Operators	Ordering Operators
box_ops	box	&& &> &< &<| >> << <<| <@ @> @ |&> |>> ~ ~=	
circle_ops	circle	&& &> &< &<| >> << <<| <@ @> @ |&> |>> ~ ~=	
inet_ops	inet, cidr	&& >> >>= > >= <> << <<= < <= =	
point_ops	point	>> >^ << <@ <@ <@ <^ ~=	<->
poly_ops	polygon	&& &> &< &<| >> << <<| <@ @> @ |&> |>> ~ ~=	

---

1. http://gist.cs.berkeley.edu/
2. http://www.sai.msu.su/~megera/postgres/gist/papers/concurrency/access-methods-for-next-generation.pdf.gz
3. http://www.sai.msu.su/~megera/postgres/gist/

Name	Indexed Data Type	Indexable Operators	Ordering Operators
range_ops	any range type	&& &> &< >> << <@ -|- = @> @>	
tsquery_ops	tsquery	<@ @>	
tsvector_ops	tsvector	@@	

For historical reasons, the inet_ops operator class is not the default class for types inet and cidr. To use it, mention the class name in CREATE INDEX, for example

```
CREATE INDEX ON my_table USING gist (my_inet_column inet_ops);
```

56.3. Extensibility

Traditionally, implementing a new index access method meant a lot of difficult work. It was necessary to understand the inner workings of the database, such as the lock manager and Write-Ahead Log. The GiST interface has a high level of abstraction, requiring the access method implementer only to implement the semantics of the data type being accessed. The GiST layer itself takes care of concurrency, logging and searching the tree structure.

This extensibility should not be confused with the extensibility of the other standard search trees in terms of the data they can handle. For example, PostgreSQL supports extensible B-trees and hash indexes. That means that you can use PostgreSQL to build a B-tree or hash over any data type you want. But B-trees only support range predicates ($<$, $=$, $>$), and hash indexes only support equality queries.

So if you index, say, an image collection with a PostgreSQL B-tree, you can only issue queries such as "is imagex equal to imagey", "is imagex less than imagey" and "is imagex greater than imagey". Depending on how you define "equals", "less than" and "greater than" in this context, this could be useful. However, by using a GiST based index, you could create ways to ask domain-specific questions, perhaps "find all images of horses" or "find all over-exposed images".

All it takes to get a GiST access method up and running is to implement several user-defined methods, which define the behavior of keys in the tree. Of course these methods have to be pretty fancy to support fancy queries, but for all the standard queries (B-trees, R-trees, etc.) they're relatively straightforward. In short, GiST combines extensibility along with generality, code reuse, and a clean interface.

There are seven methods that an index operator class for GiST must provide, and an eighth that is optional. Correctness of the index is ensured by proper implementation of the same, consistent and union methods, while efficiency (size and speed) of the index will depend on the penalty and picksplit methods. The remaining two basic methods are compress and decompress, which allow an index to have internal tree data of a different type than the data it indexes. The leaves are to be of the indexed data type, while the other tree nodes can be of any C struct (but you still have to follow PostgreSQL data type rules here, see about varlena for variable sized data). If the tree's internal data type exists at the SQL level, the STORAGE option of the CREATE OPERATOR CLASS command can be used. The optional eighth method is distance, which is needed if the operator class wishes to support ordered scans (nearest-neighbor searches).

```
consistent
```

Given an index entry p and a query value q, this function determines whether the index entry is "consistent" with the query; that is, could the predicate "*indexed_column indexable_operator q*" be true for any row represented by the index entry? For a leaf index entry this is equivalent to testing the indexable condition, while for an internal tree node this determines whether it is necessary to scan the subtree of the index represented by the tree node. When the result is true, a recheck flag must also be returned. This indicates whether the predicate is certainly true or only possibly true. If recheck = false then the index has tested the predicate condition exactly, whereas if recheck = true the row is only a candidate match. In that case the system will automatically evaluate the *indexable_operator* against the actual row value to see if it is really a match. This convention allows GiST to support both lossless and lossy index structures.

The SQL declaration of the function must look like this:

```
CREATE OR REPLACE FUNCTION my_consistent(internal, data_type, smallint, oid
RETURNS bool
AS 'MODULE_PATHNAME'
LANGUAGE C STRICT;
```

And the matching code in the C module could then follow this skeleton:

```
Datum       my_consistent(PG_FUNCTION_ARGS);
PG_FUNCTION_INFO_V1(my_consistent);

Datum
my_consistent(PG_FUNCTION_ARGS)
{
    GISTENTRY   *entry = (GISTENTRY *) PG_GETARG_POINTER(0);
    data_type   *query = PG_GETARG_DATA_TYPE_P(1);
    StrategyNumber strategy = (StrategyNumber) PG_GETARG_UINT16(2);
    /* Oid subtype = PG_GETARG_OID(3); */
    bool        *recheck = (bool *) PG_GETARG_POINTER(4);
    data_type   *key = DatumGetDataType(entry->key);
    bool         retval;

    /*
     * determine return value as a function of strategy, key and query.
     *
     * Use GIST_LEAF(entry) to know where you're called in the index tree,
     * which comes handy when supporting the = operator for example (you co
     * check for non empty union() in non-leaf nodes and equality in leaf
     * nodes).
     */

    *recheck = true;        /* or false if check is exact */

    PG_RETURN_BOOL(retval);
}
```

Here, key is an element in the index and query the value being looked up in the index. The StrategyNumber parameter indicates which operator of your operator class is being applied — it matches one of the operator numbers in the CREATE OPERATOR CLASS command. Depending on what operators you have included in the class, the data type of query could vary with the operator, but the above skeleton assumes it doesn't.

`union`

This method consolidates information in the tree. Given a set of entries, this function generates a new index entry that represents all the given entries.

The SQL declaration of the function must look like this:

```
CREATE OR REPLACE FUNCTION my_union(internal, internal)
RETURNS internal
AS 'MODULE_PATHNAME'
LANGUAGE C STRICT;
```

And the matching code in the C module could then follow this skeleton:

```
Datum          my_union(PG_FUNCTION_ARGS);
PG_FUNCTION_INFO_V1(my_union);

Datum
my_union(PG_FUNCTION_ARGS)
{
    GistEntryVector *entryvec = (GistEntryVector *) PG_GETARG_POINTER(0);
    GISTENTRY   *ent = entryvec->vector;
    data_type   *out,
                *tmp,
                *old;
    int          numranges,
                 i = 0;

    numranges = entryvec->n;
    tmp = DatumGetDataType(ent[0].key);
    out = tmp;

    if (numranges == 1)
    {
        out = data_type_deep_copy(tmp);

        PG_RETURN_DATA_TYPE_P(out);
    }

    for (i = 1; i < numranges; i++)
    {
        old = out;
        tmp = DatumGetDataType(ent[i].key);
        out = my_union_implementation(out, tmp);
    }

    PG_RETURN_DATA_TYPE_P(out);
}
```

As you can see, in this skeleton we're dealing with a data type where `union(X, Y, Z) = union(union(X, Y), Z)`. It's easy enough to support data types where this is not the case, by implementing the proper union algorithm in this GiST support method.

The `union` implementation function should return a pointer to newly `palloc()`ed memory. You can't just return whatever the input is.

compress

Converts the data item into a format suitable for physical storage in an index page.

The SQL declaration of the function must look like this:

```
CREATE OR REPLACE FUNCTION my_compress(internal)
RETURNS internal
AS 'MODULE_PATHNAME'
LANGUAGE C STRICT;
```

And the matching code in the C module could then follow this skeleton:

```
Datum       my_compress(PG_FUNCTION_ARGS);
PG_FUNCTION_INFO_V1(my_compress);

Datum
my_compress(PG_FUNCTION_ARGS)
{
    GISTENTRY   *entry = (GISTENTRY *) PG_GETARG_POINTER(0);
    GISTENTRY   *retval;

    if (entry->leafkey)
    {
        /* replace entry->key with a compressed version */
        compressed_data_type *compressed_data = palloc(sizeof(compressed_da

        /* fill *compressed_data from entry->key ... */

        retval = palloc(sizeof(GISTENTRY));
        gistentryinit(*retval, PointerGetDatum(compressed_data),
                    entry->rel, entry->page, entry->offset, FALSE);
    }
    else
    {
        /* typically we needn't do anything with non-leaf entries */
        retval = entry;
    }

    PG_RETURN_POINTER(retval);
}
```

You have to adapt *compressed_data_type* to the specific type you're converting to in order to compress your leaf nodes, of course.

Depending on your needs, you could also need to care about compressing NULL values in there, storing for example (Datum) 0 like gist_circle_compress does.

decompress

The reverse of the compress method. Converts the index representation of the data item into a format that can be manipulated by the database.

The SQL declaration of the function must look like this:

```
CREATE OR REPLACE FUNCTION my_decompress(internal)
RETURNS internal
AS 'MODULE_PATHNAME'
```

```
LANGUAGE C STRICT;
```
And the matching code in the C module could then follow this skeleton:
```
Datum          my_decompress(PG_FUNCTION_ARGS);
PG_FUNCTION_INFO_V1(my_decompress);

Datum
my_decompress(PG_FUNCTION_ARGS)
{
    PG_RETURN_POINTER(PG_GETARG_POINTER(0));
}
```
The above skeleton is suitable for the case where no decompression is needed.

`penalty`

> Returns a value indicating the "cost" of inserting the new entry into a particular branch of the tree. Items will be inserted down the path of least `penalty` in the tree. Values returned by `penalty` should be non-negative. If a negative value is returned, it will be treated as zero.
>
> The SQL declaration of the function must look like this:
> ```
> CREATE OR REPLACE FUNCTION my_penalty(internal, internal, internal)
> RETURNS internal
> AS 'MODULE_PATHNAME'
> LANGUAGE C STRICT;  -- in some cases penalty functions need not be strict
> ```
> And the matching code in the C module could then follow this skeleton:
> ```
> Datum          my_penalty(PG_FUNCTION_ARGS);
> PG_FUNCTION_INFO_V1(my_penalty);
>
> Datum
> my_penalty(PG_FUNCTION_ARGS)
> {
>     GISTENTRY   *origentry = (GISTENTRY *) PG_GETARG_POINTER(0);
>     GISTENTRY   *newentry = (GISTENTRY *) PG_GETARG_POINTER(1);
>     float       *penalty = (float *) PG_GETARG_POINTER(2);
>     data_type   *orig = DatumGetDataType(origentry->key);
>     data_type   *new = DatumGetDataType(newentry->key);
>
>     *penalty = my_penalty_implementation(orig, new);
>     PG_RETURN_POINTER(penalty);
> }
> ```
>
> The `penalty` function is crucial to good performance of the index. It'll get used at insertion time to determine which branch to follow when choosing where to add the new entry in the tree. At query time, the more balanced the index, the quicker the lookup.

`picksplit`

> When an index page split is necessary, this function decides which entries on the page are to stay on the old page, and which are to move to the new page.
>
> The SQL declaration of the function must look like this:
> ```
> CREATE OR REPLACE FUNCTION my_picksplit(internal, internal)
> RETURNS internal
> AS 'MODULE_PATHNAME'
> LANGUAGE C STRICT;
> ```

And the matching code in the C module could then follow this skeleton:

```
Datum        my_picksplit(PG_FUNCTION_ARGS);
PG_FUNCTION_INFO_V1(my_picksplit);

Datum
my_picksplit(PG_FUNCTION_ARGS)
{
    GistEntryVector *entryvec = (GistEntryVector *) PG_GETARG_POINTER(0);
    OffsetNumber maxoff = entryvec->n - 1;
    GISTENTRY  *ent = entryvec->vector;
    GIST_SPLITVEC *v = (GIST_SPLITVEC *) PG_GETARG_POINTER(1);
    int         i,
                nbytes;
    OffsetNumber *left,
                *right;
    data_type  *tmp_union;
    data_type  *unionL;
    data_type  *unionR;
    GISTENTRY **raw_entryvec;

    maxoff = entryvec->n - 1;
    nbytes = (maxoff + 1) * sizeof(OffsetNumber);

    v->spl_left = (OffsetNumber *) palloc(nbytes);
    left = v->spl_left;
    v->spl_nleft = 0;

    v->spl_right = (OffsetNumber *) palloc(nbytes);
    right = v->spl_right;
    v->spl_nright = 0;

    unionL = NULL;
    unionR = NULL;

    /* Initialize the raw entry vector. */
    raw_entryvec = (GISTENTRY **) malloc(entryvec->n * sizeof(void *));
    for (i = FirstOffsetNumber; i <= maxoff; i = OffsetNumberNext(i))
        raw_entryvec[i] = &(entryvec->vector[i]);

    for (i = FirstOffsetNumber; i <= maxoff; i = OffsetNumberNext(i))
    {
        int         real_index = raw_entryvec[i] - entryvec->vector;

        tmp_union = DatumGetDataType(entryvec->vector[real_index].key);
        Assert(tmp_union != NULL);

        /*
         * Choose where to put the index entries and update unionL and unio
         * accordingly. Append the entries to either v_spl_left or
         * v_spl_right, and care about the counters.
         */

        if (my_choice_is_left(unionL, curl, unionR, curr))
```

```
            {
                if (unionL == NULL)
                    unionL = tmp_union;
                else
                    unionL = my_union_implementation(unionL, tmp_union);

                *left = real_index;
                ++left;
                ++(v->spl_nleft);
            }
            else
            {
                /*
                 * Same on the right
                 */
            }
        }

        v->spl_ldatum = DataTypeGetDatum(unionL);
        v->spl_rdatum = DataTypeGetDatum(unionR);
        PG_RETURN_POINTER(v);
    }
```

Like `penalty`, the `picksplit` function is crucial to good performance of the index. Designing suitable `penalty` and `picksplit` implementations is where the challenge of implementing well-performing GiST indexes lies.

`same`

Returns true if two index entries are identical, false otherwise.

The SQL declaration of the function must look like this:

```
CREATE OR REPLACE FUNCTION my_same(internal, internal, internal)
RETURNS internal
AS 'MODULE_PATHNAME'
LANGUAGE C STRICT;
```

And the matching code in the C module could then follow this skeleton:

```
Datum       my_same(PG_FUNCTION_ARGS);
PG_FUNCTION_INFO_V1(my_same);

Datum
my_same(PG_FUNCTION_ARGS)
{
    prefix_range *v1 = PG_GETARG_PREFIX_RANGE_P(0);
    prefix_range *v2 = PG_GETARG_PREFIX_RANGE_P(1);
    bool        *result = (bool *) PG_GETARG_POINTER(2);

    *result = my_eq(v1, v2);
    PG_RETURN_POINTER(result);
}
```

For historical reasons, the `same` function doesn't just return a Boolean result; instead it has to store the flag at the location indicated by the third argument.

`distance`

Given an index entry p and a query value q, this function determines the index entry's "distance" from the query value. This function must be supplied if the operator class contains any ordering operators. A query using the ordering operator will be implemented by returning index entries with the smallest "distance" values first, so the results must be consistent with the operator's semantics. For a leaf index entry the result just represents the distance to the index entry; for an internal tree node, the result must be the smallest distance that any child entry could have.

The SQL declaration of the function must look like this:

```
CREATE OR REPLACE FUNCTION my_distance(internal, data_type, smallint, oid)
RETURNS float8
AS 'MODULE_PATHNAME'
LANGUAGE C STRICT;
```

And the matching code in the C module could then follow this skeleton:

```
Datum       my_distance(PG_FUNCTION_ARGS);
PG_FUNCTION_INFO_V1(my_distance);

Datum
my_distance(PG_FUNCTION_ARGS)
{
    GISTENTRY   *entry = (GISTENTRY *) PG_GETARG_POINTER(0);
    data_type   *query = PG_GETARG_DATA_TYPE_P(1);
    StrategyNumber strategy = (StrategyNumber) PG_GETARG_UINT16(2);
    /* Oid subtype = PG_GETARG_OID(3); */
    data_type   *key = DatumGetDataType(entry->key);
    double      retval;

    /*
     * determine return value as a function of strategy, key and query.
     */

    PG_RETURN_FLOAT8(retval);
}
```

The arguments to the `distance` function are identical to the arguments of the `consistent` function, except that no recheck flag is used. The distance to a leaf index entry must always be determined exactly, since there is no way to re-order the tuples once they are returned. Some approximation is allowed when determining the distance to an internal tree node, so long as the result is never greater than any child's actual distance. Thus, for example, distance to a bounding box is usually sufficient in geometric applications. The result value can be any finite `float8` value. (Infinity and minus infinity are used internally to handle cases such as nulls, so it is not recommended that `distance` functions return these values.)

All the GiST support methods are normally called in short-lived memory contexts; that is, `CurrentMemoryContext` will get reset after each tuple is processed. It is therefore not very important to worry about pfree'ing everything you palloc. However, in some cases it's useful for a support method to cache data across repeated calls. To do that, allocate the longer-lived data in `fcinfo->flinfo->fn_mcxt`, and keep a pointer to it in `fcinfo->flinfo->fn_extra`. Such data will survive for the life of the index operation (e.g., a single GiST index scan, index build, or index tuple insertion). Be careful to pfree the previous value when replacing a `fn_extra` value, or the leak will accumulate for the duration of the operation.

56.4. Implementation

56.4.1. GiST buffering build

Building large GiST indexes by simply inserting all the tuples tends to be slow, because if the index tuples are scattered across the index and the index is large enough to not fit in cache, the insertions need to perform a lot of random I/O. Beginning in version 9.2, PostgreSQL supports a more efficient method to build GiST indexes based on buffering, which can dramatically reduce the number of random I/Os needed for non-ordered data sets. For well-ordered data sets the benefit is smaller or non-existent, because only a small number of pages receive new tuples at a time, and those pages fit in cache even if the index as whole does not.

However, buffering index build needs to call the `penalty` function more often, which consumes some extra CPU resources. Also, the buffers used in the buffering build need temporary disk space, up to the size of the resulting index. Buffering can also influence the quality of the resulting index, in both positive and negative directions. That influence depends on various factors, like the distribution of the input data and the operator class implementation.

By default, a GiST index build switches to the buffering method when the index size reaches effective_cache_size. It can be manually turned on or off by the `BUFFERING` parameter to the CREATE INDEX command. The default behavior is good for most cases, but turning buffering off might speed up the build somewhat if the input data is ordered.

56.5. Examples

The PostgreSQL source distribution includes several examples of index methods implemented using GiST. The core system currently provides text search support (indexing for `tsvector` and `tsquery`) as well as R-Tree equivalent functionality for some of the built-in geometric data types (see `src/backend/access/gist/gistproc.c`). The following `contrib` modules also contain GiST operator classes:

`btree_gist`

    B-tree equivalent functionality for several data types

`cube`

    Indexing for multidimensional cubes

`hstore`

    Module for storing (key, value) pairs

`intarray`

    RD-Tree for one-dimensional array of int4 values

`ltree`

    Indexing for tree-like structures

`pg_trgm`

Text similarity using trigram matching

`seg`

Indexing for "float ranges"

Chapter 57. SP-GiST Indexes

57.1. Introduction

SP-GiST is an abbreviation for space-partitioned GiST. SP-GiST supports partitioned search trees, which facilitate development of a wide range of different non-balanced data structures, such as quad-trees, k-d trees, and radix trees (tries). The common feature of these structures is that they repeatedly divide the search space into partitions that need not be of equal size. Searches that are well matched to the partitioning rule can be very fast.

These popular data structures were originally developed for in-memory usage. In main memory, they are usually designed as a set of dynamically allocated nodes linked by pointers. This is not suitable for direct storing on disk, since these chains of pointers can be rather long which would require too many disk accesses. In contrast, disk-based data structures should have a high fanout to minimize I/O. The challenge addressed by SP-GiST is to map search tree nodes to disk pages in such a way that a search need access only a few disk pages, even if it traverses many nodes.

Like GiST, SP-GiST is meant to allow the development of custom data types with the appropriate access methods, by an expert in the domain of the data type, rather than a database expert.

Some of the information here is derived from Purdue University's SP-GiST Indexing Project web site[1]. The SP-GiST implementation in PostgreSQL is primarily maintained by Teodor Sigaev and Oleg Bartunov, and there is more information on their web site[2].

57.2. Built-in Operator Classes

The core PostgreSQL distribution includes the SP-GiST operator classes shown in Table 57-1.

Table 57-1. Built-in SP-GiST Operator Classes

Name	Indexed Data Type	Indexable Operators
kd_point_ops	point	<< <@ <^ >> >^ ~=
quad_point_ops	point	<< <@ <^ >> >^ ~=
range_ops	any range type	&& &< &> -|- << <@ = >> @>
text_ops	text	< <= = > >= ~<=~ ~<~ ~>=~ ~>~

Of the two operator classes for type point, quad_point_ops is the default. kd_point_ops supports the same operators but uses a different index data structure which may offer better performance in some

---

1. http://www.cs.purdue.edu/spgist/
2. http://www.sai.msu.su/~megera/wiki/spgist_dev

applications.

57.3. Extensibility

SP-GiST offers an interface with a high level of abstraction, requiring the access method developer to implement only methods specific to a given data type. The SP-GiST core is responsible for efficient disk mapping and searching the tree structure. It also takes care of concurrency and logging considerations.

Leaf tuples of an SP-GiST tree contain values of the same data type as the indexed column. Leaf tuples at the root level will always contain the original indexed data value, but leaf tuples at lower levels might contain only a compressed representation, such as a suffix. In that case the operator class support functions must be able to reconstruct the original value using information accumulated from the inner tuples that are passed through to reach the leaf level.

Inner tuples are more complex, since they are branching points in the search tree. Each inner tuple contains a set of one or more *nodes*, which represent groups of similar leaf values. A node contains a downlink that leads to either another, lower-level inner tuple, or a short list of leaf tuples that all lie on the same index page. Each node has a *label* that describes it; for example, in a radix tree the node label could be the next character of the string value. Optionally, an inner tuple can have a *prefix* value that describes all its members. In a radix tree this could be the common prefix of the represented strings. The prefix value is not necessarily really a prefix, but can be any data needed by the operator class; for example, in a quad-tree it can store the central point that the four quadrants are measured with respect to. A quad-tree inner tuple would then also contain four nodes corresponding to the quadrants around this central point.

Some tree algorithms require knowledge of level (or depth) of the current tuple, so the SP-GiST core provides the possibility for operator classes to manage level counting while descending the tree. There is also support for incrementally reconstructing the represented value when that is needed.

> **Note:** The SP-GiST core code takes care of null entries. Although SP-GiST indexes do store entries for nulls in indexed columns, this is hidden from the index operator class code: no null index entries or search conditions will ever be passed to the operator class methods. (It is assumed that SP-GiST operators are strict and so cannot succeed for null values.) Null values are therefore not discussed further here.

There are five user-defined methods that an index operator class for SP-GiST must provide. All five follow the convention of accepting two `internal` arguments, the first of which is a pointer to a C struct containing input values for the support method, while the second argument is a pointer to a C struct where output values must be placed. Four of the methods just return `void`, since all their results appear in the output struct; but `leaf_consistent` additionally returns a `boolean` result. The methods must not modify any fields of their input structs. In all cases, the output struct is initialized to zeroes before calling the user-defined method.

The five user-defined methods are:

config

> Returns static information about the index implementation, including the data type OIDs of the prefix and node label data types.

The SQL declaration of the function must look like this:

```
CREATE FUNCTION my_config(internal, internal) RETURNS void ...
```

The first argument is a pointer to a `spgConfigIn` C struct, containing input data for the function. The second argument is a pointer to a `spgConfigOut` C struct, which the function must fill with result data.

```
typedef struct spgConfigIn
{
    Oid         attType;        /* Data type to be indexed */
} spgConfigIn;

typedef struct spgConfigOut
{
    Oid         prefixType;     /* Data type of inner-tuple prefixes */
    Oid         labelType;      /* Data type of inner-tuple node labels */
    bool        canReturnData;  /* Opclass can reconstruct original data */
    bool        longValuesOK;   /* Opclass can cope with values > 1 page */
} spgConfigOut;
```

`attType` is passed in order to support polymorphic index operator classes; for ordinary fixed-data-type operator classes, it will always have the same value and so can be ignored.

For operator classes that do not use prefixes, `prefixType` can be set to `VOIDOID`. Likewise, for operator classes that do not use node labels, `labelType` can be set to `VOIDOID`. `canReturnData` should be set true if the operator class is capable of reconstructing the originally-supplied index value. `longValuesOK` should be set true only when the `attType` is of variable length and the operator class is capable of segmenting long values by repeated suffixing (see Section 57.4.1).

choose

Chooses a method for inserting a new value into an inner tuple.

The SQL declaration of the function must look like this:

```
CREATE FUNCTION my_choose(internal, internal) RETURNS void ...
```

The first argument is a pointer to a `spgChooseIn` C struct, containing input data for the function. The second argument is a pointer to a `spgChooseOut` C struct, which the function must fill with result data.

```
typedef struct spgChooseIn
{
    Datum       datum;          /* original datum to be indexed */
    Datum       leafDatum;      /* current datum to be stored at leaf */
    int         level;          /* current level (counting from zero) */

    /* Data from current inner tuple */
    bool        allTheSame;     /* tuple is marked all-the-same? */
    bool        hasPrefix;      /* tuple has a prefix? */
    Datum       prefixDatum;    /* if so, the prefix value */
    int         nNodes;         /* number of nodes in the inner tuple */
    Datum       *nodeLabels;    /* node label values (NULL if none) */
} spgChooseIn;

typedef enum spgChooseResultType
{
    spgMatchNode = 1,           /* descend into existing node */
```

```
    spgAddNode,                      /* add a node to the inner tuple */
    spgSplitTuple                    /* split inner tuple (change its prefix) */
} spgChooseResultType;

typedef struct spgChooseOut
{
    spgChooseResultType resultType;      /* action code, see above */
    union
    {
        struct                       /* results for spgMatchNode */
        {
            int        nodeN;        /* descend to this node (index from 0) */
            int        levelAdd;     /* increment level by this much */
            Datum      restDatum;    /* new leaf datum */
        }          matchNode;
        struct                       /* results for spgAddNode */
        {
            Datum      nodeLabel;    /* new node's label */
            int        nodeN;        /* where to insert it (index from 0) */
        }          addNode;
        struct                       /* results for spgSplitTuple */
        {
            /* Info to form new inner tuple with one node */
            bool       prefixHasPrefix;   /* tuple should have a prefix? */
            Datum      prefixPrefixDatum; /* if so, its value */
            Datum      nodeLabel;         /* node's label */

            /* Info to form new lower-level inner tuple with all old nodes */
            bool       postfixHasPrefix;  /* tuple should have a prefix? */
            Datum      postfixPrefixDatum; /* if so, its value */
        }          splitTuple;
    }          result;
} spgChooseOut;
```

datum is the original datum that was to be inserted into the index. leafDatum is initially the same as datum, but can change at lower levels of the tree if the choose or picksplit methods change it. When the insertion search reaches a leaf page, the current value of leafDatum is what will be stored in the newly created leaf tuple. level is the current inner tuple's level, starting at zero for the root level. allTheSame is true if the current inner tuple is marked as containing multiple equivalent nodes (see Section 57.4.3). hasPrefix is true if the current inner tuple contains a prefix; if so, prefixDatum is its value. nNodes is the number of child nodes contained in the inner tuple, and nodeLabels is an array of their label values, or NULL if there are no labels.

The choose function can determine either that the new value matches one of the existing child nodes, or that a new child node must be added, or that the new value is inconsistent with the tuple prefix and so the inner tuple must be split to create a less restrictive prefix.

If the new value matches one of the existing child nodes, set resultType to spgMatchNode. Set nodeN to the index (from zero) of that node in the node array. Set levelAdd to the increment in level caused by descending through that node, or leave it as zero if the operator class does not use levels. Set restDatum to equal datum if the operator class does not modify datums from one level to the next, or otherwise set it to the modified value to be used as leafDatum at the next level.

If a new child node must be added, set `resultType` to `spgAddNode`. Set `nodeLabel` to the label to be used for the new node, and set `nodeN` to the index (from zero) at which to insert the node in the node array. After the node has been added, the `choose` function will be called again with the modified inner tuple; that call should result in an `spgMatchNode` result.

If the new value is inconsistent with the tuple prefix, set `resultType` to `spgSplitTuple`. This action moves all the existing nodes into a new lower-level inner tuple, and replaces the existing inner tuple with a tuple having a single node that links to the new lower-level inner tuple. Set `prefixHasPrefix` to indicate whether the new upper tuple should have a prefix, and if so set `prefixPrefixDatum` to the prefix value. This new prefix value must be sufficiently less restrictive than the original to accept the new value to be indexed, and it should be no longer than the original prefix. Set `nodeLabel` to the label to be used for the node that will point to the new lower-level inner tuple. Set `postfixHasPrefix` to indicate whether the new lower-level inner tuple should have a prefix, and if so set `postfixPrefixDatum` to the prefix value. The combination of these two prefixes and the additional label must have the same meaning as the original prefix, because there is no opportunity to alter the node labels that are moved to the new lower-level tuple, nor to change any child index entries. After the node has been split, the `choose` function will be called again with the replacement inner tuple. That call will usually result in an `spgAddNode` result, since presumably the node label added in the split step will not match the new value; so after that, there will be a third call that finally returns `spgMatchNode` and allows the insertion to descend to the leaf level.

pricksplit

Decides how to create a new inner tuple over a set of leaf tuples.

The SQL declaration of the function must look like this:

```
CREATE FUNCTION my_picksplit(internal, internal) RETURNS void ...
```
The first argument is a pointer to a `spgPickSplitIn` C struct, containing input data for the function. The second argument is a pointer to a `spgPickSplitOut` C struct, which the function must fill with result data.

```
typedef struct spgPickSplitIn
{
    int         nTuples;        /* number of leaf tuples */
    Datum       *datums;        /* their datums (array of length nTuples) *
    int         level;          /* current level (counting from zero) */
} spgPickSplitIn;

typedef struct spgPickSplitOut
{
    bool        hasPrefix;      /* new inner tuple should have a prefix? */
    Datum       prefixDatum;    /* if so, its value */

    int         nNodes;         /* number of nodes for new inner tuple */
    Datum       *nodeLabels;    /* their labels (or NULL for no labels) */

    int         *mapTuplesToNodes;  /* node index for each leaf tuple */
    Datum       *leafTupleDatums;   /* datum to store in each new leaf tupl
} spgPickSplitOut;
```
`nTuples` is the number of leaf tuples provided. `datums` is an array of their datum values. `level` is the current level that all the leaf tuples share, which will become the level of the new inner tuple.

Set `hasPrefix` to indicate whether the new inner tuple should have a prefix, and if so set `prefixDatum` to the prefix value. Set `nNodes` to indicate the number of nodes that the new inner tuple will contain, and set `nodeLabels` to an array of their label values. (If the nodes do not require labels, set `nodeLabels` to NULL; see Section 57.4.2 for details.) Set `mapTuplesToNodes` to an array that gives the index (from zero) of the node that each leaf tuple should be assigned to. Set `leafTupleDatums` to an array of the values to be stored in the new leaf tuples (these will be the same as the input `datums` if the operator class does not modify datums from one level to the next). Note that the `picksplit` function is responsible for palloc'ing the `nodeLabels`, `mapTuplesToNodes` and `leafTupleDatums` arrays.

If more than one leaf tuple is supplied, it is expected that the `picksplit` function will classify them into more than one node; otherwise it is not possible to split the leaf tuples across multiple pages, which is the ultimate purpose of this operation. Therefore, if the `picksplit` function ends up placing all the leaf tuples in the same node, the core SP-GiST code will override that decision and generate an inner tuple in which the leaf tuples are assigned at random to several identically-labeled nodes. Such a tuple is marked `allTheSame` to signify that this has happened. The `choose` and `inner_consistent` functions must take suitable care with such inner tuples. See Section 57.4.3 for more information.

`picksplit` can be applied to a single leaf tuple only in the case that the `config` function set `longValuesOK` to true and a larger-than-a-page input value has been supplied. In this case the point of the operation is to strip off a prefix and produce a new, shorter leaf datum value. The call will be repeated until a leaf datum short enough to fit on a page has been produced. See Section 57.4.1 for more information.

inner_consistent

Returns set of nodes (branches) to follow during tree search.

The SQL declaration of the function must look like this:

```
CREATE FUNCTION my_inner_consistent(internal, internal) RETURNS void ...
```
The first argument is a pointer to a `spgInnerConsistentIn` C struct, containing input data for the function. The second argument is a pointer to a `spgInnerConsistentOut` C struct, which the function must fill with result data.

```
typedef struct spgInnerConsistentIn
{
    ScanKey     scankeys;          /* array of operators and comparison values
    int         nkeys;             /* length of array */

    Datum       reconstructedValue;    /* value reconstructed at parent */
    int         level;             /* current level (counting from zero) */
    bool        returnData;        /* original data must be returned? */

    /* Data from current inner tuple */
    bool        allTheSame;        /* tuple is marked all-the-same? */
    bool        hasPrefix;         /* tuple has a prefix? */
    Datum       prefixDatum;       /* if so, the prefix value */
    int         nNodes;            /* number of nodes in the inner tuple */
    Datum       *nodeLabels;       /* node label values (NULL if none) */
} spgInnerConsistentIn;

typedef struct spgInnerConsistentOut
```

```
{
    int         nNodes;             /* number of child nodes to be visited */
    int         *nodeNumbers;       /* their indexes in the node array */
    int         *levelAdds;         /* increment level by this much for each */
    Datum       *reconstructedValues;   /* associated reconstructed values
} spgInnerConsistentOut;
```

The array `scankeys`, of length `nkeys`, describes the index search condition(s). These conditions are combined with AND — only index entries that satisfy all of them are interesting. (Note that `nkeys` = 0 implies that all index entries satisfy the query.) Usually the consistent function only cares about the `sk_strategy` and `sk_argument` fields of each array entry, which respectively give the indexable operator and comparison value. In particular it is not necessary to check `sk_flags` to see if the comparison value is NULL, because the SP-GiST core code will filter out such conditions. `reconstructedValue` is the value reconstructed for the parent tuple; it is `(Datum) 0` at the root level or if the `inner_consistent` function did not provide a value at the parent level. `level` is the current inner tuple's level, starting at zero for the root level. `returnData` is `true` if reconstructed data is required for this query; this will only be so if the `config` function asserted `canReturnData`. `allTheSame` is true if the current inner tuple is marked "all-the-same"; in this case all the nodes have the same label (if any) and so either all or none of them match the query (see Section 57.4.3). `hasPrefix` is true if the current inner tuple contains a prefix; if so, `prefixDatum` is its value. `nNodes` is the number of child nodes contained in the inner tuple, and `nodeLabels` is an array of their label values, or NULL if the nodes do not have labels.

`nNodes` must be set to the number of child nodes that need to be visited by the search, and `nodeNumbers` must be set to an array of their indexes. If the operator class keeps track of levels, set `levelAdds` to an array of the level increments required when descending to each node to be visited. (Often these increments will be the same for all the nodes, but that's not necessarily so, so an array is used.) If value reconstruction is needed, set `reconstructedValues` to an array of the values reconstructed for each child node to be visited; otherwise, leave `reconstructedValues` as NULL. Note that the `inner_consistent` function is responsible for palloc'ing the `nodeNumbers`, `levelAdds` and `reconstructedValues` arrays.

`leaf_consistent`

Returns true if a leaf tuple satisfies a query.

The SQL declaration of the function must look like this:

```
CREATE FUNCTION my_leaf_consistent(internal, internal) RETURNS bool ...
```

The first argument is a pointer to a `spgLeafConsistentIn` C struct, containing input data for the function. The second argument is a pointer to a `spgLeafConsistentOut` C struct, which the function must fill with result data.

```
typedef struct spgLeafConsistentIn
{
    ScanKey     scankeys;           /* array of operators and comparison values
    int         nkeys;              /* length of array */

    Datum       reconstructedValue;     /* value reconstructed at parent */
    int         level;              /* current level (counting from zero) */
    bool        returnData;         /* original data must be returned? */

    Datum       leafDatum;          /* datum in leaf tuple */
} spgLeafConsistentIn;
```

```
typedef struct spgLeafConsistentOut
{
    Datum       leafValue;      /* reconstructed original data, if any */
    bool        recheck;        /* set true if operator must be rechecked *
} spgLeafConsistentOut;
```

The array `scankeys`, of length `nkeys`, describes the index search condition(s). These conditions are combined with AND — only index entries that satisfy all of them satisfy the query. (Note that `nkeys` = 0 implies that all index entries satisfy the query.) Usually the consistent function only cares about the `sk_strategy` and `sk_argument` fields of each array entry, which respectively give the indexable operator and comparison value. In particular it is not necessary to check `sk_flags` to see if the comparison value is NULL, because the SP-GiST core code will filter out such conditions. `reconstructedValue` is the value reconstructed for the parent tuple; it is `(Datum)` 0 at the root level or if the `inner_consistent` function did not provide a value at the parent level. `level` is the current leaf tuple's level, starting at zero for the root level. `returnData` is `true` if reconstructed data is required for this query; this will only be so if the `config` function asserted `canReturnData`. `leafDatum` is the key value stored in the current leaf tuple.

The function must return `true` if the leaf tuple matches the query, or `false` if not. In the `true` case, if `returnData` is `true` then `leafValue` must be set to the value originally supplied to be indexed for this leaf tuple. Also, `recheck` may be set to `true` if the match is uncertain and so the operator(s) must be re-applied to the actual heap tuple to verify the match.

All the SP-GiST support methods are normally called in a short-lived memory context; that is, `CurrentMemoryContext` will be reset after processing of each tuple. It is therefore not very important to worry about pfree'ing everything you palloc. (The `config` method is an exception: it should try to avoid leaking memory. But usually the `config` method need do nothing but assign constants into the passed parameter struct.)

If the indexed column is of a collatable data type, the index collation will be passed to all the support methods, using the standard `PG_GET_COLLATION()` mechanism.

57.4. Implementation

This section covers implementation details and other tricks that are useful for implementers of SP-GiST operator classes to know.

57.4.1. SP-GiST Limits

Individual leaf tuples and inner tuples must fit on a single index page (8KB by default). Therefore, when indexing values of variable-length data types, long values can only be supported by methods such as radix trees, in which each level of the tree includes a prefix that is short enough to fit on a page, and the final leaf level includes a suffix also short enough to fit on a page. The operator class should set `longValuesOK` to TRUE only if it is prepared to arrange for this to happen. Otherwise, the SP-GiST core will reject any request to index a value that is too large to fit on an index page.

Likewise, it is the operator class's responsibility that inner tuples do not grow too large to fit on an index page; this limits the number of child nodes that can be used in one inner tuple, as well as the maximum size of a prefix value.

Another limitation is that when an inner tuple's node points to a set of leaf tuples, those tuples must all be in the same index page. (This is a design decision to reduce seeking and save space in the links that chain such tuples together.) If the set of leaf tuples grows too large for a page, a split is performed and an intermediate inner tuple is inserted. For this to fix the problem, the new inner tuple *must* divide the set of leaf values into more than one node group. If the operator class's `picksplit` function fails to do that, the SP-GiST core resorts to extraordinary measures described in Section 57.4.3.

57.4.2. SP-GiST Without Node Labels

Some tree algorithms use a fixed set of nodes for each inner tuple; for example, in a quad-tree there are always exactly four nodes corresponding to the four quadrants around the inner tuple's centroid point. In such a case the code typically works with the nodes by number, and there is no need for explicit node labels. To suppress node labels (and thereby save some space), the `picksplit` function can return NULL for the `nodeLabels` array. This will in turn result in `nodeLabels` being NULL during subsequent calls to `choose` and `inner_consistent`. In principle, node labels could be used for some inner tuples and omitted for others in the same index.

When working with an inner tuple having unlabeled nodes, it is an error for `choose` to return `spgAddNode`, since the set of nodes is supposed to be fixed in such cases. Also, there is no provision for generating an unlabeled node in `spgSplitTuple` actions, since it is expected that an `spgAddNode` action will be needed as well.

57.4.3. "All-the-same" Inner Tuples

The SP-GiST core can override the results of the operator class's `picksplit` function when `picksplit` fails to divide the supplied leaf values into at least two node categories. When this happens, the new inner tuple is created with multiple nodes that each have the same label (if any) that `picksplit` gave to the one node it did use, and the leaf values are divided at random among these equivalent nodes. The `allTheSame` flag is set on the inner tuple to warn the `choose` and `inner_consistent` functions that the tuple does not have the node set that they might otherwise expect.

When dealing with an `allTheSame` tuple, a `choose` result of `spgMatchNode` is interpreted to mean that the new value can be assigned to any of the equivalent nodes; the core code will ignore the supplied `nodeN` value and descend into one of the nodes at random (so as to keep the tree balanced). It is an error for `choose` to return `spgAddNode`, since that would make the nodes not all equivalent; the `spgSplitTuple` action must be used if the value to be inserted doesn't match the existing nodes.

When dealing with an `allTheSame` tuple, the `inner_consistent` function should return either all or none of the nodes as targets for continuing the index search, since they are all equivalent. This may or may not require any special-case code, depending on how much the `inner_consistent` function normally assumes about the meaning of the nodes.

57.5. Examples

The PostgreSQL source distribution includes several examples of index operator classes for SP-GiST. The core system currently provides radix trees over text columns and two types of trees over points: quad-tree and k-d tree. Look into `src/backend/access/spgist/` to see the code.

Chapter 58. GIN Indexes

58.1. Introduction

GIN stands for Generalized Inverted Index. GIN is designed for handling cases where the items to be indexed are composite values, and the queries to be handled by the index need to search for element values that appear within the composite items. For example, the items could be documents, and the queries could be searches for documents containing specific words.

We use the word *item* to refer to a composite value that is to be indexed, and the word *key* to refer to an element value. GIN always stores and searches for keys, not item values per se.

A GIN index stores a set of (key, posting list) pairs, where a *posting list* is a set of row IDs in which the key occurs. The same row ID can appear in multiple posting lists, since an item can contain more than one key. Each key value is stored only once, so a GIN index is very compact for cases where the same key appears many times.

GIN is generalized in the sense that the GIN access method code does not need to know the specific operations that it accelerates. Instead, it uses custom strategies defined for particular data types. The strategy defines how keys are extracted from indexed items and query conditions, and how to determine whether a row that contains some of the key values in a query actually satisfies the query.

One advantage of GIN is that it allows the development of custom data types with the appropriate access methods, by an expert in the domain of the data type, rather than a database expert. This is much the same advantage as using GiST.

The GIN implementation in PostgreSQL is primarily maintained by Teodor Sigaev and Oleg Bartunov. There is more information about GIN on their website[1].

58.2. Built-in Operator Classes

The core PostgreSQL distribution includes the GIN operator classes shown in Table 58-1. (Some of the optional modules described in Appendix F provide additional GIN operator classes.)

Table 58-1. Built-in GIN Operator Classes

Name	Indexed Data Type	Indexable Operators
_abstime_ops	abstime[]	&& <@ = @>
_bit_ops	bit[]	&& <@ = @>
_bool_ops	boolean[]	&& <@ = @>
_bpchar_ops	character[]	&& <@ = @>
_bytea_ops	bytea[]	&& <@ = @>

---

1. http://www.sai.msu.su/~megera/wiki/Gin

Name	Indexed Data Type	Indexable Operators
_char_ops	"char"[]	&& <@ = @>
_cidr_ops	cidr[]	&& <@ = @>
_date_ops	date[]	&& <@ = @>
_float4_ops	float4[]	&& <@ = @>
_float8_ops	float8[]	&& <@ = @>
_inet_ops	inet[]	&& <@ = @>
_int2_ops	smallint[]	&& <@ = @>
_int4_ops	integer[]	&& <@ = @>
_int8_ops	bigint[]	&& <@ = @>
_interval_ops	interval[]	&& <@ = @>
_macaddr_ops	macaddr[]	&& <@ = @>
_money_ops	money[]	&& <@ = @>
_name_ops	name[]	&& <@ = @>
_numeric_ops	numeric[]	&& <@ = @>
_oid_ops	oid[]	&& <@ = @>
_oidvector_ops	oidvector[]	&& <@ = @>
_reltime_ops	reltime[]	&& <@ = @>
_text_ops	text[]	&& <@ = @>
_time_ops	time[]	&& <@ = @>
_timestamp_ops	timestamp[]	&& <@ = @>
_timestamptz_ops	timestamp with time zone[]	&& <@ = @>
_timetz_ops	time with time zone[]	&& <@ = @>
_tinterval_ops	tinterval[]	&& <@ = @>
_varbit_ops	bit varying[]	&& <@ = @>
_varchar_ops	character varying[]	&& <@ = @>
jsonb_ops	jsonb	? ?& ?| @>
jsonb_path_ops	jsonb	@>
tsvector_ops	tsvector	@@ @@@

Of the two operator classes for type jsonb, jsonb_ops is the default. jsonb_path_ops supports fewer operators but offers better performance for those operators. See Section 8.14.4 for details.

58.3. Extensibility

The GIN interface has a high level of abstraction, requiring the access method implementer only to implement the semantics of the data type being accessed. The GIN layer itself takes care of concurrency, logging and searching the tree structure.

All it takes to get a GIN access method working is to implement a few user-defined methods, which define the behavior of keys in the tree and the relationships between keys, indexed items, and indexable queries. In short, GIN combines extensibility with generality, code reuse, and a clean interface.

There are three methods that an operator class for GIN must provide:

`int compare(Datum a, Datum b)`

> Compares two keys (not indexed items!) and returns an integer less than zero, zero, or greater than zero, indicating whether the first key is less than, equal to, or greater than the second. Null keys are never passed to this function.

`Datum *extractValue(Datum itemValue, int32 *nkeys, bool **nullFlags)`

> Returns a palloc'd array of keys given an item to be indexed. The number of returned keys must be stored into `*nkeys`. If any of the keys can be null, also palloc an array of `*nkeys bool` fields, store its address at `*nullFlags`, and set these null flags as needed. `*nullFlags` can be left `NULL` (its initial value) if all keys are non-null. The return value can be `NULL` if the item contains no keys.

`Datum *extractQuery(Datum query, int32 *nkeys, StrategyNumber n, bool **pmatch, Pointer **extra_data, bool **nullFlags, int32 *searchMode)`

> Returns a palloc'd array of keys given a value to be queried; that is, `query` is the value on the right-hand side of an indexable operator whose left-hand side is the indexed column. `n` is the strategy number of the operator within the operator class (see Section 35.14.2). Often, `extractQuery` will need to consult `n` to determine the data type of `query` and the method it should use to extract key values. The number of returned keys must be stored into `*nkeys`. If any of the keys can be null, also palloc an array of `*nkeys bool` fields, store its address at `*nullFlags`, and set these null flags as needed. `*nullFlags` can be left `NULL` (its initial value) if all keys are non-null. The return value can be `NULL` if the `query` contains no keys.

> `searchMode` is an output argument that allows `extractQuery` to specify details about how the search will be done. If `*searchMode` is set to `GIN_SEARCH_MODE_DEFAULT` (which is the value it is initialized to before call), only items that match at least one of the returned keys are considered candidate matches. If `*searchMode` is set to `GIN_SEARCH_MODE_INCLUDE_EMPTY`, then in addition to items containing at least one matching key, items that contain no keys at all are considered candidate matches. (This mode is useful for implementing is-subset-of operators, for example.) If `*searchMode` is set to `GIN_SEARCH_MODE_ALL`, then all non-null items in the index are considered candidate matches, whether they match any of the returned keys or not. (This mode is much slower than the other two choices, since it requires scanning essentially the entire index, but it may be necessary to implement corner cases correctly. An operator that needs this mode in most cases is probably not a good candidate for a GIN operator class.) The symbols to use for setting this mode are defined in `access/gin.h`.

> `pmatch` is an output argument for use when partial match is supported. To use it, `extractQuery` must allocate an array of `*nkeys` booleans and store its address at `*pmatch`. Each element of the array should be set to TRUE if the corresponding key requires partial match, FALSE if not. If `*pmatch` is set to `NULL` then GIN assumes partial match is not required. The variable is initialized to `NULL` before call, so this argument can simply be ignored by operator classes that do not support partial match.

> `extra_data` is an output argument that allows `extractQuery` to pass additional data to the `consistent` and `comparePartial` methods. To use it, `extractQuery` must allocate an array of `*nkeys` Pointers and store its address at `*extra_data`, then store whatever it wants to into the individual pointers. The variable is initialized to `NULL` before call, so this argument can simply be

ignored by operator classes that do not require extra data. If `*extra_data` is set, the whole array is passed to the `consistent` method, and the appropriate element to the `comparePartial` method.

An operator class must also provide a function to check if an indexed item matches the query. It comes in two flavors, a boolean `consistent` function, and a ternary `triConsistent` function. `triConsistent` covers the functionality of both, so providing triConsistent alone is sufficient. However, if the boolean variant is significantly cheaper to calculate, it can be advantageous to provide both. If only the boolean variant is provided, some optimizations that depend on refuting index items before fetching all the keys are disabled.

```
bool consistent(bool check[], StrategyNumber n, Datum query, int32 nkeys,
Pointer extra_data[], bool *recheck, Datum queryKeys[], bool nullFlags[])
```

> Returns TRUE if an indexed item satisfies the query operator with strategy number n (or might satisfy it, if the recheck indication is returned). This function does not have direct access to the indexed item's value, since GIN does not store items explicitly. Rather, what is available is knowledge about which key values extracted from the query appear in a given indexed item. The `check` array has length `nkeys`, which is the same as the number of keys previously returned by `extractQuery` for this `query` datum. Each element of the `check` array is TRUE if the indexed item contains the corresponding query key, i.e., if (check[i] == TRUE) the i-th key of the `extractQuery` result array is present in the indexed item. The original `query` datum is passed in case the `consistent` method needs to consult it, and so are the `queryKeys[]` and `nullFlags[]` arrays previously returned by `extractQuery`. `extra_data` is the extra-data array returned by `extractQuery`, or NULL if none.
>
> When `extractQuery` returns a null key in `queryKeys[]`, the corresponding `check[]` element is TRUE if the indexed item contains a null key; that is, the semantics of `check[]` are like IS NOT DISTINCT FROM. The `consistent` function can examine the corresponding `nullFlags[]` element if it needs to tell the difference between a regular value match and a null match.
>
> On success, `*recheck` should be set to TRUE if the heap tuple needs to be rechecked against the query operator, or FALSE if the index test is exact. That is, a FALSE return value guarantees that the heap tuple does not match the query; a TRUE return value with `*recheck` set to FALSE guarantees that the heap tuple does match the query; and a TRUE return value with `*recheck` set to TRUE means that the heap tuple might match the query, so it needs to be fetched and rechecked by evaluating the query operator directly against the originally indexed item.

```
GinTernaryValue triConsistent(GinTernaryValue check[], StrategyNumber n,
Datum query, int32 nkeys, Pointer extra_data[], Datum queryKeys[], bool
nullFlags[])
```

> `triConsistent` is similar to `consistent`, but instead of a boolean `check[]`, there are three possible values for each key: GIN_TRUE, GIN_FALSE and GIN_MAYBE. GIN_FALSE and GIN_TRUE have the same meaning as regular boolean values. GIN_MAYBE means that the presence of that key is not known. When GIN_MAYBE values are present, the function should only return GIN_TRUE if the item matches whether or not the index item contains the corresponding query keys. Likewise, the function must return GIN_FALSE only if the item does not match, whether or not it contains the GIN_MAYBE keys. If the result depends on the GIN_MAYBE entries, i.e. the match cannot be confirmed or refuted based on the known query keys, the function must return GIN_MAYBE.
>
> When there are no GIN_MAYBE values in the `check` vector, GIN_MAYBE return value is equivalent of setting `recheck` flag in the boolean `consistent` function.

Optionally, an operator class for GIN can supply the following method:

```
int comparePartial(Datum partial_key, Datum key, StrategyNumber n, Pointer
extra_data)
```

Compare a partial-match query key to an index key. Returns an integer whose sign indicates the result: less than zero means the index key does not match the query, but the index scan should continue; zero means that the index key does match the query; greater than zero indicates that the index scan should stop because no more matches are possible. The strategy number n of the operator that generated the partial match query is provided, in case its semantics are needed to determine when to end the scan. Also, extra_data is the corresponding element of the extra-data array made by extractQuery, or NULL if none. Null keys are never passed to this function.

To support "partial match" queries, an operator class must provide the comparePartial method, and its extractQuery method must set the pmatch parameter when a partial-match query is encountered. See Section 58.4.2 for details.

The actual data types of the various Datum values mentioned above vary depending on the operator class. The item values passed to extractValue are always of the operator class's input type, and all key values must be of the class's STORAGE type. The type of the query argument passed to extractQuery, consistent and triConsistent is whatever is specified as the right-hand input type of the class member operator identified by the strategy number. This need not be the same as the item type, so long as key values of the correct type can be extracted from it.

58.4. Implementation

Internally, a GIN index contains a B-tree index constructed over keys, where each key is an element of one or more indexed items (a member of an array, for example) and where each tuple in a leaf page contains either a pointer to a B-tree of heap pointers (a "posting tree"), or a simple list of heap pointers (a "posting list") when the list is small enough to fit into a single index tuple along with the key value.

As of PostgreSQL 9.1, null key values can be included in the index. Also, placeholder nulls are included in the index for indexed items that are null or contain no keys according to extractValue. This allows searches that should find empty items to do so.

Multicolumn GIN indexes are implemented by building a single B-tree over composite values (column number, key value). The key values for different columns can be of different types.

58.4.1. GIN Fast Update Technique

Updating a GIN index tends to be slow because of the intrinsic nature of inverted indexes: inserting or updating one heap row can cause many inserts into the index (one for each key extracted from the indexed item). As of PostgreSQL 8.4, GIN is capable of postponing much of this work by inserting new tuples into a temporary, unsorted list of pending entries. When the table is vacuumed, or if the pending list becomes too large (larger than work_mem), the entries are moved to the main GIN data structure using the same bulk insert techniques used during initial index creation. This greatly improves GIN index update speed, even counting the additional vacuum overhead. Moreover the overhead work can be done by a background process instead of in foreground query processing.

The main disadvantage of this approach is that searches must scan the list of pending entries in addition to searching the regular index, and so a large list of pending entries will slow searches significantly. Another disadvantage is that, while most updates are fast, an update that causes the pending list to become "too large" will incur an immediate cleanup cycle and thus be much slower than other updates. Proper use of autovacuum can minimize both of these problems.

If consistent response time is more important than update speed, use of pending entries can be disabled by turning off the FASTUPDATE storage parameter for a GIN index. See CREATE INDEX for details.

58.4.2. Partial Match Algorithm

GIN can support "partial match" queries, in which the query does not determine an exact match for one or more keys, but the possible matches fall within a reasonably narrow range of key values (within the key sorting order determined by the compare support method). The extractQuery method, instead of returning a key value to be matched exactly, returns a key value that is the lower bound of the range to be searched, and sets the pmatch flag true. The key range is then scanned using the comparePartial method. comparePartial must return zero for a matching index key, less than zero for a non-match that is still within the range to be searched, or greater than zero if the index key is past the range that could match.

58.5. GIN Tips and Tricks

Create vs. insert

    Insertion into a GIN index can be slow due to the likelihood of many keys being inserted for each item. So, for bulk insertions into a table it is advisable to drop the GIN index and recreate it after finishing bulk insertion.

    As of PostgreSQL 8.4, this advice is less necessary since delayed indexing is used (see Section 58.4.1 for details). But for very large updates it may still be best to drop and recreate the index.

maintenance_work_mem

    Build time for a GIN index is very sensitive to the maintenance_work_mem setting; it doesn't pay to skimp on work memory during index creation.

work_mem

    During a series of insertions into an existing GIN index that has FASTUPDATE enabled, the system will clean up the pending-entry list whenever the list grows larger than work_mem. To avoid fluctuations in observed response time, it's desirable to have pending-list cleanup occur in the background (i.e., via autovacuum). Foreground cleanup operations can be avoided by increasing work_mem or making autovacuum more aggressive. However, enlarging work_mem means that if a foreground cleanup does occur, it will take even longer.

gin_fuzzy_search_limit

    The primary goal of developing GIN indexes was to create support for highly scalable full-text search in PostgreSQL, and there are often situations when a full-text search returns a very large set of results.

Moreover, this often happens when the query contains very frequent words, so that the large result set is not even useful. Since reading many tuples from the disk and sorting them could take a lot of time, this is unacceptable for production. (Note that the index search itself is very fast.)

To facilitate controlled execution of such queries, GIN has a configurable soft upper limit on the number of rows returned: the `gin_fuzzy_search_limit` configuration parameter. It is set to 0 (meaning no limit) by default. If a non-zero limit is set, then the returned set is a subset of the whole result set, chosen at random.

"Soft" means that the actual number of returned results could differ somewhat from the specified limit, depending on the query and the quality of the system's random number generator.

From experience, values in the thousands (e.g., 5000 — 20000) work well.

58.6. Limitations

GIN assumes that indexable operators are strict. This means that `extractValue` will not be called at all on a null item value (instead, a placeholder index entry is created automatically), and `extractQuery` will not be called on a null query value either (instead, the query is presumed to be unsatisfiable). Note however that null key values contained within a non-null composite item or query value are supported.

58.7. Examples

The PostgreSQL source distribution includes GIN operator classes for `tsvector` and for one-dimensional arrays of all internal types. Prefix searching in `tsvector` is implemented using the GIN partial match feature. The following `contrib` modules also contain GIN operator classes:

`btree_gin`

B-tree equivalent functionality for several data types

`hstore`

Module for storing (key, value) pairs

`intarray`

Enhanced support for `int[]`

`pg_trgm`

Text similarity using trigram matching

Chapter 59. Database Physical Storage

This chapter provides an overview of the physical storage format used by PostgreSQL databases.

59.1. Database File Layout

This section describes the storage format at the level of files and directories.

Traditionally, the configuration and data files used by a database cluster are stored together within the cluster's data directory, commonly referred to as PGDATA (after the name of the environment variable that can be used to define it). A common location for PGDATA is /var/lib/pgsql/data. Multiple clusters, managed by different server instances, can exist on the same machine.

The PGDATA directory contains several subdirectories and control files, as shown in Table 59-1. In addition to these required items, the cluster configuration files postgresql.conf, pg_hba.conf, and pg_ident.conf are traditionally stored in PGDATA, although it is possible to place them elsewhere.

Table 59-1. Contents of PGDATA

Item	Description
PG_VERSION	A file containing the major version number of PostgreSQL
base	Subdirectory containing per-database subdirectories
global	Subdirectory containing cluster-wide tables, such as pg_database
pg_clog	Subdirectory containing transaction commit status data
pg_dynshmem	Subdirectory containing files used by the dynamic shared memory subsystem
pg_logical	Subdirectory containing status data for logical decoding
pg_multixact	Subdirectory containing multitransaction status data (used for shared row locks)
pg_notify	Subdirectory containing LISTEN/NOTIFY status data
pg_replslot	Subdirectory containing replication slot data
pg_serial	Subdirectory containing information about committed serializable transactions
pg_snapshots	Subdirectory containing exported snapshots
pg_stat	Subdirectory containing permanent files for the statistics subsystem

Item	Description
pg_stat_tmp	Subdirectory containing temporary files for the statistics subsystem
pg_subtrans	Subdirectory containing subtransaction status data
pg_tblspc	Subdirectory containing symbolic links to tablespaces
pg_twophase	Subdirectory containing state files for prepared transactions
pg_xlog	Subdirectory containing WAL (Write Ahead Log) files
postgresql.auto.conf	A file used for storing configuration parameters that are set by ALTER SYSTEM
postmaster.opts	A file recording the command-line options the server was last started with
postmaster.pid	A lock file recording the current postmaster process ID (PID), cluster data directory path, postmaster start timestamp, port number, Unix-domain socket directory path (empty on Windows), first valid listen_address (IP address or *, or empty if not listening on TCP), and shared memory segment ID (this file is not present after server shutdown)

For each database in the cluster there is a subdirectory within PGDATA/base, named after the database's OID in pg_database. This subdirectory is the default location for the database's files; in particular, its system catalogs are stored there.

Each table and index is stored in a separate file. For ordinary relations, these files are named after the table or index's *filenode* number, which can be found in pg_class.relfilenode. But for temporary relations, the file name is of the form t*BBB_FFF*, where *BBB* is the backend ID of the backend which created the file, and *FFF* is the filenode number. In either case, in addition to the main file (a/k/a main fork), each table and index has a *free space map* (see Section 59.3), which stores information about free space available in the relation. The free space map is stored in a file named with the filenode number plus the suffix _fsm. Tables also have a *visibility map*, stored in a fork with the suffix _vm, to track which pages are known to have no dead tuples. The visibility map is described further in Section 59.4. Unlogged tables and indexes have a third fork, known as the initialization fork, which is stored in a fork with the suffix _init (see Section 59.5).

Caution

Note that while a table's filenode often matches its OID, this is *not* necessarily the case; some operations, like TRUNCATE, REINDEX, CLUSTER and some forms of ALTER TABLE, can change the filenode while preserving the OID. Avoid assuming that filenode and table OID are the same. Also, for certain system catalogs including pg_class itself, pg_class.relfilenode contains zero. The actual filenode number of these catalogs is stored in a lower-level data structure, and can be obtained using the pg_relation_filenode() function.

When a table or index exceeds 1 GB, it is divided into gigabyte-sized *segments*. The first segment's file name is the same as the filenode; subsequent segments are named filenode.1, filenode.2, etc. This arrangement avoids problems on platforms that have file size limitations. (Actually, 1 GB is just the default segment size. The segment size can be adjusted using the configuration option `--with-segsize` when building PostgreSQL.) In principle, free space map and visibility map forks could require multiple segments as well, though this is unlikely to happen in practice.

A table that has columns with potentially large entries will have an associated *TOAST* table, which is used for out-of-line storage of field values that are too large to keep in the table rows proper. `pg_class.reltoastrelid` links from a table to its TOAST table, if any. See Section 59.2 for more information.

The contents of tables and indexes are discussed further in Section 59.6.

Tablespaces make the scenario more complicated. Each user-defined tablespace has a symbolic link inside the `PGDATA/pg_tblspc` directory, which points to the physical tablespace directory (i.e., the location specified in the tablespace's `CREATE TABLESPACE` command). This symbolic link is named after the tablespace's OID. Inside the physical tablespace directory there is a subdirectory with a name that depends on the PostgreSQL server version, such as `PG_9.0_201008051`. (The reason for using this subdirectory is so that successive versions of the database can use the same `CREATE TABLESPACE` location value without conflicts.) Within the version-specific subdirectory, there is a subdirectory for each database that has elements in the tablespace, named after the database's OID. Tables and indexes are stored within that directory, using the filenode naming scheme. The `pg_default` tablespace is not accessed through `pg_tblspc`, but corresponds to `PGDATA/base`. Similarly, the `pg_global` tablespace is not accessed through `pg_tblspc`, but corresponds to `PGDATA/global`.

The `pg_relation_filepath()` function shows the entire path (relative to `PGDATA`) of any relation. It is often useful as a substitute for remembering many of the above rules. But keep in mind that this function just gives the name of the first segment of the main fork of the relation — you may need to append a segment number and/or `_fsm`, `_vm`, or `_init` to find all the files associated with the relation.

Temporary files (for operations such as sorting more data than can fit in memory) are created within `PGDATA/base/pgsql_tmp`, or within a `pgsql_tmp` subdirectory of a tablespace directory if a tablespace other than `pg_default` is specified for them. The name of a temporary file has the form `pgsql_tmpPPP.NNN`, where `PPP` is the PID of the owning backend and `NNN` distinguishes different temporary files of that backend.

59.2. TOAST

This section provides an overview of TOAST (The Oversized-Attribute Storage Technique).

PostgreSQL uses a fixed page size (commonly 8 kB), and does not allow tuples to span multiple pages. Therefore, it is not possible to store very large field values directly. To overcome this limitation, large field values are compressed and/or broken up into multiple physical rows. This happens transparently to the user, with only small impact on most of the backend code. The technique is affectionately known as TOAST (or "the best thing since sliced bread").

Only certain data types support TOAST — there is no need to impose the overhead on data types that cannot produce large field values. To support TOAST, a data type must have a variable-length (*varlena*) representation, in which the first 32-bit word of any stored value contains the total length of the value in bytes (including itself). TOAST does not constrain the rest of the representation. All the C-level functions supporting a TOAST-able data type must be careful to handle TOASTed input values. (This is normally done by invoking PG_DETOAST_DATUM before doing anything with an input value, but in some cases more efficient approaches are possible.)

TOAST usurps two bits of the varlena length word (the high-order bits on big-endian machines, the low-order bits on little-endian machines), thereby limiting the logical size of any value of a TOAST-able data type to 1 GB (2^{30} - 1 bytes). When both bits are zero, the value is an ordinary un-TOASTed value of the data type, and the remaining bits of the length word give the total datum size (including length word) in bytes. When the highest-order or lowest-order bit is set, the value has only a single-byte header instead of the normal four-byte header, and the remaining bits give the total datum size (including length byte) in bytes. As a special case, if the remaining bits are all zero (which would be impossible for a self-inclusive length), the value is a pointer to out-of-line data stored in a separate TOAST table. (The size of a TOAST pointer is given in the second byte of the datum.) Values with single-byte headers aren't aligned on any particular boundary, either. Lastly, when the highest-order or lowest-order bit is clear but the adjacent bit is set, the content of the datum has been compressed and must be decompressed before use. In this case the remaining bits of the length word give the total size of the compressed datum, not the original data. Note that compression is also possible for out-of-line data but the varlena header does not tell whether it has occurred — the content of the TOAST pointer tells that, instead.

If any of the columns of a table are TOAST-able, the table will have an associated TOAST table, whose OID is stored in the table's pg_class.reltoastrelid entry. Out-of-line TOASTed values are kept in the TOAST table, as described in more detail below.

The compression technique used is a fairly simple and very fast member of the LZ family of compression techniques. See src/backend/utils/adt/pg_lzcompress.c for the details.

Out-of-line values are divided (after compression if used) into chunks of at most TOAST_MAX_CHUNK_SIZE bytes (by default this value is chosen so that four chunk rows will fit on a page, making it about 2000 bytes). Each chunk is stored as a separate row in the TOAST table for the owning table. Every TOAST table has the columns chunk_id (an OID identifying the particular TOASTed value), chunk_seq (a sequence number for the chunk within its value), and chunk_data (the actual data of the chunk). A unique index on chunk_id and chunk_seq provides fast retrieval of the values. A pointer datum representing an out-of-line TOASTed value therefore needs to store the OID of the TOAST table in which to look and the OID of the specific value (its chunk_id). For convenience, pointer datums also store the logical datum size (original uncompressed data length) and actual stored size (different if compression was applied). Allowing for the varlena header bytes, the total size of a TOAST pointer datum is therefore 18 bytes regardless of the actual size of the represented value.

The TOAST code is triggered only when a row value to be stored in a table is wider than TOAST_TUPLE_THRESHOLD bytes (normally 2 kB). The TOAST code will compress and/or move field values out-of-line until the row value is shorter than TOAST_TUPLE_TARGET bytes (also normally 2 kB) or no more gains can be had. During an UPDATE operation, values of unchanged fields are normally preserved as-is; so an UPDATE of a row with out-of-line values incurs no TOAST costs if none of the out-of-line values change.

The TOAST code recognizes four different strategies for storing TOAST-able columns:

- PLAIN prevents either compression or out-of-line storage; furthermore it disables use of single-byte headers for varlena types. This is the only possible strategy for columns of non-TOAST-able data types.

- EXTENDED allows both compression and out-of-line storage. This is the default for most TOAST-able data types. Compression will be attempted first, then out-of-line storage if the row is still too big.

- EXTERNAL allows out-of-line storage but not compression. Use of EXTERNAL will make substring operations on wide text and bytea columns faster (at the penalty of increased storage space) because these operations are optimized to fetch only the required parts of the out-of-line value when it is not compressed.

- MAIN allows compression but not out-of-line storage. (Actually, out-of-line storage will still be performed for such columns, but only as a last resort when there is no other way to make the row small enough to fit on a page.)

Each TOAST-able data type specifies a default strategy for columns of that data type, but the strategy for a given table column can be altered with ALTER TABLE SET STORAGE.

This scheme has a number of advantages compared to a more straightforward approach such as allowing row values to span pages. Assuming that queries are usually qualified by comparisons against relatively small key values, most of the work of the executor will be done using the main row entry. The big values of TOASTed attributes will only be pulled out (if selected at all) at the time the result set is sent to the client. Thus, the main table is much smaller and more of its rows fit in the shared buffer cache than would be the case without any out-of-line storage. Sort sets shrink also, and sorts will more often be done entirely in memory. A little test showed that a table containing typical HTML pages and their URLs was stored in about half of the raw data size including the TOAST table, and that the main table contained only about 10% of the entire data (the URLs and some small HTML pages). There was no run time difference compared to an un-TOASTed comparison table, in which all the HTML pages were cut down to 7 kB to fit.

59.3. Free Space Map

Each heap and index relation, except for hash indexes, has a Free Space Map (FSM) to keep track of available space in the relation. It's stored alongside the main relation data in a separate relation fork, named after the filenode number of the relation, plus a _fsm suffix. For example, if the filenode of a relation is 12345, the FSM is stored in a file called 12345_fsm, in the same directory as the main relation file.

The Free Space Map is organized as a tree of FSM pages. The bottom level FSM pages store the free space available on each heap (or index) page, using one byte to represent each such page. The upper levels aggregate information from the lower levels.

Within each FSM page is a binary tree, stored in an array with one byte per node. Each leaf node represents a heap page, or a lower level FSM page. In each non-leaf node, the higher of its children's values is stored. The maximum value in the leaf nodes is therefore stored at the root.

See src/backend/storage/freespace/README for more details on how the FSM is structured, and how it's updated and searched. The pg_freespacemap module can be used to examine the information stored in free space maps.

59.4. Visibility Map

Each heap relation has a Visibility Map (VM) to keep track of which pages contain only tuples that are known to be visible to all active transactions. It's stored alongside the main relation data in a separate relation fork, named after the filenode number of the relation, plus a _vm suffix. For example, if the filenode of a relation is 12345, the VM is stored in a file called 12345_vm, in the same directory as the main relation file. Note that indexes do not have VMs.

The visibility map simply stores one bit per heap page. A set bit means that all tuples on the page are known to be visible to all transactions. This means that the page does not contain any tuples that need to be vacuumed. This information can also be used by *index-only scans* to answer queries using only the index tuple.

The map is conservative in the sense that we make sure that whenever a bit is set, we know the condition is true, but if a bit is not set, it might or might not be true. Visibility map bits are only set by vacuum, but are cleared by any data-modifying operations on a page.

59.5. The Initialization Fork

Each unlogged table, and each index on an unlogged table, has an initialization fork. The initialization fork is an empty table or index of the appropriate type. When an unlogged table must be reset to empty due to a crash, the initialization fork is copied over the main fork, and any other forks are erased (they will be recreated automatically as needed).

59.6. Database Page Layout

This section provides an overview of the page format used within PostgreSQL tables and indexes.[1] Sequences and TOAST tables are formatted just like a regular table.

In the following explanation, a *byte* is assumed to contain 8 bits. In addition, the term *item* refers to an individual data value that is stored on a page. In a table, an item is a row; in an index, an item is an index entry.

Every table and index is stored as an array of *pages* of a fixed size (usually 8 kB, although a different page size can be selected when compiling the server). In a table, all the pages are logically equivalent, so a particular item (row) can be stored in any page. In indexes, the first page is generally reserved as a *metapage* holding control information, and there can be different types of pages within the index, depending on the index access method.

Table 59-2 shows the overall layout of a page. There are five parts to each page.

Table 59-2. Overall Page Layout

Item	Description

---

1. Actually, index access methods need not use this page format. All the existing index methods do use this basic format, but the data kept on index metapages usually doesn't follow the item layout rules.

Item	Description
PageHeaderData	24 bytes long. Contains general information about the page, including free space pointers.
ItemIdData	Array of (offset,length) pairs pointing to the actual items. 4 bytes per item.
Free space	The unallocated space. New item pointers are allocated from the start of this area, new items from the end.
Items	The actual items themselves.
Special space	Index access method specific data. Different methods store different data. Empty in ordinary tables.

The first 24 bytes of each page consists of a page header (PageHeaderData). Its format is detailed in Table 59-3. The first two fields track the most recent WAL entry related to this page. Next is a 2-byte field containing flag bits. This is followed by three 2-byte integer fields (`pd_lower`, `pd_upper`, and `pd_special`). These contain byte offsets from the page start to the start of unallocated space, to the end of unallocated space, and to the start of the special space. The next 2 bytes of the page header, `pd_pagesize_version`, store both the page size and a version indicator. Beginning with PostgreSQL 8.3 the version number is 4; PostgreSQL 8.1 and 8.2 used version number 3; PostgreSQL 8.0 used version number 2; PostgreSQL 7.3 and 7.4 used version number 1; prior releases used version number 0. (The basic page layout and header format has not changed in most of these versions, but the layout of heap row headers has.) The page size is basically only present as a cross-check; there is no support for having more than one page size in an installation. The last field is a hint that shows whether pruning the page is likely to be profitable: it tracks the oldest un-pruned XMAX on the page.

Table 59-3. PageHeaderData Layout

Field	Type	Length	Description
pd_lsn	XLogRecPtr	8 bytes	LSN: next byte after last byte of xlog record for last change to this page
pd_checksum	uint16	2 bytes	Page checksum
pd_flags	uint16	2 bytes	Flag bits
pd_lower	LocationIndex	2 bytes	Offset to start of free space
pd_upper	LocationIndex	2 bytes	Offset to end of free space
pd_special	LocationIndex	2 bytes	Offset to start of special space
pd_pagesize_version	uint16	2 bytes	Page size and layout version number information

Field	Type	Length	Description
pd_prune_xid	TransactionId	4 bytes	Oldest unpruned XMAX on page, or zero if none

All the details can be found in `src/include/storage/bufpage.h`.

Following the page header are item identifiers (`ItemIdData`), each requiring four bytes. An item identifier contains a byte-offset to the start of an item, its length in bytes, and a few attribute bits which affect its interpretation. New item identifiers are allocated as needed from the beginning of the unallocated space. The number of item identifiers present can be determined by looking at `pd_lower`, which is increased to allocate a new identifier. Because an item identifier is never moved until it is freed, its index can be used on a long-term basis to reference an item, even when the item itself is moved around on the page to compact free space. In fact, every pointer to an item (`ItemPointer`, also known as `CTID`) created by PostgreSQL consists of a page number and the index of an item identifier.

The items themselves are stored in space allocated backwards from the end of unallocated space. The exact structure varies depending on what the table is to contain. Tables and sequences both use a structure named `HeapTupleHeaderData`, described below.

The final section is the "special section" which can contain anything the access method wishes to store. For example, b-tree indexes store links to the page's left and right siblings, as well as some other data relevant to the index structure. Ordinary tables do not use a special section at all (indicated by setting `pd_special` to equal the page size).

All table rows are structured in the same way. There is a fixed-size header (occupying 23 bytes on most machines), followed by an optional null bitmap, an optional object ID field, and the user data. The header is detailed in Table 59-4. The actual user data (columns of the row) begins at the offset indicated by `t_hoff`, which must always be a multiple of the MAXALIGN distance for the platform. The null bitmap is only present if the *HEAP_HASNULL* bit is set in `t_infomask`. If it is present it begins just after the fixed header and occupies enough bytes to have one bit per data column (that is, `t_natts` bits altogether). In this list of bits, a 1 bit indicates not-null, a 0 bit is a null. When the bitmap is not present, all columns are assumed not-null. The object ID is only present if the *HEAP_HASOID* bit is set in `t_infomask`. If present, it appears just before the `t_hoff` boundary. Any padding needed to make `t_hoff` a MAXALIGN multiple will appear between the null bitmap and the object ID. (This in turn ensures that the object ID is suitably aligned.)

Table 59-4. HeapTupleHeaderData Layout

Field	Type	Length	Description
t_xmin	TransactionId	4 bytes	insert XID stamp
t_xmax	TransactionId	4 bytes	delete XID stamp
t_cid	CommandId	4 bytes	insert and/or delete CID stamp (overlays with t_xvac)
t_xvac	TransactionId	4 bytes	XID for VACUUM operation moving a row version

Field	Type	Length	Description
t_ctid	ItemPointerData	6 bytes	current TID of this or newer row version
t_infomask2	uint16	2 bytes	number of attributes, plus various flag bits
t_infomask	uint16	2 bytes	various flag bits
t_hoff	uint8	1 byte	offset to user data

All the details can be found in `src/include/access/htup.h`.

Interpreting the actual data can only be done with information obtained from other tables, mostly `pg_attribute`. The key values needed to identify field locations are `attlen` and `attalign`. There is no way to directly get a particular attribute, except when there are only fixed width fields and no null values. All this trickery is wrapped up in the functions *heap_getattr*, *fastgetattr* and *heap_getsysattr*.

To read the data you need to examine each attribute in turn. First check whether the field is NULL according to the null bitmap. If it is, go to the next. Then make sure you have the right alignment. If the field is a fixed width field, then all the bytes are simply placed. If it's a variable length field (attlen = -1) then it's a bit more complicated. All variable-length data types share the common header structure `struct varlena`, which includes the total length of the stored value and some flag bits. Depending on the flags, the data can be either inline or in a TOAST table; it might be compressed, too (see Section 59.2).

Chapter 60. BKI Backend Interface

Backend Interface (BKI) files are scripts in a special language that is understood by the PostgreSQL backend when running in the "bootstrap" mode. The bootstrap mode allows system catalogs to be created and filled from scratch, whereas ordinary SQL commands require the catalogs to exist already. BKI files can therefore be used to create the database system in the first place. (And they are probably not useful for anything else.)

initdb uses a BKI file to do part of its job when creating a new database cluster. The input file used by initdb is created as part of building and installing PostgreSQL by a program named `genbki.pl`, which reads some specially formatted C header files in the `src/include/catalog/` directory of the source tree. The created BKI file is called `postgres.bki` and is normally installed in the `share` subdirectory of the installation tree.

Related information can be found in the documentation for initdb.

60.1. BKI File Format

This section describes how the PostgreSQL backend interprets BKI files. This description will be easier to understand if the `postgres.bki` file is at hand as an example.

BKI input consists of a sequence of commands. Commands are made up of a number of tokens, depending on the syntax of the command. Tokens are usually separated by whitespace, but need not be if there is no ambiguity. There is no special command separator; the next token that syntactically cannot belong to the preceding command starts a new one. (Usually you would put a new command on a new line, for clarity.) Tokens can be certain key words, special characters (parentheses, commas, etc.), numbers, or double-quoted strings. Everything is case sensitive.

Lines starting with # are ignored.

60.2. BKI Commands

create *tablename tableoid* [bootstrap] [shared_relation] [without_oids] [rowtype_oid *oid*] (*name1* = *type1* [, *name2* = *type2*, ...])

Create a table named *tablename*, and having the OID *tableoid*, with the columns given in parentheses.

The following column types are supported directly by `bootstrap.c`: bool, bytea, char (1 byte), name, int2, int4, regproc, regclass, regtype, text, oid, tid, xid, cid, int2vector, oidvector, _int4 (array), _text (array), _oid (array), _char (array), _aclitem (array). Although it is possible to create tables containing columns of other types, this cannot be done until after pg_type has been created and filled with appropriate entries. (That effectively means that only these column types can be used in bootstrapped tables, but non-bootstrap catalogs can contain any built-in type.)

When `bootstrap` is specified, the table will only be created on disk; nothing is entered into `pg_class`, `pg_attribute`, etc, for it. Thus the table will not be accessible by ordinary SQL operations until such entries are made the hard way (with `insert` commands). This option is used for creating `pg_class` etc themselves.

The table is created as shared if `shared_relation` is specified. It will have OIDs unless `without_oids` is specified. The table's row type OID (`pg_type` OID) can optionally be specified via the `rowtype_oid` clause; if not specified, an OID is automatically generated for it. (The `rowtype_oid` clause is useless if `bootstrap` is specified, but it can be provided anyway for documentation.)

open *tablename*

Open the table named *tablename* for insertion of data. Any currently open table is closed.

close [*tablename*]

Close the open table. The name of the table can be given as a cross-check, but this is not required.

insert [OID *= oid_value*] (*value1 value2* ...)

Insert a new row into the open table using *value1*, *value2*, etc., for its column values and *oid_value* for its OID. If *oid_value* is zero (0) or the clause is omitted, and the table has OIDs, then the next available OID is assigned.

NULL values can be specified using the special key word _null_. Values containing spaces must be double quoted.

declare [unique] index *indexname indexoid* on *tablename* using *amname* (*opclass1 name1* [, ...])

Create an index named *indexname*, having OID *indexoid*, on the table named *tablename*, using the *amname* access method. The fields to index are called *name1*, *name2* etc., and the operator classes to use are *opclass1*, *opclass2* etc., respectively. The index file is created and appropriate catalog entries are made for it, but the index contents are not initialized by this command.

declare toast *toasttableoid toastindexoid* on *tablename*

Create a TOAST table for the table named *tablename*. The TOAST table is assigned OID *toasttableoid* and its index is assigned OID *toastindexoid*. As with `declare index`, filling of the index is postponed.

build indices

Fill in the indices that have previously been declared.

60.3. Structure of the Bootstrap BKI File

The `open` command cannot be used until the tables it uses exist and have entries for the table that is to be opened. (These minimum tables are `pg_class`, `pg_attribute`, `pg_proc`, and `pg_type`.) To allow those tables themselves to be filled, `create` with the `bootstrap` option implicitly opens the created table for data insertion.

Also, the `declare index` and `declare toast` commands cannot be used until the system catalogs they need have been created and filled in.

Thus, the structure of the `postgres.bki` file has to be:

1. `create bootstrap` one of the critical tables

2. `insert` data describing at least the critical tables

3. `close`

4. Repeat for the other critical tables.

5. `create` (without `bootstrap`) a noncritical table

6. `open`

7. `insert` desired data

8. `close`

9. Repeat for the other noncritical tables.

10. Define indexes and toast tables.

11. `build indices`

There are doubtless other, undocumented ordering dependencies.

60.4. Example

The following sequence of commands will create the table `test_table` with OID 420, having two columns `cola` and `colb` of type `int4` and `text`, respectively, and insert two rows into the table:

```
create test_table 420 (cola = int4, colb = text)
open test_table
insert OID=421 ( 1 "value1" )
insert OID=422 ( 2 _null_ )
close test_table
```

Chapter 61. How the Planner Uses Statistics

This chapter builds on the material covered in Section 14.1 and Section 14.2 to show some additional details about how the planner uses the system statistics to estimate the number of rows each part of a query might return. This is a significant part of the planning process, providing much of the raw material for cost calculation.

The intent of this chapter is not to document the code in detail, but to present an overview of how it works. This will perhaps ease the learning curve for someone who subsequently wishes to read the code.

61.1. Row Estimation Examples

The examples shown below use tables in the PostgreSQL regression test database. The outputs shown are taken from version 8.3. The behavior of earlier (or later) versions might vary. Note also that since ANALYZE uses random sampling while producing statistics, the results will change slightly after any new ANALYZE.

Let's start with a very simple query:

```
EXPLAIN SELECT * FROM tenk1;

                          QUERY PLAN
-------------------------------------------------------------
 Seq Scan on tenk1  (cost=0.00..458.00 rows=10000 width=244)
```

How the planner determines the cardinality of tenk1 is covered in Section 14.2, but is repeated here for completeness. The number of pages and rows is looked up in pg_class:

```
SELECT relpages, reltuples FROM pg_class WHERE relname = 'tenk1';

 relpages | reltuples
----------+-----------
      358 |     10000
```

These numbers are current as of the last VACUUM or ANALYZE on the table. The planner then fetches the actual current number of pages in the table (this is a cheap operation, not requiring a table scan). If that is different from relpages then reltuples is scaled accordingly to arrive at a current number-of-rows estimate. In this case the value of relpages is up-to-date so the rows estimate is the same as reltuples.

Let's move on to an example with a range condition in its WHERE clause:

```
EXPLAIN SELECT * FROM tenk1 WHERE unique1 < 1000;

                                  QUERY PLAN
-------------------------------------------------------------------------------
 Bitmap Heap Scan on tenk1  (cost=24.06..394.64 rows=1007 width=244)
   Recheck Cond: (unique1 < 1000)
   ->  Bitmap Index Scan on tenk1_unique1  (cost=0.00..23.80 rows=1007 width=0)
```

```
Index Cond: (unique1 < 1000)
```

The planner examines the WHERE clause condition and looks up the selectivity function for the operator < in pg_operator. This is held in the column oprrest, and the entry in this case is scalarltsel. The scalarltsel function retrieves the histogram for unique1 from pg_statistics. For manual queries it is more convenient to look in the simpler pg_stats view:

```
SELECT histogram_bounds FROM pg_stats
WHERE tablename='tenk1' AND attname='unique1';
```

```
                     histogram_bounds
-----------------------------------------------------------
 {0,993,1997,3050,4040,5036,5957,7057,8029,9016,9995}
```

Next the fraction of the histogram occupied by "< 1000" is worked out. This is the selectivity. The histogram divides the range into equal frequency buckets, so all we have to do is locate the bucket that our value is in and count *part* of it and *all* of the ones before. The value 1000 is clearly in the second bucket (993-1997). Assuming a linear distribution of values inside each bucket, we can calculate the selectivity as:

```
selectivity = (1 + (1000 - bucket[2].min)/(bucket[2].max - bucket[2].min))/num_
            = (1 + (1000 - 993)/(1997 - 993))/10
            = 0.100697
```

that is, one whole bucket plus a linear fraction of the second, divided by the number of buckets. The estimated number of rows can now be calculated as the product of the selectivity and the cardinality of tenk1:

```
rows = rel_cardinality * selectivity
     = 10000 * 0.100697
     = 1007   (rounding off)
```

Next let's consider an example with an equality condition in its WHERE clause:

```
EXPLAIN SELECT * FROM tenk1 WHERE stringu1 = 'CRAAAA';
```

```
                     QUERY PLAN
-----------------------------------------------------------
 Seq Scan on tenk1  (cost=0.00..483.00 rows=30 width=244)
   Filter: (stringu1 = 'CRAAAA'::name)
```

Again the planner examines the WHERE clause condition and looks up the selectivity function for =, which is eqsel. For equality estimation the histogram is not useful; instead the list of *most common values* (MCVs) is used to determine the selectivity. Let's have a look at the MCVs, with some additional columns that will be useful later:

```
SELECT null_frac, n_distinct, most_common_vals, most_common_freqs FROM pg_stats
WHERE tablename='tenk1' AND attname='stringu1';
```

```
null_frac          | 0
n_distinct         | 676
```

```
most_common_vals  | {EJAAAA,BBAAAA,CRAAAA,FCAAAA,FEAAAA,GSAAAA,JOAAAA,MCAAAA,NA
most_common_freqs | {0.00333333,0.003,0.003,0.003,0.003,0.003,0.003,0.003,0.003
```

Since `CRAAAA` appears in the list of MCVs, the selectivity is merely the corresponding entry in the list of most common frequencies (MCFs):

```
selectivity = mcf[3]
            = 0.003
```

As before, the estimated number of rows is just the product of this with the cardinality of `tenk1`:

```
rows = 10000 * 0.003
     = 30
```

Now consider the same query, but with a constant that is not in the MCV list:

```
EXPLAIN SELECT * FROM tenk1 WHERE stringu1 = 'xxx';

                       QUERY PLAN
-----------------------------------------------------------
 Seq Scan on tenk1  (cost=0.00..483.00 rows=15 width=244)
   Filter: (stringu1 = 'xxx'::name)
```

This is quite a different problem: how to estimate the selectivity when the value is *not* in the MCV list. The approach is to use the fact that the value is not in the list, combined with the knowledge of the frequencies for all of the MCVs:

```
selectivity = (1 - sum(mvf))/(num_distinct - num_mcv)
            = (1 - (0.00333333 + 0.003 + 0.003 + 0.003 + 0.003 + 0.003 +
                   0.003 + 0.003 + 0.003 + 0.003))/(676 - 10)
            = 0.0014559
```

That is, add up all the frequencies for the MCVs and subtract them from one, then divide by the number of *other* distinct values. This amounts to assuming that the fraction of the column that is not any of the MCVs is evenly distributed among all the other distinct values. Notice that there are no null values so we don't have to worry about those (otherwise we'd subtract the null fraction from the numerator as well). The estimated number of rows is then calculated as usual:

```
rows = 10000 * 0.0014559
     = 15   (rounding off)
```

The previous example with `unique1 < 1000` was an oversimplification of what `scalarltsel` really does; now that we have seen an example of the use of MCVs, we can fill in some more detail. The example was correct as far as it went, because since `unique1` is a unique column it has no MCVs (obviously, no value is any more common than any other value). For a non-unique column, there will normally be both a histogram and an MCV list, and *the histogram does not include the portion of the column population represented by the MCVs*. We do things this way because it allows more precise estimation. In this situation `scalarltsel` directly applies the condition (e.g., "< 1000") to each value of the MCV list, and adds up the frequencies of the MCVs for which the condition is true. This gives an exact estimate of the selectivity within the portion of the table that is MCVs. The histogram is then used in the same way as above to estimate the selectivity in the portion of the table that is not MCVs, and then the two numbers are combined to estimate the overall selectivity. For example, consider

```
EXPLAIN SELECT * FROM tenk1 WHERE stringu1 < 'IAAAAA';

                          QUERY PLAN
------------------------------------------------------------
 Seq Scan on tenk1  (cost=0.00..483.00 rows=3077 width=244)
   Filter: (stringu1 < 'IAAAAA'::name)
```

We already saw the MCV information for `stringu1`, and here is its histogram:

```
SELECT histogram_bounds FROM pg_stats
WHERE tablename='tenk1' AND attname='stringu1';

                          histogram_bounds
------------------------------------------------------------------------------
 {AAAAAA,CQAAAA,FRAAAA,IBAAAA,KRAAAA,NFAAAA,PSAAAA,SGAAAA,VAAAAA,XLAAAA,ZZAAAA}
```

Checking the MCV list, we find that the condition `stringu1 < 'IAAAAA'` is satisfied by the first six entries and not the last four, so the selectivity within the MCV part of the population is

```
selectivity = sum(relevant mvfs)
            = 0.00333333 + 0.003 + 0.003 + 0.003 + 0.003 + 0.003
            = 0.01833333
```

Summing all the MCFs also tells us that the total fraction of the population represented by MCVs is 0.03033333, and therefore the fraction represented by the histogram is 0.96966667 (again, there are no nulls, else we'd have to exclude them here). We can see that the value `IAAAAA` falls nearly at the end of the third histogram bucket. Using some rather cheesy assumptions about the frequency of different characters, the planner arrives at the estimate 0.298387 for the portion of the histogram population that is less than `IAAAAA`. We then combine the estimates for the MCV and non-MCV populations:

```
selectivity = mcv_selectivity + histogram_selectivity * histogram_fraction
            = 0.01833333 + 0.298387 * 0.96966667
            = 0.307669

rows        = 10000 * 0.307669
            = 3077  (rounding off)
```

In this particular example, the correction from the MCV list is fairly small, because the column distribution is actually quite flat (the statistics showing these particular values as being more common than others are mostly due to sampling error). In a more typical case where some values are significantly more common than others, this complicated process gives a useful improvement in accuracy because the selectivity for the most common values is found exactly.

Now let's consider a case with more than one condition in the `WHERE` clause:

```
EXPLAIN SELECT * FROM tenk1 WHERE unique1 < 1000 AND stringu1 = 'xxx';

                          QUERY PLAN
------------------------------------------------------------------------------
```

```
Bitmap Heap Scan on tenk1  (cost=23.80..396.91 rows=1 width=244)
   Recheck Cond: (unique1 < 1000)
   Filter: (stringu1 = 'xxx'::name)
   -> Bitmap Index Scan on tenk1_unique1  (cost=0.00..23.80 rows=1007 width=0)
         Index Cond: (unique1 < 1000)
```

The planner assumes that the two conditions are independent, so that the individual selectivities of the clauses can be multiplied together:

```
selectivity = selectivity(unique1 < 1000) * selectivity(stringu1 = 'xxx')
            = 0.100697 * 0.0014559
            = 0.0001466

rows        = 10000 * 0.0001466
            = 1  (rounding off)
```

Notice that the number of rows estimated to be returned from the bitmap index scan reflects only the condition used with the index; this is important since it affects the cost estimate for the subsequent heap fetches.

Finally we will examine a query that involves a join:

```
EXPLAIN SELECT * FROM tenk1 t1, tenk2 t2
WHERE t1.unique1 < 50 AND t1.unique2 = t2.unique2;

                              QUERY PLAN
--------------------------------------------------------------------------------
Nested Loop  (cost=4.64..456.23 rows=50 width=488)
   -> Bitmap Heap Scan on tenk1 t1  (cost=4.64..142.17 rows=50 width=244)
         Recheck Cond: (unique1 < 50)
         -> Bitmap Index Scan on tenk1_unique1  (cost=0.00..4.63 rows=50 width
               Index Cond: (unique1 < 50)
   -> Index Scan using tenk2_unique2 on tenk2 t2  (cost=0.00..6.27 rows=1 wid
         Index Cond: (unique2 = t1.unique2)
```

The restriction on tenk1, unique1 < 50, is evaluated before the nested-loop join. This is handled analogously to the previous range example. This time the value 50 falls into the first bucket of the unique1 histogram:

```
selectivity = (0 + (50 - bucket[1].min)/(bucket[1].max - bucket[1].min))/num_bu
            = (0 + (50 - 0)/(993 - 0))/10
            = 0.005035

rows        = 10000 * 0.005035
            = 50  (rounding off)
```

The restriction for the join is t2.unique2 = t1.unique2. The operator is just our familiar =, however the selectivity function is obtained from the oprjoin column of pg_operator, and is eqjoinsel. eqjoinsel looks up the statistical information for both tenk2 and tenk1:

```
SELECT tablename, null_frac,n_distinct, most_common_vals FROM pg_stats
WHERE tablename IN ('tenk1', 'tenk2') AND attname='unique2';
```

```
tablename  | null_frac | n_distinct | most_common_vals
-----------+-----------+------------+------------------
 tenk1     |         0 |         -1 |
 tenk2     |         0 |         -1 |
```

In this case there is no MCV information for `unique2` because all the values appear to be unique, so we use an algorithm that relies only on the number of distinct values for both relations together with their null fractions:

```
selectivity = (1 - null_frac1) * (1 - null_frac2) * min(1/num_distinct1, 1/num_
            = (1 - 0) * (1 - 0) / max(10000, 10000)
            = 0.0001
```

This is, subtract the null fraction from one for each of the relations, and divide by the maximum of the numbers of distinct values. The number of rows that the join is likely to emit is calculated as the cardinality of the Cartesian product of the two inputs, multiplied by the selectivity:

```
rows = (outer_cardinality * inner_cardinality) * selectivity
     = (50 * 10000) * 0.0001
     = 50
```

Had there been MCV lists for the two columns, `eqjoinsel` would have used direct comparison of the MCV lists to determine the join selectivity within the part of the column populations represented by the MCVs. The estimate for the remainder of the populations follows the same approach shown here.

Notice that we showed `inner_cardinality` as 10000, that is, the unmodified size of `tenk2`. It might appear from inspection of the `EXPLAIN` output that the estimate of join rows comes from 50 * 1, that is, the number of outer rows times the estimated number of rows obtained by each inner index scan on `tenk2`. But this is not the case: the join relation size is estimated before any particular join plan has been considered. If everything is working well then the two ways of estimating the join size will produce about the same answer, but due to round-off error and other factors they sometimes diverge significantly.

For those interested in further details, estimation of the size of a table (before any `WHERE` clauses) is done in `src/backend/optimizer/util/plancat.c`. The generic logic for clause selectivities is in `src/backend/optimizer/path/clausesel.c`. The operator-specific selectivity functions are mostly found in `src/backend/utils/adt/selfuncs.c`.